The History of the Origins of Christianity

Book VII - Marcus-Aurelius

By Joseph Ernest Renan

Edited by Anthony Uyl

Devoted Publishing

Woodstock, Ontario, 2017

The History of the Origins of Christianity Book VII - Marcus-Aurelius

By Joseph Ernest Renan

Member of the French Academy

Edited by Anthony Uyl

Originally Published by:
London: Mathieson & Company 25, Paternoster Square. E.C.

What kind of philosophies do you have? Let us know!

Contact us at: devotedpub@hotmail.com
Visit us on Facebook: @DevotedPublishing
Get more products via our website: www.devotedpublishing.com

Published in Woodstock, Ontario, Canada 2017

For bulk educational rates, please contact us at the email address above.

ISBN: 978-1-988297-75-0

Table of Contents

PREFACE

This volume closes the series of essays which I have dedicated to the History of the Origins of Christianity. It contains the exhibition of the development of the Church during the reign of Marcus-Aurelius, and the parallel picture of the efforts of philosophy to improve civil society. The second century of our era has had the double glory of definitely founding Christianity--that is to say, the grand principle which has wrought the reformation of manners by faith in the supernatural, and of unrolling, thanks to stoical teaching and without any element of the marvellous, the finest attempt of the laic school of virtue which the world has known till now. These two attempts were strangers to each other, and rather contradict than aid each other reciprocally; but the triumph of Christianity is only explicable when we have taken account of what there was of force and of insufficiency in the philosophical attempt. Marcus-Aurelius is on this point the subject of study to which we must constantly refer. He sums up all that there was of good in the ancient world, and he offers criticism this advantage, of presenting himself to it unveiled, thanks to a writing of an uncontested sincerity and authenticity.

More than ever do I think that the period of the beginning, if we might so express it, closed at the death of Marcus-Aurelius, in 180. At that data the child had all its organs: it is separated from its mother; it shall henceforth live its own life. The death of Marcus-Aurelius could have been considered as marking the end of ancient civilisation. What good has been done after that, has been done by the Helleno-Roman principle; the Judæo-Syrian principle gains, and, although more than a hundred years shall pass away before its final triumph, we see well already that the future is its own. The third century is the agony of a world, which, in the second century, is still full of life and energy.

Far from me be the thought of lowering the ages which follow the epoch with which I have closed my work. These are sad days in history: there are no days barren and without interest. The development of Christianity remains a spectacle highly interesting, while the Christian Churches count such men as St. Irenæus, Clement of Alexandria, Tertullian, and Origen. The development of Christianity, which was wrought at Rome and in Africa, in the time of St. Cyprian, and of Pope Cornelius, ought to be studied with the most extreme care. The martyrs of the time of Decius and Diocletian do not yield in heroism to those of Rome, Smyrna, and Lyons the first and second centuries. But it is there we have what is called Ecclesiastical History--a history eminently curious and worthy of being written with love and all the refinements of the most attentive science, but essentially distinct, nevertheless, from the history of Christian origins--that is to say, of the analysis of the successive transformations which the germ laid by Jesus in the bosom of humanity has submitted to before becoming a complete and durable Church. Its needs methods quite different to treat the different ages of a grand formation, whether religious or political. The investigation of these origins supposes a philosophical mind--a lively intuition of what is certain, probable, or plausible--a profound sentiment of life and metamorphoses, a special art in drawing from rare texts all they possess, all that which, in fact, they include of revelations as to psychological situations far removed from us. In the history of an already complete institution, such as is the Christian Church in the third century, and with greater reasons in the following ages, the qualities of judgment and solid erudition of a Tillemont nearly suffice. That is why the seventeenth century, which has made such great progress in ecclesiastical history, has never taken up the problem of its origin. The seventeenth century had no taste but for that which can be expressed with the appearances of certainty. Such a search, of which the result cannot but be to meet possibilities, flying clouds--such a narration, which is forbidden to tell how a thing has passed, but which is limited to say: "These are one or two of the ways in which it can be imagined that the thing has taken place," could not be to its taste. In presence of the questions of origin, the seventeenth century either took all with an artless credulity, or suppressed what it felt to be half fabulous. The knowledge of obscure conditions, anterior to the clear reflection, that is to say, rightly of conditions where the human conscience shows itself especially creative and fertile, is the intellectual question of the nineteenth century. I have sought, without any other motive than a very lively curiosity, to make the application of the methods of criticism which have prevailed in our days in those delicate matters in the most important religious appearance which had a place in history. Since my youth I have been preparing this work. The edition of seven volumes to compose, which has taken me twenty years. The general index which will appear at the same time as this volume will permit these being found easily in a work which it did not depend on me to render less complex and less charged with details.

I thank the infinite Goodness for the time and necessary ardour to accomplish this difficult purpose. If there should remain to me some years of work, I shall dedicate them to complete from another side the subject which I have made the centre of my reflections. To be strictly logical, I should have begun a History of the Origin of Christianity by a history of the Jewish people. Christianity commences in the eighth century B.C., at the moment when the great prophets, taking up the people of Israel, made of it the people of God, charged to inaugurate in the world the pure religion. Up till then the worship of Israel had not essentially differed from that egotistical, self-interested cult which was that of all the tribes and nations, and which is revealed to us in the inscription of King Mesha, for example. A revolution was accomplished when an imprisoned man, not belonging to the priesthood, said: "Can we believe God will be pleased with the smoke of your victims or with the fat of your bullocks? Leave then these sacrifices, which only disgrace, and do good." Isaiah is in that sense the first founder of Christianity. Jesus has not really said, in popular and charming language, what 750 years before him had been said in the Hebrew classic. To show how the religion of Israel, which in its origin had not perhaps any superiority over the religion of Ammon or Moab, became a moral religion, and how the religious history of the Jews has been a constant progress towards worship in spirit and in truth, that is what would need to be shown before introducing Jesus upon the scene of the facts. But life is short, and its duration uncertain. I therefore betook myself to the most pressing of them: I threw myself into the midst of the subject, and commenced with the Life of Jesus, holding for well-known the former revolutions of the Jewish religion. Now that it has been given me to treat, with all the care I desired, that part on which I laid the greatest value, it shall be my care to go back to the earlier history, and dedicate to it what still remains to me of force and energy.

CHAPTER I

ADVENT OF MARCUS-AURELIUS

Antoninus died 7th March, 161, in his palace of Lorium, with the calmness of an accomplished sage. When he felt death approaching, he, like a plain individual, put his family affairs in order, and commanded to be transferred into the chamber of his adopted son, Marcus-Aurelius, the golden statue of Fortune which had hitherto always stood in the apartment of the emperor. To the Tribune in attendance he gave the watchword Æquanimitas; then, turning himself, he appeared to fall asleep. Every order of the State rivalled each other in doing homage to his memory. There were established in his honour priesthoods, games, and societies. His piety, his clemency, and his holiness were the subjects of unusual eulogiums.

It was remarked that during the whole of his reign he had not caused to be shed a drop of Roman blood, nor a drop of blood of foreigners. In piety, in his religious observance of ceremonies, as well as in the happiness and security he had been able to give to the empire, he was compared to Numa.

Antoninus would have had the reputation of being the best of sovereigns if he had not designated for his successor a man equal to himself in goodness and in modesty--one who joined to these shining qualities talent, and a charm which make an image to live in the recollection of mankind. Simple, amiable, full of sweet gaiety, Antoninus was a philosopher without pretending to be so, and almost without knowing it. Marcus-Aurelius was a philosopher whose humanity and sincerity were admirable, but yet reflective. In this respect Antoninus was the greater. His kindness did not lead him to commit mistakes. He was not tormented by the evil instincts which gnawed at the heart of his adopted son. That extraneous evil, that restless study of self, that demon of scrupulousness, that fever of perfection, are the indications of a nature less strong than distinguished. The most beautiful thoughts are those which men do not commit to writing; but let it be added that we should have known nothing of Antoninus if Marcus-Aurelius had not handed down to us that exquisite portrait of his adopted father, in which he seems, by reason of humility, to have applied himself to paint an image superior to what he himself was, Antoninus resembled a Christ who would not have had an Evangel; Marcus-Aurelius a Christ who would have written his own.

It is the glory of sovereignty that two models of irreproachable virtue are to be found in its ranks, and that the most beautiful lessons of patience and disinterestedness could proceed from a condition which we may suppose was unreservedly exposed to all the seductions of pleasure and vanity. The throne sometimes is an aid to virtue; and Marcus-Aurelius certainly would not have been what he was if it had not been that he exercised supreme power. It is the faculties which such an exceptional position alone puts into exercise, alongside of the reality, which make it appear to better advantage. It is disadvantageous to fame when the sovereign, the servant of all, cannot allow his genius to have free scope; but such a situation, when there is brought to bear on it an elevated soul, is very favourable to the development of the individual genius and talent which constitute the moralist. The sovereign really worthy of the name observes humanity from his exalted position in the most complete manner. His point of view resembles that of the philosophical historian--that which results from those sweeping glances cast over our poor species; it is a sweet sentiment mixed with resignation, piety, and hope. The cold severity of an artist cannot belong to a sovereign. The first condition of art is freedom; but the sovereign, subjected as he is to the prejudices of middle-class society, is the least free of men. He has not the right to his own opinions; he has hardly any right to his own tastes. A crowned Goethe even could not avow that royal disdain for bourgeois ideas, that haughty indifference to practical results, which are the essential characteristics of the artist; but one can imagine the mind of a good sovereign like that of a sympathetic Goethe, a Goethe converted to the good, brought to see that there is something greater than art, led to estimate men by the habitual nobleness of his thoughts and by the feeling of his own happiness.

Such were these two admirable sovereigns, Antoninus the Pious and Marcus-Aurelius, at the head of the greatest empire that ever existed. History only presents another example of this heredity of wisdom upon the throne, in the persons of the three great Mogul emperors, Baber, Humaïoun, Akbar, the latter of whom shows, when compared with Marcus-Aurelius, some traits of striking resemblance. The salutary principle of adoption had made of the imperial court, in the second century, a true nursery of virtue. The noble and learned Nerva, in establishing that principle, assured the happiness of the human species for nearly three hundred years, and gave to the world the most beautiful century of progress which has been conserved by the memory of man.

It is Marcus-Aurelius himself who has sketched for us in the first book of his Thoughts this latter admirable plan, in which we see moving, in a celestial light, the noble and pure features of his father, mother, ancestors and masters. Thanks to him, we can comprehend what the old Roman families, who had witnessed the reign of the bad emperors, guarded still of honesty, dignity, right, the civil spirit, and, if I may say so, republican. People lived there in the admiration of Cato, of Brutus, of Thraseas, and of the great Stoics, whose souls had not been subjugated by tyranny. The reign of Domitian was there abhorred. The sages who opposed him without flinching were honoured as heroes. The advent of the Antonines was only the succession to power of the society whose just colours Tacitus has handed down to us, a society of sages brought into existence by the league of all those who had revolted against the despotism of the first Cæsars.

Neither the oriental pomps of some oriental royalties, founded upon the baseness and the stupidity of men, nor the pedantic pride of the royalties of the middle ages, founded upon an exaggerated sentiment of heredity, and upon the simple faith of the Germanic races in the rights of blood, can give us an idea of this wholly republican sovereignty of Nerva, of Trajan, of Hadrian, of Antoninus, and of Marcus-Aurelius. There was nothing of the hereditary prince or of right divine; none of the military captain; it was a kind of grand civil magistrature, with nothing which resembled a court, nor which stripped the emperor of his individual character. Marcus-Aurelius was neither little nor much of a king in the proper sense of the term; his fortune was immense, but consisted wholly of patrimony; his aversion to the Cæsars (the emperors before Nerva), whom he regarded as a species of Sardanapalus, magnificent, debauched and cruel, appeared at every minute of his life. The civility of his manners was perfection; he gave back to the Senate the whole of its ancient importance; when he was at Rome he never missed a sitting, nor quitted his place until the Consul had pronounced the formula: Nihil vos moramur, Patres conscripti.

The sovereignty thus possessed in common by a group of the élite of men, which bound them together or separated them, according to the exigencies of the moment, lost a part of that attraction which renders it so dangerous. One reached the throne without having to canvass for it, but also without owing it to birth or to a kind of abstract right; one attained to it undeceived, wearied of men, prepared by long authority. The empire was a burden, which one accepted when one's hour came, without one's dreaming of precipitating that hour. Marcus-Aurelius was designated for it so young that the idea of reigning had hardly any commencement, and did not exercise over his mind a moment's seduction. At eight years old, when he was already proesul of the Salic priests, Hadrian remarked this brooding, sweet child, and loved him for his good nature, his docility, and his incapacity to lie. At ten years old, the empire was assured to him. He waited patiently for it for twenty-two years. The evening on which Antoninus felt himself to be dying, and caused to be carried into his chamber the statue of Fortune, had for him neither surprise nor joy. He had for a long time been surfeited by the joys which he had never tasted; he had, by reason of the profoundness of his philosophy, perceived their absolute vanity.

His youth had been tranquil and pleasant, divided between the pleasures of the country, exercises in Latin rhetoric in the slightly frivolous manner of his master Fronto, and philosophical meditations. Greek pedagogy had attained its perfection, and, as happens in these sort of things, perfection was approaching decadence. The lettered men and the philosophers were divided in opinion, and were engaged in ardent combat. The rhetoricians dreamed only of affected ornaments of discourse; philosophers favoured almost baldness and negligence of expression. In spite of his friendship for Fronto, and his adjurations against the latter, Marcus-Aurelius was soon an adept in philosophy. Junius Rusticus became his favourite master, and won him wholly over to the severe discipline which he opposed to the ostentation of the rhetoricians. Rusticus continued to be the confidant and the intimate counsellor of his august pupil, who acknowledged having received from him his taste for a simple style, for a demeanour noble and serious, not to mention a still superior benefit, to wit: "I am indebted to him for my knowledge of he Conversations of Epictetus,' which he lent me from his own library." Claudius Severus, the peripatetic, laboured to the same end, and ultimately led young Marcus to philosophy. Marcus had a habit of calling him his brother, and appeared to have had for him a deep attachment.

Philosophy was at that time a kind of religious profession, implying mortification and rules almost monastic. From the age of twelve Marcus assumed the philosophic mantle, learned to sleep upon a hard bed and to practise all the austerities of ascetic stoicism. It required his mother on several occasions to induce him to spread a few skins upon his couch. His health was more than once affected by this excessive rigour. But that did not prevent him from presiding at feasts, or from fulfilling his duties as a youthful prince, with that affable air which in him was the result of the greatest disinterestedness.

His hours were as strict as those of a religious recluse. In spite of his feeble health, he could, thanks to the sobriety of his régime and to the strictness of his morals, lead a life of labour and fatigue. He had not what is called esprit, and he had very little passion. Esprit rarely succeeds apart from a certain amount of malignity. It is accustomed to do this by turns which are neither wholly good-natured nor troublesome. Marcus understood nothing perfectly--except duty. What he lacked was the kissing of a fairy at his birth, a thing quite philosophical in its way; I mean, the art of unbending to nature and to gaiety, which teaches that abstinence and sustenance are not everything, and that life might as well be summed up in "laughter and mirth."

In every art he had for masters the most eminent professors. Claudius Severus instructed him in peripateticism; Apollonius of Chalcis was brought expressly from the East by Antoninus to take charge of his adopted son, who appears to have been a perfect preceptor; Sextus of Cheronea, the nephew of Plutarch, the accomplished stoic; Diognetus, who trained him to love asceticism; Claudius Maximus, always brimful of fine sentences; Alexander of Cotyus, who taught him Greek; Herodus Atticus, who recited to him the ancient harangues of Athens. His exterior was that of his masters themselves; habits simple and modest, beard almost neglected, body attenuated and reduced to a shadow, eyes twitching with hard labour. No study, not even that of painting, was strange to him. With Greek he was familiar; when he reflected on philosophical subjects he thought in that language; but his solid mind discovered the folly of literary exercises, in which Hellenic education was lost; his Greek style, though correct, has something artificial which smells of the midnight oil. Morality was to him the last word of existence, and he brought to bear on it constant application.

How did these respectable pedagogues, none of them of any consequence, succeed in forming such a man? This is a question which one asks himself with some surprise. To judge of it by the ordinary analogies, it had all the appearance that an education so overdone would turn out to be the very worst. But to speak the truth, superior to all these masters who had been selected from every corner of the globe, Marcus had a single master whom he revered above them all; and that was Antoninus. The moral value of the man is in proportion to his faculty of admiration. It was because Marcus-Aurelius had by his side the most beautiful model of a perfect life, and one whom he understood and loved, that he became what he was.

Beware of "Cæarising" or losing your true colour; that approaches. Preserve thyself simple, good, pure, grave, the enemy of pomp, the friend of justice and religion, benevolent, human, firm in the practice of duties. Make every effort to remain such as philosophy would have thee do; revere the gods, watch the preservation of men. Life is short, the only fruit of earthly life is to maintain one's soul in a holy frame, to do actions useful to society. Act always like a disciple of Antoninus; recall to thyself his constancy in the accomplishments of the prescriptions of reason, the equanimity of his disposition in all situations, his holiness, his serenity of countenance, his extreme gentleness, his contempt for vain-glory, his determination to penetrate the meaning of things; how he never allowed anything to pass before he had examined and well understood it; how he bore unjust reproaches without recriminating; how he did nothing with precipitation; how he would not listen to detractors; how carefully he studied character and action; neither spiteful nor fastidious, nor suspicious, nor sophistical: content with so little as to house, sleep, garments, food, service; laborious, patient, sober, so much so that he could occupy himself till night in the same business without having to leave for his necessary wants, except at the usual hours. And that friendship always constant, equable, and that goodness in supporting contradiction, and that joy in receiving counsel better than his own: and that piety without superstition! Think of these things, so that the last hour may find thee like him, with a consciousness of good accomplished.

The consequence of this austere philosophy might have produced stiffness and severity. But here it was that the rare goodness of the nature of Marcus-Aurelius shone out in all its brilliancy. His severity was confined only to himself. The fruit of this great tension of mind is inexhaustible benevolence. His whole life was a study of how to render good for evil. After some sad experience of human perversity, he can only contrive in the evening to note down the following: "If thou canst do it, correct them; in the contrary case, remember thou how thou must act towards those who had bestowed kindness on thee. The gods themselves are benevolent to these creatures; they aid them (so great is their bounty!), bestow on them health, riches, and glory; to thee it is permitted to do as the gods." Another day men were very wicked; for here is what he writes on his tablets: "Such is the order of nature: some men of that sort must, of necessity, act thus. To wish that it be otherwise is to wish that the fig-tree should produce no figs. Remember thou, in a word, this: In a very short time thou and he will die; soon after, your names will be remembered no more." These reflections on universal forgiveness recur continually.

It is on rare occasions that he mixes with that superlative kindness an imperceptible smile. "The best way to revenge oneself on the wicked is not to render them like for like," or, with a soft emphasis of pride: "It is a royal thing, when one does good, to remember the evil that is in himself." One day he has to reproach himself: "Thou hast forgotten that this holy relationship re-unites each man with the human species; a relationship not of blood and of birth, but a participation in the same intelligence. Thou hast forgotten that the reasonable soul of each person is a god, a thing derived from the Supreme Being."

In the business of life he must have been exquisite, though, no doubt, a little simple, like the majority of men who are very good. He was sincerely humble, without hypocrisy, make-believe, or studied deceit. One of the maxims of the excellent emperor was that the wicked are unhappy, that one is wicked only in spite of himself and through ignorance; he grieves for those who are not like himself; he did not believe in the right of imposing on them.

He perceived clearly the baseness of men, but he did not avow it. This habit of blinding oneself willingly was the defect of the hearts of the élite. The world not being such as they would wish it, they deceived themselves in order to see it otherwise than it was. Hence he was a little lenient in his judgments. With Marcus-Aurelius, this pliableness produces in us sometimes a cause of irritation. If we were to believe him, his masters, several of whom were mediocre enough, must have been without exception superior men. We should have to admit that everybody about him was virtuous. It is at such a point as this that we are compelled to ask if that brother, upon whom he has made so great an eulogium in his acts of thanks to the gods, was not his brother by adoption, the debauched Lucius Verus. It is certain that the good emperor was capable of gross illusions when the matter in hand was the rendering to others their proper meed of virtue.

No person of sense will deny that his was a great soul. But had he a great mind? Yes; since he saw into the infinite depths of duty and of conscience. He lacked decision only in one point. He never dared deny absolutely the supernatural. We certainly can share his dread of atheism; we understand perfectly what he meant when he speaks to us of his horror of a world without God and without Providence. But that which we little comprehend is when he speaks to us seriously of the gods intervening in human affairs through the will of particular persons. The meagreness of his scientific education can alone explain such weakness. To protect himself from vulgar errors, he had neither the nimbleness of Hadrian nor the adroitness of Lucian. But it must be added that those errors were in him of no consequence. The supernatural was not the base of his piety. His religion was limited to some medical superstitions, and to a patriotic condescension for old usages. The initiations of Eleusis did not appear to have occupied a large place in his moral life. His virtue, like that of the present day, rested on reason and upon nature. Saint Louis was a very virtuous man, and, according to the ideas of his time, a very good sovereign, because he was a Christian. Marcus-Aurelius was the most pious of men, not because he was a pagan, but because he was an accomplished man. He was the embodiment of human nature, and not of a fixed religion. Whatever may be the religious and philosophical revolutions of the future, his grandeur will not suffer any reproach, for it rests entirely upon that which can never perish--upon excellence of heart.

To live with the gods! He who lives with the gods here shows always a mind contented with the lot which has fallen to him, and is obedient to the genius which Jupiter has separated, even as it were a part of himself, to serve as our director and guide. This genius is the intelligence and the reasoning faculty of each one.

The world is either but chaos--successive aggregation or segregation--or it is providence, order, and unity. In the first case, why should we desire to remain in such a cloaca? The segregation alone will know how to reach me. In the latter case, I adore, I rest myself, I have confidence in him who governs.

CHAPTER II

PROGRESS AND REFORMS. THE ROMAN LAW

Considered as a sovereign, Marcus-Aurelius was the embodiment of the liberal politician. Respect for mankind formed the basis of his conduct. He recognised that in the interest of good itself, we ought not to impose this good on others in an arbitrary manner, the free play of freedom being the first condition of human life. He desired the amelioration of mind and not merely physical obedience to the law; he sought for the public felicity, but such felicity not to be procured through servitude, which is the greatest of errors. His ideal of government was wholly republican. The prince was the first subject under the law. He was only the lessee and tenant of the wealth of the State. He must indulge no useless luxury; be strictly economical; his charity real and inexhaustible; easily accessible and affable of speech; pursuing in everything the public good, and not public applause.

Some historians, more or less imbued with this polity, which was regarded as superior because it assuredly had no connection with any philosophy, have endeavoured to prove that a man so accomplished as Marcus-Aurelius could but be a bad administrator and a mediocre sovereign. It might be, indeed, that Marcus-Aurelius sinned more than once through being too indulgent. However, apart from the evils which it was absolutely impossible to foresee or to prevent, his reign stands out to us as being great and prosperous. The improvement in manners was considerable. Many of the secret aims which instinctively pursued Christianity were legally attained. The general political system had some grave defects; but the wisdom of the good emperor covered all with a temporary palliative. It was a singular thing that this virtuous prince, who never once made the least concession to false popularity, was adored by the people. He was democratic in the best sense of the word. The old Roman aristocracy inspired him with antipathy. He had no regard for birth, nor even for education and manners; he only looked to merit. As he could not find amongst the patricians fit subjects to second his ideas of wise government, he entrusted those functions to men whose only nobility was their honesty.

Public assistance, established by Nerva and Trajan, developed by Antoninus, reached, under Marcus-Aurelius, the highest point it had ever attained. The principle that the State has in some sort paternal duties to perform towards its members (a principle which ought to be remembered with gratitude, even when we have got beyond it)--that principle, I say, was proclaimed in the world for the first time in the second century. The education of children in a liberal manner had become, on account of the insufficiency of morals, and in consequence of the defective economical principles upon which society reposed, one of the great pre-occupations of statesmen. Since the time of Trajan it had been endowed by hypothecating sums of money, the revenues from which were managed by the procurators. Marcus Aurelius made the procurators functionaries of the first rank; he selected them with the greatest care from amongst the consuls and prætors, and increased their powers. His great private fortune rendered it easy for him to place these largesses on a secure basis. He himself created a great number of endowments for the succour of the youth of both sexes. The institute of the Young female Faustinas dated from Antoninus. After the death of the second Faustina, Marcus-Aurelius founded New female Faustinas. An elegant bas-relief represents these young women pressing around the empress, who drops wheat into a fold of their robes.

Stoicism, since the reign of Hadrian, had permeated the Roman law with its broad maxims and had made of it a natural law, a philosophical law, so that reason might conceive it as applicable to all men. The perpetual edict of Salvius Julianus was the first complete expression of that new law destined to become the universal law. It was the triumph of the Greek mind over the Latin mind. The strict law yielded to equity; mildness turned the scale on severity; justice seemed inseparable from beneficence. The great jurisconsulates of Antoninus, Salvius Valens, Ulpius Marcellus, Javolenus, Volusius Moecianus continued the same work. The last was the master of Marcus-Aurelius in the matter of jurisprudence, and, to speak the truth, the work of the two holy emperors ought not to have been separated. From them dates the majority of the sensible and humane laws which modify the rigour of the ancient law and form, from legislation primarily narrow and implacable, a code susceptible of being adopted by all civilised peoples.

The weak individual, in ancient societies, was somewhat dependent. Marcus-Aurelius constituted himself in a fashion the tutor of all those who had not one. The wants of the poor child and the sick child were assured. The tutelary Prætor was created to give guarantees for the orphaned. The civil law and the registration of births were commenced. A multitude of ordinances, completely just, introduced into the whole administration a remarkable spirit of mildness and of humanity. The expenses of the cures were diminished. Thanks to a better system of provisioning, famines in Italy were rendered impossible. In the order of judicature many reforms of an excellent character dated in like manner from the reign of Marcus. The regulation of manners, notably that which had reference to indiscriminate baths, was made more strict. It was to the slaves especially that Antoninus and Marcus-Aurelius showed themselves beneficent. Some of the greatest monstrosities of slavery were corrected. It was henceforward admitted that the master could commit an injustice to a slave. From the time of the new legislation corporal punishments were regulated. To kill a slave became a crime; to treat him with excessive cruelty was a misdemeanour, and drew upon the master the necessity of selling the unfortunate whom he had tortured. The slave, in time, resorted to the tribunals, became a somebody, and a member of the city. He was proprietor of his own substance, had his family, and it was not allowable to sell separately husband, wife, and children. The application of the question to servile persons was limited. The master might not, except in certain cases, sell his slaves to make them fight with wild beasts in the amphitheatres. The servant, sold under the condition ne prostituatur, was preserved from the bordelles. There was what was called favor libertatis; in case of doubt, interpretation the most favourable to liberty was admitted. People placed humanity against the rigour of the law, often even against the letter of the statute. In point of fact, from the time of Antoninus, the jurisconsulate, imbued with Stoicism, considered slavery as a violation of the rights of nature, and were inclined to restrict it. Enfranchisement was favoured in every way. Marcus-Aurelius went further and recognised within certain limits the right of slaves to the goods of the master. If a person did not present himself to claim the heritage of a testator, slaves were authorised to divide the goods amongst themselves; when one only or several were admitted to the adjudication the result was the same. The enfranchised person was in like manner protected by the most stringent enactments against slavery, which had a thousand different devices for seizing on him again.

The son, the wife, the minor were the objects of legislation at once intelligent and humane. The son was obliged to maintain his father, but ceased to be under his control. The most odious excesses, which the ancient Roman law regarded as quite natural to permit to paternal authority, were abolished or restrained. The father had duties towards his children, and could get nothing back for having fulfilled them; the son, on his side, owed to his kindred alimentary succour, in proportion to his fortune.

The laws, up to this time, of tutelage and trusteeship had been most incomplete; Marcus-Aurelius made them models of administrative foresight. By the ancient law the mother made hardly any part of the family of her husband and of her children. The Tertullian Senatus consultum (in the year 158), and the Orphitian Senatus consultum (178) established to the mother the right of succession, from the mother to the child and from the child to the mother. Sentiment and natural law took precedence. The excellent laws in regard to banks, to the sale of slaves, to informers and slanderers, put an end to a multitude of abuses. The fiscal laws had always been severe, exacting. It was henceforward settled in principle that in doubtful cases it should be the treasury that was wrong. Imposts of a vexatious character were abolished. The length of processes was diminished. The criminal law became less cruel, and the inculpated person was given valuable guarantees; still, it was the personal characteristic of Marcus-Aurelius to diminish, in application, the established penalties. In cases of folly punishment was remitted. The great stoical principle, that culpability resided in the motive, not in the deed, became the soul of laws.

Thus was definitely established that great marvel the Roman law, a sort of revelation in its way which ignorance has placed to the honour of the compilers of Justinian, but which in reality was the work of the great emperors of the second century, and admirably interpreted and continued by the eminent jurisconsulates of the third century. The Roman law had a less clamorous triumph than Christianity, but in a sense a more durable one. Wiped out first by barbarism, it was resuscitated about the close of the Middle Ages, was the law of the world of the Renaissance, and became once more in a modified form the law of modern peoples. It was hence that the great Stoical school in the second century attempted to reform the world, after having to appearance miserably failed, and achieved in reality a complete victory. Compiled by the classical jurisconsults of the times of Severus, mutilated and altered by Tribonian, the texts survived, and these texts became later the code of the entire world. Now these texts were the work of the eminent legalists who, grouped about Hadrian, Antoninus, and Marcus-Aurelius, caused the law to enter definitely into its philosophic age. The labour was continued under the Syrian emperors; the frightful political decadence of the third century did not prevent that vast edifice from continuing its slow and splendid growth.

It was not that Marcus-Aurelius made a parade of the innovating spirit. On the contrary, he conducted himself in such a manner as to give to the reforms a conservative appearance. He treated man always as a moral being; he never affected, as did often the pretended transcendental politicians, to treat him as a machine or a means to an end. If he could not change the atrocious penal code of the times he mitigated it in its application. A fund was established for the obsequies of the poor citizens; funeral colleges were authorised to receive legacies and to become civil societies, having the right to possess property, slaves, franchises. Seneca had said: "All men, if we go back to the origin of things, have gods for fathers." On the morrow Ulpian will say: "By the law of nature all men are born free and equal."

Marcus-Aurelius wished to suppress the hideous scenes which made the amphitheatres actual places of horror for whoever possessed a moral sense. But he did not succeed; these abominable representations were a part of the life of the people. When Marcus-Aurelius armed the gladiators for the great Germanic war, there was almost a revolution. "He wishes to take away from us our amusements," cried the multitude, "and to constrain us to philosophy." The habitués of the amphitheatres were the only persons who did not love him. Compelled to yield to an opinion which was stronger than he, Marcus-Aurelius protested nevertheless in every possible way. He brought some alleviation to evils he was not able to suppress; we hear of rope-dancers having mattresses placed under them, and of people not being allowed to fight unless their arms were covered. The emperor visited the spectacles as seldom as he could help, and only out of complaisance. He affected during the representation to read, to give audiences, to sign despatches, without making himself the object of the raillery of the public. One day a lion that a slave had pricked for the purpose of devouring some men made so much of his master that on every side the public clamoured for his manumission. The emperor, who during this time had turned his head, responded with temper: "This man has done nothing worthy of liberty." He issued several edicts to prevent precipitate manumissions, called for under the excitement of popular plaudits, which seemed to him a first reward for cruelty.

CHAPTER III

THE REIGN OF THE PHILOSOPHERS

The problem of the happiness of humanity had never before been known to have been pursued with so much assiduousness and heartiness. The ideal of Plato was realised; the world was governed by the philosophers. All that had been in the form of a beautiful sentiment in the great soul of Seneca had come to be a reality. Though railed at for two hundred years by the brutal Romans, the Greek philosophy, by dint of patience, triumphed. We have seen already under Antoninus philosophers privileged, pensioned, enjoying almost the position of public functionaries; now the emperor is wholly surrounded with them. His old masters have become his ministers, his men of state. He showers honours upon them with profusion, raises statues to them, places their monuments among his household gods, and, on the anniversary of their death, goes to sacrifice at their tombs, which he always keeps decked with flowers. The consulship, which until now had been reserved for the Roman aristocracy, is invaded by the rhetoricians and the philosophers. Herodus Atticus, Fronto, Junius Rusticus, Claudius Severus, Proculus, became in their day consuls or proconsuls. Marcus-Aurelius had in particular for Rusticus the most tender affection. He made him twice consul, and always embraced him before saluting the prefect of the prætorium. The important functions of the prefect of Rome were for some years as if placed immutably in his hands.

It was inevitable that this sudden favour, accorded by the emperor to a class of men who combined all that was excellent and contemptible, should lead to many abuses. From all parts of the world the good Marcus-Aurelius had caused to be brought philosophers of renown. Among the proud mendicants, clad in ragged blouses, which that large call had put in movement, there were more than one person of mediocrity, more than one charlatan. That which implied an exterior profession provoked always a comparison between real manners and those which habit engendered. These parvenus were accused of greediness, of avariciousness, of gormandising, of impertinence, and of rancour. People sometimes laughed at the weaknesses which their mantles could shelter. Their badly combed hair, their beards, their nails were the objects of raillery. "His beard is worth to him ten thousand sestercias," said some people, "it will soon be necessary to salary also goats." Their vanity gave often occasion to these pleasantries. Peregrinus, sacrificing himself upon Mount Olympus (in 166), showed how far the necessity of the tragic could lead a fool who was infatuated with his rôle and eager to have himself spoken of.

Their pretended absolute self-sufficiency called forth stinging rebukes. People repeated the phrase attributed to Demonax, upon Apollonius of Chalcis, departing from Rome with his suite: "Here comes Apollonius and his argonauts." These Greeks, these Syrians, flocking to the assault of Rome, seemed to be setting out for the conquest of a new fleece of gold. The pensions and the exemptions which they enjoyed meant that they were in charge of the republic; and Marcus-Aurelius was compelled to justify himself on this point. People complained especially of their maltreatment of certain individuals. The ordinary insolences of the cynics only too far justified those accusations. These miserable snarling dogs possessed neither shame nor respect, and they were very numerous.

Marcus-Aurelius did not dissimulate the defects of his friends; but his perfect sagacity led him to make a distinction between the doctrine and the weaknesses of those whom he taught. He knew that there were few or none of the philosophers really practical in what they advised. Experience had taught him that the majority of them were greedy, quarrelsome, vain, insolent; that they sought only disputation, that they were possessed solely by a spirit of pride, malignity, and jealousy. But he was too judicious to expect perfection in men. As St. Louis was not disturbed for a moment in his faith by the disorders of the clericals, so Marcus-Aurelius was never disgusted with philosophy--with what were the vices of the philosophers. "I esteem the true philosophers, indulgently exempt from blame the pretended philosophers, without, however, ever being duped by them," was what he remarked in Antoninus, and the rule he himself observed. He went and listened in their schools to Apollonius and to Sextus of Cheronea, and was not made angry by people laughing at him. Like Antoninus, he had a faculty for supporting the ill-natured remarks of vain and badly educated people, which those honours probably exaggerated and rendered impertinent. Alexander saw him walking in the streets without courtiers, without a guard, clad in the mantle of the philosopher and living like one of them. At Athens he instituted chairs for all the sciences, and endowed them liberally; and he was able to give to the institution called the university of that city an éclat superior even to that which she had received from Hadrian.

It was natural that the representatives of what still remained of solidity, endurance, and of strength in the ancient Roman nature should exhibit some impatience at that invasion of the high places in the republic by people without family renown, without military audacity, belonging for the most part to those oriental races which the true Roman contemned. Such was especially the position unfortunately taken by Avedius Cassius, a true soldier and statesman, an enlightened man even, and sympathising fully with Marcus-Aurelius, but one who was persuaded that government existed for another purpose than philosophy. By reason of calling the emperor in jest "a good female philosopher," he was led into embracing the most fatal of ideas, to wit, revolt. The great reproach that he laid at the door of Marcus-Aurelius was the confiding of the highest positions to men who, whether as regards fortune, antecedents, and even education, could offer no guarantees, Bassæus and Pompeian, for example. The good emperor went, in fact, so far as innocently to desire that Pompeian should marry his daughter Lucilla, the, widow of Lucius Verus, and to pretend that Lucilla loved Pompeian, because he was the most virtuous man in the empire. This unfortunate idea was one of the principal causes which corrupted his internal government; for Faustina supported the resistance of his daughter, and that was one of the causes which threw her into the opposition against her husband.

If Marcus-Aurelius had not united to his goodness a rare degree of practical sense, his infatuation for a class of persons, who were not always worth that which his profession would have made one suppose, would have led him into errors. Religion has had its absurdities; philosophy has had its also. Those people who crowded the public places, armed with truncheons, parading their long beards, their wallets, and their threadbare cloaks, these shoe-makers, these artisans who abandoned their benches to lead the idle life of begging cynics, exciting amongst people of mind the same antipathy which later on the Capuchin vagabond excited amongst the well-educated bourgeoisie. But, in general, despite the somewhat exaggerated respect which he had à priori for the costumes of the philosophers, Marcus-Aurelius exercised in his discernment of men a very perfect tact. The whole group of sages who had seized power on all sides presented a very venerable aspect; the emperor regarded them less as masters or friends than as brothers, who were associated with him in the government. The philosophers, as Seneca had dreamed, had become a power in the State, a certain constitutional institution, a privy council, whose influence in the affairs of State was of first importance.

This curious phenomenon, which has been witnessed but once in history, partook certainly of the character of the emperor; but it partook also of the nature of the empire, and of the Roman conception of the State, a conception wholly rationalistic, into which there entered no theocratic idea. The law was the expression of reason; it was hence natural that men of reason should attain one day or other to power. Like judges in cases of conscience, the philosophers had a rôle which was in a manner legal. For centuries the Greek philosophy had constituted the education of the highest Roman society; almost all the preceptors were Greeks; education was imparted wholly in Greek. Greece could not name a more splendid victory than that which she had thus gained through her pedagogues and professors. Philosophy took more and more the character of a religion; she had her preachers, her missionaries, her directors of consciences, her casuists. The great personages conversed with one another in a familiar philosophy, which was at the same time their intimate friend, their monitor, the guardian of their souls. It was hence a philosophy which had its thorns, and the first conditions of which were a venerable exterior, a fine beard, and a fashion of wearing a cloak with dignity.

Rubellius Plautus had near him, it is said, "two doctors of wisdom," Coeranus and Musonius, the one Greek, the other Etruscan, in order to furnish him with the grounds for being able to await death with courage. Before death, people conversed with some sage, similar to what is called with us a priest, so that the last breath drawn might have a moral religious character. Canus Julius walked to the scaffold accompanied by "his philosopher." Thraseus died assisted by the cynic Demetrius.

People hold it to be the first duty of a philosopher to enlighten men, to sustain them and to direct them. In great afflictions we send for a philosopher to give consolation, and often the philosophers, like our priests invoked in extremis, complain that they have only been sent for at the last minute when it is too late. We only purchase remedies when we are very sick; we neglect the philosopher in like manner, except when we are very unfortunate. We see a man rich, enjoying good health, and having a wife bien portants, but should he lose his fortune, or his health, should his wife, or his son, or his brother be struck down dead, then it is that the philosopher is sent for; he is called in to administer some consolation, to explain to the rich man in what manner one can support so much misfortune.

It was the conscience of the sovereign in particular that the philosophers, like the Jesuits later, sought to gain over to the right. "The sovereign is good and wise for the benefit of others;" in bettering him the philosopher accomplished more than if he had seduced into the paths of wisdom hundreds of isolated individuals. Areus was to Augustus a director, a kind of confessor, to whom the emperor unfolded all his thoughts, even to his most secret movements. When Livy lost his son Drusus it was

Areus who condoled with him. Seneca played at intervals a similar part to Nero. The philosopher in the times of Epictetus, though he was still treated with great rudeness by the unpolished personages in Italy, became the comes of the prince, his most intimate friend, he whom he received at all times. It might be said of these species of almoners that they had functions and received regular treatment. Dion Chrysostom wrote for Trajan his discourses on the duties of royalty. Hadrian has been represented to us as being surrounded with Sophists.

The public had, like the princes, its regular lessons in philosophy. There were in important cities an eclectic official teacher, lessons, conferences. All the ancient denominations of the school subsisted. There were yet Platonists, Pythagoreans, Cynics, Epicureans, Peripaticians, drawing equal salaries, on the sole condition of their proving that their teaching was in full accord with that of Plato, Pythagoras, Diogenes, Epicurus, and Aristotle. The scoffers even pretended that certain professors taught at once several philosophies, and were paid for playing divers parts. A sophist presented himself at Athens as being acquainted with all the philosophies: "When Aristotle calls me to the Lyceum," said he, "I am he; when Plato invites me to the Academy I enter it; if Zeno calls me, I make myself the guest of the Portico; at one word of Pythagoras I am silent." "Suppose that Pythagoras were to call thee?" responded Demonax.

It is too often forgotten that the second century had a veritable Pagan preaching, similar to that of Christianity, and in many respects in accord with the latter. It was not uncommon at the circus, at the theatre, or in the assemblies to see a sophist get up, like a divine messenger, in the name of eternal truth. Dionysius Chrysostom had already furnished the model of these homilies, borrowed from a polytheism greatly mitigated by philosophy, and which recalls the teachings of the Fathers of the Church. The Cynic Theagenus, at Rome, attracted the multitude to the course of lectures he gave in the gymnasium of Trajan. Maximus of Tyre in his Sermons presents to us a theology, at bottom monotheistic, in which the representations set forth are conserved only as the necessary symbols of human weakness, and which could satisfy alone the sages. All cults, according to that sometimes eloquent thinker, are an impotent effort in the direction of a unique ideal. The varieties which they present are insignificant, and ought not to be any impediment to the veritable worshipper.

Thus there was realised a veritable historical miracle, what might be called the reign of philosophers. This is the moment to study that which such a régime favoured, that which it contemned. It assisted marvellously the social and moral progress; humanity, the softening of manners, increased exceedingly; the idea of a state being governed by wisdom, benevolence, and reason was established for ever. On the other hand, the military force, art, and literature underwent a certain decadence. Philosophy and letters were far from being the same thing. The philosophers regarded with pity the frivolity of lettered persons and their taste for applause. The lettered laughed at the barbarousness of the style of the philosophers, their lack of manners, their beards, and their mantles. Marcus-Aurelius, after hesitating between the two factions, decided boldly for the philosophers. He neglected Latin, ceased to encourage the necessity of writing in that language, preferred the Greek, which was the language of his favourite authors.

The utter ruin of the Latin literature was then decided. The West decayed rapidly, whilst the East became day by day more brilliant; the dawn of Constantine was already apparent. The plastic arts, so greatly loved by Hadrian, must have appeared to Marcus-Aurelius a sort of semi-vanity. That which remains of his arch is insipid enough; everybody, even the barbarians, are given in it a dignified air; the horses have tender and philanthropic eyes. The Antonine column is a curious work, but is without delicacy in the execution, greatly inferior to the temple of Antoninus and Faustina, erected under the preceding reign. The equestrian statue of the Capitol charms us by the exact image it presents to us of the excellent emperor; but the artist has not the right to give up all boasting on this point. We feel that the total ruin of the art of design, which was accomplished in fifty years, has some profound causes. Christianity and philosophy equally contributed to it. The world began to be too indifferent to form and beauty; it asked no more than what improves the lot of the weak and sweetens the strong.

The dominant philosophy was moral in the highest degree, but it was not very scientific; it did not urge research. Such a philosophy had nothing in it incompatible with cults so little dogmatic as were those of that time. Philosophers were often invested with sacerdotal functions in their respective towns. Thus Stoicism, which contributed so powerfully to spiritual improvement, was weak against superstition; it elevated the heart, not the intellect. The number of truly learned was very small. Galienus himself is not a practical spirit; he admits medical dreams and many superstitions of the time. In spite of the laws, the most mischievous magicians succeeded. The East overflowed with its mass of chimeras. In the province every folly found followers.

Bæotia had a semi-god, a certain Sostratus, a kind of colossal idiot, leading a savage life, in whom everybody saw Hercules resuscitated. He was considered to be the good genius of the country, and they consulted him from all quarters.

A most incredible thing! the stupid religion of Alexander of Abonoticos, which we saw emerging from the depths of the Paphlagonian folly, found some adherents in the higher ranks of Roman society and among the friends of Marcus-Aurelius. Severian, legate of Cappadocia, allowed himself to be taken in by it. At Rome the people desired to see the impostor; a consular personage, Publius Mummius Sisenna Rutilianus, became his apostle, and when sixty years old found himself honoured by marrying a girl whom this base rogue pretended to have had by the moon. At Rome Alexander established certain mysteries which lasted three days; the first day they celebrated the birth of Apollo and Æsculapius; the second day the epiphany of Glycon; the third, the birth of Alexander; each one with pompous processions and dances by torchlight. There were enacted in these mysteries scenes of revolting immorality. During the plague of 166 the talismanic formulas of Alexander, engraved on the doors of houses, were believed by the superstitious multitude to be preservatives against it. At the time of the great war of Pannonia (169-171), Alexander still spoke of his serpent, and it was by his orders that two live lions were thrown into the Danube with solemn sacrifices. Marcus-Aurelius personally presided over the ceremony, attired as pontiff, surrounded by personages clothed in long robes. The two lions were beaten to death by blows of the bludgeon on the other bank, and the Romans cut in pieces. These exhibitions did not at all hurt the impostor, who, protected by Rutilianus, was able to escape all that the defenders of the good public feeling attempted to do to arrest his career. He died in his glory; statues of him were, about 178, the object of public worship, especially at Parium, where his tomb decorated the public square. Nicomedia stamped Glycon on its coins; Pergamos also honoured him. Some Latin inscriptions, found in Dacia and in Upper Mysia, prove that Glycon had a large number of devotees, and that Alexander had recognised him as a god.

This uncouth theology had even its development. They gave the serpent a female, the Dracena; they connected Glycon with the agathodemon Chnoubis and the mystic Iao. Nicomedia kept the serpent with the human head upon its coins till about 240. In 252 the religion of Glycon still flourished at Ionopolis. The name substituted by the impostor for Abonoticos has been more lasting than a thousand changes better justified. It continues in our day under the Turkish-looking name Ineboli.

Peregrinus, after his extraordinary suicide at Olympia, also obtained at Parium statues and a worship. He pronounced oracles, and sick people were cured by his intercession.

Thus intellectual progress did not advance at the same pace as social progress. Attachment to the State religion only nourished superstition, and prevented the establishment of good public education. But that was not the emperor's fault. He did what he could. The object he had in view--the improvement of men--needed centuries. Those centuries Christianity had before it; the empire had not.

The universal cause, said the emperor, is a torrent which carries everything along with it. What wretched politicians are those little men who pretend to rule the world by the maxims of philosophy; they are babies whose noses require to be wiped with a pocket-handkerchief. Man, what would you do? Do that which nature demands at the present moment. Go before it if you can and don't disturb yourself by seeking to know whether anyone occupies himself with what you are doing. Do not hope ever to have a republic like Plato's; let it he sufficient for you to improve some things, and do not regard this as a success of inconsiderable importance. How, in fact, can the inward dispositions of men be changed? And, without this change in their thoughts, what are they but slaves fastened to the yoke, people affecting a hypocritical persuasion? Come then, and tell me about Alexander, Philip, Demetrius of Phaleria. If they have only played the part of tragic actors, no one has condemned me to imitate them. The work of philosophy is simple and modest; do not persuade me therefore with a dead-house full of pretension. (Thoughts, ix. 29.)

CHAPTER IV

PERSECUTIONS AGAINST THE CHRISTIANS

The philosophy, which had so thoroughly conquered the mind of Marcus-Aurelius, was hostile to Christianity. Fronton, his tutor, seems to have been full of prejudice against the Christians; and we know that Marcus-Aurelius guarded like a religion the recollections of his youth, and the impression made by his teachers. In general, the Greek pedagogues as a class were opposed to the new culture. Proud in looking at himself as the father of his family, the preceptor considered himself injured by the illiterate catechists who acted as spies clandestinely upon his functions, and put their pupils on their guard against him. These pedants, in the world of the Antonines, enjoyed a perhaps exaggerated favour. Often the denunciations against the Christians came from conscientious teachers, who considered themselves bound to save the young people confided to their care from an indiscreet propaganda, opposed to the opinions of their families. Littérateurs of the style of Ælius Aristides did not show themselves less severe. Jews and Christians are to them impious people, who deny the gods, enemies of society, disturbers of the peace of families, intriguers who seek to intrude everywhere, to draw everything to themselves, tormenting, presumptuous, and malevolent brawlers. Some men like Galienus, of practical mind as well as philosophers or rhetoricians, showed less partiality, and without reserve praised the purity, the austerity, the pleasant manners of the inoffensive sectaries whom calumny had succeeded in transforming into odious malefactors.

The emperor's principle was to maintain the ancient Roman maxims in their integrity. It could not therefore be but that the new reign should be little favourable to the Church. Roman tradition is a dogma for Marcus-Aurelius; it incites him to virtue "like a man, like a Roman." The prejudices of the Stoic doubled themselves with those of patriot, and it has been recorded that the best of men will commit the most awkward faults by excess of earnestness, of sedulousness and conservative mind. Ah! if he had possessed something of the thoughtlessness of Hadrian or the laughter of Lucian.

Marcus-Aurelius certainly knew many Christians. He had them among his servants; he conceived little esteem for them. The kind of supernatural which formed the basis of Christianity was repugnant to him, and he had the feelings of all the Romans against the Jews. It does not appear that any edition of the Gospel text came under his eyes; the name of Jesus was, perhaps, unknown to him; that which struck him as a Stoic was the courage of the martyr. But one feature shocked him, that was their air of triumph, their way of acting in the face of death. This bravado against the law appeared hateful; as chief of the state he saw in it a danger. Stoicism, besides, did not teach one to seek death, but to endure it. Had Epictetus not represented the heroism of the "Galileans" as the effect of an obdurate fanaticism? Ælius Aristides expressed himself nearly in the same manner. Those voluntary deaths appeared to the august moralist as little rational as the theatrical suicide of Peregrinus. We find this note among his memoranda of thoughts: "A disposition of the soul always ready to be separated from the body, whether to be annihilated, to be dispersed, or to continue. When I say ready, I mean that this should be the effect of a proper judgment, not out of pure opposition, as among the Christians; it must be a reflective act, grave, capable of persuading others, without any mingling of tragic display." He was right, but the true liberal must refuse everything to fanatics, even the pleasure of being martyrs.

Marcus-Aurelius changed nothing of the established rules against the Christians. The persecutions were the result of the fundamental principles of the empire brought into combination. Marcus-Aurelius, far from exaggerating the former legislation, mitigated it with all his energy, and one of the glories of his reign is the extension he gave to the rights of colleges. His decree, pronouncing banishment on superstitious agitations, applied even more to political prophecies or to knaves who traded on the public credulity than to established religions. Yet he did not quite go to the root; he did not completely abolish the laws against the collegia illicita, and there resulted from this some application of these in the provinces infinitely to be regretted. The reproach that might be brought against him is the very same that might be addressed to the sovereigns of our day, who do not suppress, by a stroke of the pen, all the restrictive laws concerning freedom of meeting, association, the press. At the distance we are removed from him, we can see that Marcus-Aurelius, in being more thoroughly liberal, was wiser. Perhaps Christianity, left free, would have developed in a less disastrous way the theocratic and absolute principle which was in it. But we cannot reproach a statesman with having promoted a radical

17

revolution by a foresight of the events which should occur many years afterwards. Trajan, Hadrian, and Marcus-Aurelius could not understand the principles of general history and political economy which have been realised only in the 19th century, and which our last revolutions have revealed to us.

In any case as to the application of the laws, the mildness of the emperor was safe from all reproach. We have not, on this point, the right to be harder than Tertullian, who was, in infancy and youth, an eye-witness of this fatal struggle. "Consult your annals," said he to the Roman magistrates, "and you will find that the princes who have been cruel to us are those whom it was held an honour to have as persecutors. On the contrary, of all princes who have known divine and human law, name one of them who has persecuted the Christians. We might even instance one of them who declared himself their protector, the wise Marcus-Aurelius. If he did not openly revoke the edicts against our brethren, he destroyed the effect of them by the severe penalties he instituted against their accusers." The torrent of universal admiration carried away the Christians themselves. "Great" and "good"--these were the two words in which a Christian of the 3rd century summed up the character of this mild persecutor.

It is necessary to recollect that the Roman empire was ten or twelve times larger than France, and that the responsibility of the emperor for the sentences pronounced in the provinces was very small. It must be especially remembered that Christianity demanded nothing but freedom of worship; all the other religions which were tolerated were quite free in the empire; that which gave to Christianity, and formerly to Judaism, a distinct position was their intolerance, their spirit of exclusiveness. The liberty of thought was absolute. From Nero to Constantine, not a thinker, not a scholar was disturbed in his researches.

The law was the persecutor, but the people were even more so. The evil reports spread by the Jews and kept up by malignant missionaries, a sort of commercial travellers of calumny, estranged the most moderate and sincere minds. The people held by their superstitions, and were irritated against those who attacked them by sarcasm. Even some enlightened people, such as Celsus and Apuleius, believed that the political feebleness of the age arose from the progress of unbelief in the national religion. The position of the Christians was that of a Protestant missionary settled in a very Catholic town in Spain and preaching against the saints, the Virgin, and processions. The saddest episodes of persecution under Marcus-Aurelius arose from the hatred of the people. At every famine, inundation, and epidemic, the cry "The Christians to the lion!" resounded like a gloomy menace. Never had a reign witnessed so many calamities; the people believed the gods were angry, and redoubled their devotion; they called over the expiatory acts. The attitude of the Christians, in the midst of all this, remained obstinately disdainful, or even provocative. Often they received their condemnation with an insult to the judge. Before a temple or an idol they breathed hard, as if to repulse an impure thing, or made the sign of the Cross. It was not rare to see a Christian stop before a statue of Jupiter or Apollo, and say to it as he struck it with his staff: "Ah well, you see, your god does not avenge you!" The temptation was strong in such a case to arrest the sacrilegious one and to crucify him, saying, "And does your god avenge you!" The Epicurean philosophers were not less hostile to these vulgar superstitions, and yet they did not persecute them. Never did one see a philosopher forced to offer sacrifice, to swear by the emperor, or to carry flambeaux. The philosopher could have consented to those vain formalities, and that was enough without more being asked.

All the pastors, all the grave men dissuaded the faithful from going to offer themselves as martyrs; but they could not conquer a fanaticism which saw in condemnation the grandest triumph, and in punishment a kind of pleasure. In Asia this thirst for death was infectious, and produced certain phenomena analogous to those which, later on, were developed on a large scale among the "circoncellions" of Africa. One day the proconsul of Asia, Arrius Antoninus, having ordered certain rigorous proceedings against some Christians, beheld all the believers in the town present themselves in a body at the bar of his tribunal claiming the right of their co-religionists chosen for martyrdom; Arrius Antoninus, furious, made them lead a small number to punishment, sending away the others with the words, "Be off then, you wretches! If you wish so much to die you have precipices and cords!"

When, in the heart of a great state, a faction has certain interests opposed to those of all the rest, hatred is inevitable. Now the Christians desired, at bottom, that everything should go on in the worst way. Far from making common cause with the good citizens, and seeking to exorcise dangers from their native land, the Christians rejoiced in these. The Montanists and the whole of Phrygia went to the extreme of folly in their malignant prophecies against the empire. They could imagine themselves gone back to the times of the grand Apocalypse of 69. These kinds of prophecies formed a crime forbidden by law; Roman society felt instinctively that it was growing weaker; it saw but vaguely the causes of this feebleness; it laid them, not without some reason, on Christianity. It imagined that a return to the old gods would recall fortune. These gods had made the greatness of Rome; they were supposed to be irritated now by the blasphemies of the Christians. Was the way to appease them not to kill the Christians? No doubt these latter did not suspend their mockeries as to the inanity of sacrifices, and of the means they employed to ward off the plague. What would they think in England of a sceptic bursting with laughter in public on a day of feasting and prayer commanded by the Queen?

Some atrocious calumnies, some bloody scoffs were the revenge the Pagans took. The most abominable of the calumnies was the accusation of worshipping the priests by shameful embraces. The attitude of the penitent in confession gave rise to this disgraceful report. Some odious caricatures circulated among the public, and were placed on the walls. The absurd fable, according to which the Jews adored an ass, made people imagine that it was the same thing with the Christians. Here it was, the picture of a crucified person with an ass's head receiving the adoration of a half-witted lad. In other details it was one with a long cloak and long ears, the feet in clogs, and he held a book with a devout air, while this epigram was beneath the representation, DEVS CHRISTIANORVM ONOKOITHC (the only-begotten God of the Christians). An apostate Jew, who had become an attendant in the amphitheatre, painted a great caricature at Carthage in the last years of the second century. A mysterious cock, having an aphallus for a beak, and with the inscription COTHP KOCMOU (Saviour of the world), had also a relation to the Christian beliefs.

The liking of the catechists for women and children afforded scope for a thousand jests. Opposed to the dryness of Paganism, the church produced the effect of a conventicle of effeminate persons. The tender feeling of every one towards another, showed in the aspasmos and glorified by martyrdom, created a kind of atmosphere of softness, full of attraction for gentle souls, and of danger for certain others. This movement of good women concerned about the church, the habit of calling each other brother and sister, this respect for the bishop, shown by frequently kneeling before him, had something in it repulsive, and which provoked disagreeable interpretations. The grave preceptor, who saw himself deprived of his pupils by this womanish attraction, conceived for it a profound hatred, and believed that he was serving the State by seeking to revenge himself on it. Children, in fact, allowed themselves to be easily drawn by the words of mystic tenderness which reached them secretly, and sometimes this drew on them severe chastisements from their parents.

Thus persecution attained a degree of energy which it had not reached till now. The distinction between the simple fact of being a Christian and certain crimes connected with the name was forgotten. To say: "I am a Christian"--that was to sign a declaration whose consequence might be a sentence of death. Terror became the habitual condition of the Christian life. Denunciations came from all sides, especially from slaves, Jews, and Pagans. The police, knowing the days and the place when and where their meetings were held, made sudden incursions into the hall. The questioning of the inculpated persons furnished to the fanatics occasions of witticisms. The Acts of these proceedings were collected by the faithful as triumphal documents; they circulated them; they read them greedily; they made out of them a kind of literature. The appearing before the judges became a pre-occupation for which they prepared with coquetry. The reading of these papers, when the best part always fell to the accused, exalted the imagination, provoked imitators, and inspired a hatred of civil society, and a condition of things where good people could be treated thus. The fearful punishments of the Roman law were applied with all their severity. The Christian as humilior, and even as a wretch, was punished by the cross, beasts, fire, the rod. For death there was sometimes substituted condemnations to the mines, and transportation to Sardinia. Cruel mitigation! The judges, in "putting the question," were guided by a thoroughly arbitrary disposition, and sometimes a perfect perversion of ideas.

There was here a wretched spectacle. No one suffered from it more than the true friend of philosophy. But what could be done? Two contradictory things could not exist at the same time. Marcus-Aurelius was a Roman, when he persecuted he acted as a Roman. For sixty years an emperor, as good-hearted, but less enlightened in mind than Marcus-Aurelius, Alexander Severus, shall carry out without regard to any Roman maxims the true principles of liberalism; he shall grant complete freedom of conscience, and shall withdraw the laws restrictive of the liberty of meeting. We approve of that thoroughly. But Alexander Severus did this because he was a Syrian, and a stranger to the imperial tradition. He failed, besides, completely in his undertaking. All the great restorers of Roman affairs, who shall appear after him, Decius, Aurelian, Diocletian, shall return to the principles established and followed by Trajan, Antoninus, and Marcus-Aurelius. The perfect peace of conscience experienced by these men should not, therefore, surprise us; it was evidently with absolute serenity of heart that Marcus, in particular, dedicates in the Capitol a temple to his favourite goddess "Goodness."

CHAPTER V

INCREASING GRANDEUR OF THE CHURCH OF ROME--PSEUDO-CLEMENTINE WRITINGS

Rome became every day more and more the capital of Christianity, and replaced Jerusalem as the religious centre of the human race. Civitas sacrosancta! That extraordinary city was at the culminating point of its grandeur; nothing could allow one to foresee the events which, in the third century, should happen to cause it to degenerate and become nothing more than the capital of the West. Greek was at last as much spoken there as Latin, and the great rupture of the East could not be guessed. Greek was exclusively the language of the Church; the liturgy, the preaching, the propaganda were carried on in Greek.

Anicet ruled the Church with a high hand. They consulted him throughout all the Christian world. It was fully admitted that the Church of Rome had been founded by Peter; it was believed that this apostle had transmitted to his church the primacy with which Jesus had invested him; there was applied to this church the strong language in which it was believed that Jesus had conferred on Cephas the position of the corner-stone in the edifice he would build up. By unparalleled effort the Church of Rome had succeeded in remaining at the same time the church of Paul. Peter and Paul reconciled--that was the grand act which founded the ecclesiastical supremacy of Rome for the future. A new mythical duality replaced that of Romulus and Remus. We have already seen the question of Easter, the struggles of Gnosticism, those of Justin and Tatian meeting at Rome. All the controversies which rent the Christian conscience followed the same path, up till Constantine dissentients demanded from the Church of Rome an arbitration, if not a judgment. Celebrated doctors considered it a duty to visit, for their instruction, that Church in which, since the disappearance of the first Church of Jerusalem, all recognised the prestige of an ancient origin.

Among the Orientals who came to Rome under Anicet, there must be named a converted Jew, called Joseph or Hegesippus, originally no doubt from Palestine. He had received a careful Rabbinical education, knew Hebrew and Syriac, and was versed in the unwritten traditions of the Jews; but he lacked critical taste. Like the majority of converted Jews he made use of the Gospel of the Hebrews. Zeal for the purity of the faith induced him to undertake long voyages and a sort of apostolate. He went from church to church conferring with the bishops, informing himself as to their faith, arranged the succession of pastors by which they were connected with the apostles. The dogmatic agreement which he found among the bishops filled him with joy. All these little churches on the borders of the Eastern Mediterranean showed a complete accord. At Corinth, in particular, Hegesippus was specially comforted by his meeting with the primate bishop and with the faithful, whom he found in the most orthodox path. He thence embarked for Rome, where he put himself in communication with Anicet and carefully remarked the condition of tradition. Anicet had a deacon Eleutherus, who later on became in his turn bishop of Rome. Hegesippus, although a Judaiser and even an Ebionite, was delighted with these churches of Paul, and he had the more merit in this because his mind was subtle and specially inclined to observed heresies. "In every succession of bishops, in every town, things are carried out as the law, the prophets, and the Lord ordain." He settled at Rome like Justin and remained there more than twenty years, much respected by all, in spite of the surprise which his Oriental Christianity and the address of his mind would excite. Like Papias he had, in the midst of the rapid transformations of the church, the effect of "an ancient man," a sort of survivor of the apostolic age.

A material cause contributed greatly to the pre-eminence which all the churches recognised in the Church of Rome. That church was extremely rich; its property, ably administered, served as a fund for help and propagandism to other churches. The confessors condemned to the mines received a subsidy from her. The common treasury of Christianity was in some sort at Rome. The Sunday collection, a constant practice in the Roman church, was already probably established. A marvellous spirit of management animated this little community, where Judea, Greece, and Latium appeared to have mingled, in view of a prodigious future, their very diverse gifts. While the Jewish monotheism furnished the immovable basis of the new formation, while Greece continued by Gnosticism its free speculation, Rome applied itself with an astonishing persistence to the work of organisation and government. All authority, all artifices, were to it good for that end. Policy did not retreat before fraud; but policy had already chosen its seat in the most secret councils of the Church of Rome. It produced about this time a new vein of apocryphal literature, by which Roman piety sought once more to impose itself on the Christian world.

The name of Clement was the fictitious guarantee which the forgers chose to serve as a cover to their pious designs. The great reputation which the old Roman pastor had left, the right which they recognised in him to give in some sort his recommendatory note to the books which were worthy of circulation, recommended him for this position. Upon the basis of the Cerygmata and Periodi of Peter, an unknown author, a Pagan born and introduced into Christianity by the Esseno-Ebionite door, built up a romance of which Clement was supposed to be at once the author and the hero. This precious document, entitled The Confessions, because of the surprises of the denouement, has reached us in two editions different enough from each other, and of which probably neither the one nor the other is the original. Both appear to be derived from a lost document, which made at the time we speak of its first appearance.

The author sets out from the hypothesis that Clement was the immediate successor of Peter in the presidency of the Church of Rome, and received from the prince of the apostles the episcopal ordination. Just as the Cerygmata were dedicated to James, just as the new romance bore as a heading an epistle where Clement recounted to James, "Bishop of bishops and chief of the Holy Church of the Hebrews at Jerusalem," the violent death of Peter, and narrates how that apostle, the first of them all, the true companion, the true friend of Jesus, constituted by Jesus the only foundation of the Church, has established him, Clement, as his successor in the episcopate of Rome, and has recommended him to write compendiously, and to address to James the record of their journeys and their preachings in common. The work does not speak of Peter's sojourn at Rome nor of the circumstances of his death. These last accounts doubtless formed the basis of a second work which was of service to him who has preserved them to us.

The Ebionite spirit, hostile to Paul, which formed the basis of the first Cerygmata, is here much effaced. Paul is not named in the whole work. It is surely not without reason that the author affects not to know other apostles than the twelve presided over by Peter and James, and that he attributes to Peter only the honour of having spread Christianity in the Pagan world. In a multitude of places the wrongs of the Judeo-Christians were still to be seen, but all is said in a half word; a disciple of Paul could scarcely read the book without being shocked. Little by little, indeed, this calumnious history of apostolic struggles, invented by a hateful school, but which had some portions made to please all the Christians, lost its sectarian colour, became almost catholic, and was adopted by the greatest number of the faithful. The allusions against St. Paul were obscure enough. Simon the Magician stands charged with everything odious in the story; the allusions his name had served to fail were forgotten; nothing more than a double of Nero in the infernal rôle of Antichrist.

The work is composed according to all the rules of ancient romance. Nothing is wanting: travels, love episodes, shipwrecks, twins which resemble each other, people taken by pirates, recognition of people separated for long years. Clement, from a confusion which arises from a very ancient epoch, was considered to belong to the imperial family. Mattidia, his mother, is a perfectly chaste Roman lady, married to the noble Faustus. Pursued with a criminal love by her brother-in-law, wishing at the same time to save her honour and the reputation of her family, she quits Rome, with her husband's permission, and goes to Athens to educate her sons, Faustinus and Faustinian. At the end of four years, not receiving news of them, Faustus embarks with his third son, Clement, to go in search of his wife and her sons. After a thousand adventures the father, the mother, and the three sons meet. They were not Christians at first, but all deserved to be, and all became so. As Pagans they had had honest morals; and charity has this privilege, that God owes it to Himself to save those who practise it by natural instinct. "If it were not an absolute rule that no one could be saved without baptism the chaste Pagan would be saved." The infidels who are converted are those who have deserved it by their regulated morals. Clement, in fact, meets the apostles, Peter and Barnabas, makes them his companions, recounts to us their preachings, their contest with Simon, and becomes for all the members of his family the occasion of a conversion, for which they were so well prepared.

This romantic framework is only a pretext for making an apology for the Christian religion, and for showing how superior it is to the philosophical and theurgic opinion of the age. St. Peter is no longer the apostle we know by the Acts and the letters of Paul; he is a skilful polemic--a master, who brings all the trickeries of the sophist's art into the service of the truth. The ascetic life he led, his rigorous xerophagy, repelled the Essenes. His wife travels with him as a deaconess. The ideas which were given of the social condition, in the midst of which Jesus and his apostles lived, had already become altogether erroneous. The most simple data of apostolic theology were unknown. It must be said, to the author's praise, that if his confidence in the credulity of the public is very naïve, he has at least a belief in discussion which does honour to his tolerance. He admits readily that one may be innocently deceived. Among the figures of the romance Simon the Magician alone is altogether sacrificed. His disciples, Apion and Anubion, represent, the first, the effort to draw from mythology something religious; the second, the misguided sincerity which shall one day be rewarded by the knowledge of the truth. Simon and Peter dispute metaphysically, Clement and Apion discuss morally. A touching shade of pity and sympathy with the erring spreads a charm over these pages, which we feel are written by one who has passed through the throes of scepticism, and knows better than any other how we may suffer and acquire merit in seeking the truth. Clement, like Justin of Neapolis, has tried all the philosophies, the lofty problems of the immortality of the soul, future rewards and punishments, Providence, the relations of man with God possess his mind; no school has satisfied him; he is despairingly about to plunge into the grossest superstitions when the voice of Christ comes to him. He finds, in the teaching which has been given as that of Christ, the reply to all his doubts; he is a Christian.

The system of refutation of Paganism which shall make the basis of the argumentation of all the Fathers is already found complete in the pseudo-Clement. The primitive meaning of mythology was lost everywhere; the old physical myths became unseemly tales, offered no food for the soul. It was easy to show that the gods of Olympus have given very bad examples, and that the man who imitates them would be a villain. Apion vainly seeks to escape by symbolic explanations. Clement establishes without difficulty the absolute powerlessness of polytheism to produce a serious morality. Clement has unconquerable demands of soul; honest, pious, candid, he wishes a religion which shall satisfy his lively sensibility. One moment the two adversaries recall the souvenirs of youth, of which they now make arms to fight. Apion had once been the guest of Clement's father. Seeing the latter sad and sick one day from the anguish which seeking the truth gave him, Apion, who had medical pretensions, asked him what was wrong. "The disease of the young. I have a disease of the soul!" replied Clement. Apion thought he was a prey to love, made him the most unseemly proposals, and composed for him a piece of erotic literature, which Clement brings into the debate with more malice than reason.

The philosophy of the book is Deism, considered as the fruit of a revelation, not of reason. The author speaks of God, of His nature, attributes, and Providence, of evil, regarded as a proof and as a source of merit for man, in the style of Glycon and Epictetus. A lucid and correct mind, opposed to the Montanist aberrations, and to the quasi-polytheism of the Gnostics, the author of the pseudo-Clementine romance is a strict monotheist, or, as might be said, a monarchist. God is the being whose essence is of Himself alone. The Son is by nature inferior to Him. These ideas, very analogous to those of the pseudo-Hermias, were long the basis of the Roman theology. Far from being revolutionary thoughts, they were at Rome the conservative ideas. It was at bottom the theology of the Nazarenes and the Ebionites, or rather of Philo and the Essenes, developed in the Gnostic sense. The world is the theatre and the struggle of good and evil. The good gains always a little upon the evil, and at last will overcome it. The partial triumphs of good are wrought by means of the appearance of successive prophets, Adam, Abel, Enoch, Abraham, Noah, Moses; or rather a single prophet, Adam, immortal and impeccable, the typical man par excellence, the perfect image of God, the Christ, ever living, ever changing in form and name, pervading the world unceasingly and fulfilling history, preaching eternally the same law in the name of the same Holy Spirit.

The true law of Moses had nearly realised the ideal of the absolute religion. But Moses wrote nothing, and his institutions were altered by his successors. The sacrifices were a victory of Paganism over the pure law. A crowd of errors have slipped into the Old Testament. David, with his harp and his bloody wars, is a prophet quite inferior. The other prophets were still less perfect, Adam-Christs. The Greek philosophy, on its side, is a tissue of chimeras--a true logomachy. The prophetic spirit, which is nothing else than the Holy Spirit manifested, the primitive man, Adam, such as God made him, has appeared now in a last Christ, in Jesus, who is Moses himself; so much so that between them there is no contest or rivalry. To believe in the one is to believe in the other--it is to believe in God. The Christian, by being a Christian, does not cease to be a Jew (Clement gave himself always this latter name; he and all his family "were Jews"). The Jew who knows Moses and does not know Jesus shall not be condemned if he practises well what he knows, and does not hate what he is ignorant of. The Christian of Pagan origin, who knows Jesus and does not know Moses, shall not be condemned if he observes the law of Jesus, and does not hate the law which has been revealed to him. Revelation, besides, is only the ray by which some truths, hidden in all men's hearts, become visible to each of them; to know this is not to apprehend--it is to comprehend.

The relation of Jesus to God has been that of all the other prophets. He has been the instrument of the Spirit, that is all. The ideal Adam, who is found more or less obscured in every man coming into this world, is, according to the prophet, master of the world, in the condition of clear knowledge and full possession. "Our Lord," says Peter, "has never said that there should be another God than He who created everything, and did not proclaim Himself God: He has only, with good reason, declared the man blessed who has proclaimed Him Son of the God who has created all." "But does it not appear," said Simon, "as if He, who comes from God, is God?" "How can that be?" said Peter. "The essence of the Father has not been begotten, the essence of the Son is begotten; therefore he who has been begotten cannot compare himself to him who has begotten himself. He who is not in everything identical with another being cannot have the same names in common with him." The author never speaks of the death of Jesus, and seems to attach no theological importance to that death.

Jesus is then a prophet, the last of the prophets, he whom Moses had announced as coming after him. His religion is only a clearer edition of that of Moses, a choice between traditions, of which some are good and others bad. His religion is perfect; it suits Jews and Greeks, educated and barbarous men alike; it satisfies alike the heart and the mind. It is continued in due course by the twelve apostles, of whom Peter is chief, and by those who hold their powers from them. The appeal to dreams, private visions, is presumptuous.

An odd mingling of Ebionism and philosophical liberalism, of strict catholicism and heresy, of exalted love for Jesus and of fear lest his part should be exaggerated, of profane instruction and of chimerical philosophy, of rationalism and faith--the book could not long satisfy orthodoxy; but it suited an age of syncretism, in which the points of the Christian faith were badly defined. It needed the prodigies of sagacity of modern criticism to recognise the satire of Paul behind the mask of Simon Magus. The book is, in short, a book of conciliation. It is the work of a moderate Ebionite, of an eclectic mind, opposed at once to the unjust judgments of the Gnostics, and of Marcion against Judaism, and to the effeminate prophesying of the disciples of Montanus. Circumcision is not commanded; yet the circumcised have a rank superior to the uncircumcised. Jesus is equal to Moses; Moses is as good as Jesus. Perfection is to see that both of them constitute only one, that the new law is the old, and the old the new. Those who have the one can do without the other. Let each one abide by his own, and let him not hate others.

It was, it will be seen, the absolute denial of the doctrine of Paul. Jesus is to our theologian a restorer rather than an innovator. In the very work of this restoration, Jesus is only the interpreter of a tradition of sages, who, in the midst of the general corruption, had never lost the true meaning of the law of Moses, which is itself nothing but the religion of Adam, the primitive religion of humanity. According to the pseudo-Clement, Jesus is Adam himself. According to St. Paul, Jesus is a second Adam, altogether opposed to the first. The idea of the fall of Adam, the basis of the theology of St. Paul, nearly disappears here. On one side especially the author shows himself more reasonable than Paul. The latter never ceases to protest that man owes to no personal merit his election and Christian calling. The Ebionite, more liberal, believes that the honest Pagan makes a way for his conversion by his virtues. He is far from thinking that all acts of unbelievers are sins. The merits of Jesus have not, in his eyes, the transcendent part they possess in the system of Paul. Jesus places man in a relation to God, but he does not substitute himself for God.

The Roman pseudo-Clementine separates himself clearly from the truly authentic writings of the first Christian inspiration by his prolixity, his rhetoric, his abstract philosophy, borrowed for the most part from the Greek schools. There is no longer here a Semitic book, shadowless, like the purely Judeo-Greek writings. A great admirer of Judaism, the author possesses a Græco-Italian mind, a political mind, preoccupied above all with the social needs, with the morale of the people. His culture is quite Hellenic; in Hellenism he only repels one thing--the religion. The author shows himself in every point quite superior to St. Justin. A considerable fraction of the Church adopted the work, and gave it a place beside the most reverenced books of the apostolic age, upon the borders of the New Testament. The gross errors which we read here as to the divinity of Jesus Christ, and as to the sacred books, are opposed to the rest of the work. But people continued to read it; the orthodox replied to exert thing by saying that Clement had written his book without a blemish, but that some heretics had altered it. Some extracts were made in which the offensive passages were omitted, and to which they readily attributed inspiration. We have seen, and we shall see, many other examples of romances invented by the heretics, forcing thus the gates of the orthodox Church, and causing themselves to be accepted by her, because they were edifying and capable of furnishing a nourishment to piety.

The fact is that this Ebionite literature, in spite of its rather childish freshness, had the Christian unction in the highest degree. The tone was that of a moving preaching; its character was essentially ecclesiastical and pastoral. The pseudo-Clement is a partisan of the hierarchy quite as enthusiastic as the pseudo-Ignatius. The community recapitulates itself in its chief; the clergy is the indispensable mediator between God and His flock. The bishop's meaning must be taken at once; one must not wait till he says "Such a man is my enemy" to shun that man. To be a friend of anyone whom the bishop does not love, to speak to one whom he shuns--that is to place oneself out of the church, to pass into the ranks of its worst enemies. The office of a bishop is so difficult! Everybody ought to labour to make it easy for him; the deacons are the eyes of the bishop, they ought to survey everything, to know everything for him. A sort of espionage is recommended; what maybe called the clerical spirit has never been expressed in stronger language.

Abstinence and Essenian practices were placed very high. Purity of manners was the principal preoccupation of these worthy sectaries. The adulterer in their eyes is worse than the homicide. "The chaste woman is the most beautiful object in the world--the most perfect reminiscence of God's primitive creation. The pious woman, who only finds her pleasure with the saints, is the ornament, the perfume, the example of the Church; she helps the pure to be pure; she delights God Himself. God loves her, is pleased with her, watches over her; she is His child, the bride of the Son of God, clothed as she is with holy light."

Those mystic images do not constitute the author a partisan of virginity. He is too much a Jew for that. He wishes the priest to marry the young people in good time, causing even the old to marry. The Christian woman loves her husband, covers him with caresses, makes much of him, serves him, seeks to please him, obeys him in all which is not a disobedience to God! To be loved by another than her husband is for her a living misery. Ah! how foolish is the man who seeks to separate his wife from the fear of God! The grand source of chastity is the Church. It is there that woman learns her duties, and hears of this judgment of God which punishes a moment of pleasure by an eternal punishment. The husband ought to compel his wife to go to hear such sermons, if he cannot succeed by persuasion.

"But what is better," adds the author, addressing himself to the husband, "is that you come yourself, leading her by the hand, that you also may be chaste, and capable of understanding the happiness of honourable marriage. To become a father, to love your children, to be loved by them, all this is at your disposal, if you desire it. He who wishes to have a chaste wife loves chastely, pays her conjugal duties, eats with her, lives with her, goes with her to the sanctifying preaching, does not grieve her or scold her without reason, seeks to please, procures for her all the pleasures he can, and makes up for those he cannot give her by caresses. Those caresses, besides, the chaste wife does not need in order that she should fulfil her duties. She looks on her husband as her master. Is he poor, she bears with his poverty; she is hungry with him, if he is hungry; if he emigrates, she emigrates; she consoles him when he is sad; when she has even a dowry larger than what her husband possesses, she takes the inferior attitude of one who has nothing. The husband, on his side, if he has a poor wife, ought to consider her wisdom as an ample dowry. The prudent woman is temperate in eating and drinking; . . . . she never remains alone with young men, she even avoids old men; she shuns boisterous laughter . . . . she delights in grave conversations, she avoids those which have not the marks of decorum."

The good Mattidia, Clement's mother, is an actual example of the practice of these pious maxims. A Pagan, she sacrifices everything to chastity; chastity preserves her from the greatest perils, and is as good to her as the knowledge of the true religion.

Christian preaching developed itself, became blended with culture. The sermon was the essential part of the sacred meeting. The Church became the mother of all edification and consolation. The rules as to ecclesiastical discipline were already multiplied. To give them authority they referred them to the apostles, and as Clement was thought the best guarantee where apostolic traditions were concerned, since he had been in intimate relations with Peter and Barnabas, it was still under the name of that revered pastor that we see dawning a whole apocryphal literature of Constitutions reputed to be founded by the College of the Twelve. The nucleus of this apocryphal compilation, the first basis of a collection of ecclesiastical canons, was preserved, very nearly without admixture, among the Syrians. Among the Greek, the collection, increased by time, sensibly altered, and became barely recognisable. It was quoted as forming part of the Sacred Scriptures, although certain reservations always rendered its authenticity doubtful. In course of time, liberty was granted to give this collection of pretended apostolic writings the form which was considered best to strike the faithful and to impress them; the name of Clement was always inscribed at the head of these various editions, which present besides marks of the strictest relationship with the romance of The Confessions. All the pseudo-Clementine literature of the second century presents thus the character of a complete unity.

What characterises it in the highest degree is the spirit of practical organisation. Already in the supposed epistle of Clement to James, which serves as a preface to The Confessions, Peter, before dying, holds a long discourse on the episcopate, its duties, its difficulties, its excellence, on the priests, the deacons, the catechists, which is like a new edition of the epistles to Titus and Timothy. The Apostolic Constitutions were a kind of codification, growing gradually larger, of these pastoral precepts. What Rome founded was not dogma; few churches were more barren in speculation, less pure as to the question of doctrine. Ebionism, Montanism, Artemonism, held the majority there, one after the other. What Rome made is discipline, is Catholicism.

At Rome probably the expression "Catholic Church" was written for the first time. Bishop, priest, layman, all these words took a fixed meaning in that Hierarchical Church. The church was a ship where each dignitary has his function concerning the safety of the passengers. Morality was severe and the cloister was already known. The mere liking for riches is condemned. The ornamentation of women is nothing but an invitation to sin. Woman is responsible for the sins of thought which she causes to be committed. Certainly, if she repels advances the evil is lessened; but is it nothing to be the cause of perdition to others? To live modestly occupied by her duties, to go her own way without mixing herself up with the gossiping of the street, to rear her children well, to administer frequent corrections to them, to forbid them dining in company with persons of their own age, to have them married in good time, not to read Pagan books (the Bible is sufficient and contains everything), not to take baths oftener than necessary and with great precautions, such were the rules for laymen. The bishops, the priests, the deacons, the widows, had more complicated duties. Besides holiness, they were to bring wisdom and sagacity into these functions. They were true magistrates--very superior to profane magistrates. Christians brought all their cases before the tribunal of the bishop, the dicaster of this last became in fact a civil jurisdiction which had its rules and its laws. The household of the bishop was already considerable; it came to be supported at the common expense of the faithful. The ideas of the ancient law as to the tithe and the offerings due to the priests were little by little restored. A strong theocracy was becoming established.

The Church, in fact, absorbed everything; civil society was disparaged and despised. To the emperor belonged the census and the official salutations, that was all. The Christian constituted thus could only live with Christians. He was recommended to attract the heathen by the charm of amiable manners, in the hope that they might be converted. But beyond this hope the relations with the unbelievers were surrounded with such precautions, and implied so much disgust, that those became very rare. A mixed society of Pagans and Christians would be impossible. It was forbidden to take part in the rejoicings of the heathen, to eat or to amuse oneself with them, to be present at their spectacles, at their games, or at any of their grand profane re-unions. Even the public markets were interdicted, save in what concerned the purchase of necessary articles. On the contrary, Christians ought to eat together as much as possible, and live together, and form a little coterie of saints. In the third century that spirit of recluseness shall produce its own results. Roman society will die of exhaustion, a concealed cause will keep itself in life. When a considerable portion of a state makes a combination apart, and ceases to work for the common good, that state is almost ready to die.

Mutual assistance was the principal duty in that society of the poor, administered by its bishops, its deacons, and its widows. The position of the rich man in the midst of small citizens and small honourable merchants, judging their affairs among themselves, scrupulous as to weights and measures, was difficult and embarrassing. The Christian life was not made for him. A brother dies, leaving orphans, boys and girls, and another brother adopts them, and marries the daughter to his son if their ages be suitable. This appeared quite simple. The rich people took with difficulty to a system so fraternal: then they were threatened with the forfeiture of their possessions, which they could not use well, and people applied to them the dictum: "What the saints have not eaten the Assyrians eat." The money of the poor was held as a sacred thing; those who were in easy circumstances paid a subsidy as large as they could; these were called "the contributions of the Lord."

Delicacy was pushed to such an extent that everybody's money was not received in the Church's treasury. They rejected the offerings of tavern-keepers and of people who practised shameful trades; especially those of the excommunicated, who sought by their generosity to return to favour. "These people there would give," it was said, "and if we refuse their alms what shall we do to assist our widows, or to nourish the poor of the people?" "Better to die of hunger," was the Ebionite fanatic's reply, "than be under an obligation to the enemies of God for gifts which are an affront in the eyes of His friends. Acceptable offerings are those which the workman takes from the fruit of his toil. When the priest is obliged to receive the money of the wicked, let him use it for the purchase of wood and coal, so that the widow and the orphan may not be condemned to live upon polluted money. The presents of the wicked are thus food for the fire, not nourishment for believers." It is thus seen what a tight chain wound about the Christian life. Such an abyss separated, in the mind of those worthy sectaries, good and evil, that the conception of a liberal society, where each one acts according to his taste, under the regulation of civil laws, without giving an account to any or exercising a surveillance over others, appeared to them the height of impiety.

CHAPTER VI

TATIAN--THE TWO SYSTEMS OF APOLOGY

Tatian, after Justin's death, remained some years at Rome. He continued there his master's school, professing for him always the loftiest admiration, but each day deviating more and more from his mind. He had some distinguished pupils, among others the Asiatic Rodon, a fertile writer who became later on one of the supports of orthodoxy against Marcion and Apelles. It was probably in the first year of the reign of Marcus-Aurelius that Tatian composed this document, hard and incorrect in style, sometimes lively and piquant, which passes rightly for one of the most original monuments of the Christian apologetics of the 2nd century.

The work is entitled "Against the Greeks." The hatred of Greece was indeed Tatian's dominant sentiment. A true Syrian, he was jealous of and hated the arts and literature which had conquered the admiration of the human race. The Pagan gods seemed to him the personification of immorality. The world of Greek statues he saw at Rome gave him no rest. Going over the personages in whose honour they had been erected, he found that nearly all, male and female, had been people of evil life. The horrors of the amphitheatre revolted him with better reason; but he confounded with the Roman cruelties the national games and the theatre of the Greeks. Euripides, Menander, appeared to him as masters of debauch, and (a desire which was too much listened to!) he wished their works to be destroyed.

Justin had taken as the basis of his apology a very wide sentiment. He had dreamed of a reconciliation of the Christian dogmas and Greek philosophy. That was assuredly a grand illusion. It did not require much effort to see that the Greek philosophy, essentially rational, and the new faith, proceeding from the supernatural, were enemies of each other, and that only one could remain on the ground. The apologetic method of St. Justin is narrow and perilous for the faith. Tatian felt that, and it is upon the very ruins of Greek philosophy that he seeks to raise the edifice of Christianity. Like his master, Tatian possessed a wide Greek erudition; like him he had no critical qualities, and mixed up, in the most arbitrary fashion, the authentic and the apocryphal, what he knew and what he did not know. Tatian's is a mind sombre, heavy, violent, full of wrath against the civilisation and against the Greek philosophy, to which he much prefers that of the East, what he calls the barbarian philosophy. An erudition of base alloy, like that which Josephus had shown in his work against Apion, came here to his help. Moses is, according to him, much more ancient than Homer. The Greeks have invented nothing of themselves; they have taken everything from other nations, notably the Orientals. They only excelled in the art of writing; for the foundation of their ideas they are as ignorant as other nations. The Grammarians are the cause of the whole evil; those are they who by their lies have embellished error and created that usurped reputation which is the principal obstacle to the triumph of the truth. The Assyrians, Phoenicians, Egyptians --those are the true authorities!

Far from ameliorating men, Greek philosophy has not known how to preserve its votaries from the greatest crimes. Diogenes was intemperate, Plato a gourmand, Aristotle servile. The philosophers have all the vices among them; they are the blind disputing with the deaf. The laws of the Greeks were worth no more than their philosophy; they differ from each other; whereas the good law ought to be common to all men. Among the Christians, on the contrary, there is no disagreement. Rich, poor, men and women have the same opinions. By a bitter irony of fate, Tatian was to die a heretic, and to prove that Christianity was not more sheltered than philosophy was from schisms and party divisions.

Justin and Tatian, although lifelong friends, represented already in the most characteristic manner the two opposing attitudes which Christian apologists shall take in regard to philosophy. The one class; at bottom Greeks, while reproaching Pagan society with the looseness of its manners, shall admit its arts, its general culture, its philosophy. The other class, Syrians or Africans, shall not see in Hellenism but a mass of wickedness and absurdities; they shall much prefer the "barbarian" to Greek wisdom; insult and sarcasm shall be their habitual arms.

The moderate school of Justin seemed at first to gain. Some writings quite analogous to those of the philosophy of Naplouse, especially the Logos paræneticos, the Logos addressed to the Greeks, and the treatise On Monarchy, characterised by numerous Pagan Sibylline and pseudo-Chaldean quotations, began to group themselves around his principal works. They were yet fresh. The unknown author of the

Logos paræneticos, the tolerant Athenagoras, the clever Minucius Felix, Clement of Alexandria, and, up to a certain point, Theophilus of Antioch, sought for all their dogmas some rational foundation. Even the most mysterious dogmas, the strangest to Greek philosophy, like the resurrection of the body, have, for these wide theologians, Greek antecedents. Christianity has, according to them, its roots in man's heart; it completes what the natural lights have begun; far from raising itself upon the ruins of reason, Christianity is only its complete development; it is the true philosophy. Everything leads us to believe that the lost apology of Melito was conceived in this spirit. The more or less Gnostic school of Alexandria, by adhering to this same sort of view, shall give it, in the third century, immense celebrity. It shall proclaim, like Justin, that the Greek philosophy is the preparation for Christianity, the ladder which leads to Christ. Platonism especially, by its idealistic tendency, is, for these phil-Hellenic Christians, the object of marked favour. Clement of Alexandria speaks of the Stoics with nothing but admiration. According to him each school of philosophy has laid hold of a particle of the truth. He goes so far as to say that, in order to know God, the Jews had had the prophets, the Greeks had had philosophy, and some inspired beings, such as the Sibyl and Hystaspes, so much so that a third Testament had created spiritual knowledge, and reduced the other two revelations to the condition of obsolete forms.

But Christian feeling shall display a lively antipathy to those concessions of an apology sacrificing the severity of dogmas to a desire to please those whom it wishes to gain. The author of the Epistle to Diognetus nearly approaches Tatian in the extreme harshness with which he judges Greek philosophy. The Sarcasm of Hermias is pitiless. The author of Philosophumena looks upon ancient philosophy as the source of all heresies. This method of apology, the only really Christian one, to speak the truth, shall be taken up by Tertullian with unparalleled talent. The rough African shall oppose to the enervating weaknesses of the Hellenic apologists the disdain of Credo quia absurdum. He is in this only the interpreter of St. Paul's idea. "They are extinguishing Christ," the great apostle would have said in view of this soft complaisance. If the philosophers could, by the natural progress of their ideas, save the world, why has Christ come? Why has he been crucified? Socrates, you say, knew Christ to some extent. It is then likewise partly by the merits of Socrates that you are justified!

The mania for demonological explanations is, with Tatian, pushed to the height of absurdity. Among the apologists his is the most barren of the philosophic mind. But his vigorous attack upon Paganism did much to condone this. The discourse against the Greeks was much praised even by men who, like Clement of Alexandria, were far from having any hatred against Greece; the charlatan-like scholarship which the author had put into his work created a school. Ælius Aristides seems to allude to this when, taking exactly the opposite of our author's idea, he represents the Jews as a sad race who have created nothing, strangers to belles-lettres and philosophy, only knowing how to disparage the Hellenic glories, arrogating to themselves the name of "philosophers" only by a complete reversal of the sense of the word.

The heavy paradoxes of Tatian against the ancient civilisation were nevertheless to triumph. That civilisation had in fact done great injury; it neglected the intellectual education of the people. The people, deprived of elementary instruction, were a prey to all the surprises of ignorance, and believed every one of the chimeras of which they were told with assurance and conviction.

As to what concerns Tatian, good sense had, at least, its revenge. This Lamennais of the second century followed, in many respects, the line of the Lamennais of our time. The exaggeration of mind and a kind of savageness which shock us in his discourse cast him out of the orthodox church. These extreme apologists became almost always an embarrassment to the cause they had defended.

Already, in the discourse against the Greeks, Tatian is moderately orthodox. Like Apelles he believes that God, absolute in Himself, produces the Word, who created matter and produces the world. Like Justin, he declares the soul to be an aggregation of elements; that of its essence it is mortal and in darkness; that it is only by its union with the Holy Spirit that it becomes luminous and immortal. Then his fanatical character threw him into the excess of a hypercriticism on nature. By the kind of errors he showed and by his style, at once spiritual and rough, Tatian was to be the prototype of Tertullian. He wrote with the fulness and enthusiasm of a sincere mind, not quite clear. More excitable than Justin, if less regulated by discipline, he cannot, like himself, reconcile his liberty with the exigencies of all. So long as his master lived he frequented the church, and the church upheld him. After Justin's martyrdom, he lived in an isolated manner, without connection with the faithful, like a sort of independent Christian, making a people quite separate. The desire to have a school led him astray, according to Jerome. That which undid him, we believe, was rather the desire to be alone.

CHAPTER VII

DECADENCE OF GNOSTICISM

Christianity, at the point we have arrived at, had, if we may thus express it, reached the complete bloom of its youth. Life with it abounded, overflowed; no contradiction arrested it; it had representatives for all tendencies, advocates for all causes. The nucleus of the Catholic Church and orthodoxy was already so strong that all sorts of fancies could be found beside her without injuring her. Apparently, the sects denounced the Church of Jesus; but these sects remained isolated without consistency, and disappeared, for the most part, after having satisfied for a moment the needs of the little group which had created them. It is not that their action was barren; the almost individual secret instructions were at the moment of their highest popularity. Heresies almost always triumphed by their very condemnation. Gnosticism especially was chased out of the church and it was everywhere; the Orthodox Church, by striking at it with its anathema, impregnated itself with it. Among the Judeo-Christians, Ebionites and Essenes, it flowed along over the banks.

When a religion begins to count a large number of partisans, it loses for a time certain of the advantages which have contributed to found it; for man is better pleased and finds more comfort in the little gathering than in the numerous church, where he is not known. As the public power did not direct its energy in the service of the Orthodox Church, the religious situation was that which England and America present at this day. The chapels, if one may say so, were multiplied in all directions. The chiefs of the sects struggled to obtain influence over the faithful, as in our times this is done by the Methodist preachers, the innumerable Dissenters of free countries. The faithful were a sort of curacy driven off by greedy sectaries, more like hungry dogs than pastors. The women especially were the coveted prey; when they were widows and in possession of property, they never were but surrounded by young and clever directors, who strove by mildness and complaisance to monopolise the cure of souls, at once fruitful and sweet.

The Gnostic doctors had, in this hunt for souls, great advantages. Affecting a higher intellectual culture and less rigid manners, they found a sure clientèle among the richer classes, who desired to be distinguished and to escape the common discipline prescribed for the poor. Contact with the Pagans, and the perpetual contraventions of police rules which a member of the church was led to commit, contraventions which exposed him constantly to martyrdom, became tremendous difficulties for a Christian occupying a certain social position. Far from pressing towards martyrdom, the Gnostics furnished means to escape it. Basilides and Heracleon protested against the immoderate honours rendered to the martyrs; the Valentinians went further: in the time of hot persecution they advised that the faith should be denied, alleging that God did not demand from His adorers the sacrifice of life, and that it was better to confess Him less before men than before the Æons.

They did not exercise less seduction among rich women, in whom their independence inspired the desire for a personal position. The Orthodox Church followed the severe rule laid down by St. Paul, which forbade all participation by the woman in the exercises of the church. In these little sects, on the contrary, women baptized, officiated, presided at the liturgy, and prophesied. As opposed as possibly could be in manners and mind, the Gnostics and the Montanists had this in common, that, by the side of their doctors, a female prophetess was found; Helen beside Simon, Philumena beside Apelles, Priscilla and Maximilla beside Montanus, and quite a galaxy of women around Markos and Marcion. Fable and calumny took possession of a circumstance which lent itself to misapprehension. Many of these dependents could only have been allegories without reality, or inventions of the orthodox. But certainly the modest position which the Catholic Church always imposed on women, and which became the cause of their ennoblement, was not quite observed in these petty sects, subjected to a less rigorous rule, and little accustomed, in spite of their apparent holiness, to practise true piety, which is self-denial.

The three great systems of Christian philosophy which had appeared under Hadrian, that of Valentinus, that of Basilides, that of Saturninus, were developed without being much improved. The chiefs of these systems still lived or had successors. Valentinus, although thrice driven from the church, was much sought after. He left Rome to return to the East; but his sect continued to flourish in the capital. He died about the year 160 in the island of Cyprus. His disciples were all over the world. There was a difference between the doctrine of the East and that of Italy. The chiefs of the former were

Ptolemy and Heracleon; Secundus and Theodotus at first, then Axiomicus and Bardesanus, directed the Oriental branch. The Valentinian school was much the most serious and Christian of all those which bore the general name of Gnostics. Heracleon and Ptolemy were learned exegetes in the Epistles of Paul, and the Gospel called that of John. Heracleon, in particular, was a real Christian doctor, by whom Clement of Alexandria and Origen profited a great deal. Clement has preserved to us from him one beautiful and elevated page on martyrdom. The writings of Theodotus were also habitually in Clement's hand, and some extracts appear to us to have come from them into the great mass of notes' made by the laborious Stromatist.

In many points of view, the Valentinians might pass for enlightened and moderate Christians, but there was at the bottom of their moderation a principle of pride. The Church was not, in their eyes, a depository of anything but a minimum of truth, barely sufficient for ordinary men. The basis of things was known to them alone. Under the pretext that they made part of the psychical world and could not fail to be saved, they gave themselves unheard-of liberties, ate of everything without distinction, went to Pagan festivals, and even to the cruellest spectacles, fled from persecution, and even spoke against martyrdom. They were people of the world, free in manners and conversation, treating as prudery and bigotry the extreme reserve of the Catholics, who feared a light word, even an imprudent thought. The direction of women, in such circumstances, presented many dangers. Some of these Valentinian pastors were plainly seducers; others affected modesty; "but soon," says Irenæus, "the sister became enceinte by the brother." They arrogated superior intelligence to themselves, and left to the simple faithful the faith, "which is very different." Their exegesis was learned but barely safe. When they were pressed with texts of Scripture, they said the Scripture had been corrupted. When apostolic tradition was contrary to them, they no longer hesitated to reject it. They had, it appeared, a gospel which they called "The Gospel of the Truth." They really ignored the Gospel of Christ. They substituted for salvation by faith or by works a salvation by gnosis, that is to say, by the knowledge of a pretended truth. If such a tendency had prevailed, Christianity would have ceased to be a moral fact, to become a cosmogony and a metaphysic without influence on the general progress of humanity.

It was not, moreover, with impunity that they flashed abstruse formulas in the people's eyes, keeping back to themselves the meaning. One single Valentinian book remains to us, "The Believer's Wisdom"; and it shows us to what a height of extravagance certain speculations had arrived--beautiful enough in the mind of their authors when they fell upon puerile minds. Jesus, after his resurrection, was reported to have passed eleven years on the earth to teach his disciples the highest truths. He told them the history of Piste Sophia; how she, enticed by her imprudent desire to seize the light she had seen at a distance, fell into the material chaos; how she was for a long time persecuted by the other Æons, who refused her rank to her; how at length she accomplished a series of proofs of repentance, until at last one sent from heaven, Jesus, descended for her from the luminous region. Sophia is saved by having believed in this Saviour before she had seen him. All this is expressed in a prolix style, with the wearisome process of amplification and hyperbole of the apocryphal gospels. Mary, Peter, Magdalene, Martha, John Parthenos, and the different Gospel personages play an almost ludicrous part. But the people, who found dryness in the restrained enough circle of the Jewish and Judeo-Christian Scriptures, took pleasure in these dreams, and many owed to such readings the opportunity of knowing Christ. The mysterious forms of the sect rested before everything on oral instruction, and its successive degrees of imitation fascinated the imagination and made them hold firmly to the revelations which they had obtained in consequence of so many trials. After Marcion, Valentinus was the heretic whose colleges were most frequented. Bardesanus, at Edessa, succeeded, by inspiring himself with it, in creating a large school of Christian instruction, such as had never been seen. We shall speak later on of this singular phenomenon.

Saturninus always had numerous disciples. Basilides had his successor, his son Isidore. There wrought, besides, in this world of sects, certain fusions and separations, which were often the outcome of the vanity of the leaders. Far from lending themselves to the exigencies of practical life, the Gnostic system became every day more crude, complicated, and chimerical. Every one wished to be the founder of a school, to have a church, with its profits; in this some one, clouded with doctors, the least Christian of men, sought to surpass the others, and added some oddity to the oddities of their predecessors.

The school of Carpocrates presented an incredible mixture of aberrations and of fine criticism. They spoke, as of a miracle of learning and eloquence, of the son of Carpocrates, named Epiphanes, a sort of infant prodigy, who died at sixteen years of age, after having astonished those who knew him by his knowledge of Greek literature, and especially by the knowledge he had of Plato's philosophy. It appears that they had raised to him a temple and altars at Samos, in the island of Cephalonia; an academy was erected in his name; they celebrated his birthday like the apotheosis of a god by sacrifices, feasts, and hymns. His book "On Justice" was much boasted of; what has been preserved to us is a sophistical and rugged discussion which recalls Prudhon and the socialists of our days. God, said Epiphanes, is just and good, for nature is equality. The light is alike for all, the sky the same to all; the sun makes no distinction between poor and rich, nor male nor female, nor bond nor free. No one can take from another his share of the sun to double his own; it is the sun which nourishes all. Nature, in other words, presents to everyone an equal happiness. It is human laws which, by violating the divine, have introduced evil; the distinction between "mine" and "thine," inequality, antagonism. Applying these principles to marriage, Epiphanes denied its justice or necessity. The desires which we all hold from nature are our rights, and no institution should put any limits to it.

Epiphanes, to tell the truth, is less a Christian than a Utopian. The idea of absolute justice bewitches him. As opposed to the lower world, he dreams of a perfect, true world of God, a world founded on the doctrine of the sages, Pythagoras, Plato, Jesus, where equality, and consequently community of goods, should reign. His mistake was to believe that such a world could have a place in reality. Led away by the Republic of Plato, which he took quite seriously, he indulged in the saddest sophisms, and although he doubtless failed to rebut the gross calumnies which they related concerning those festivals where, the lights being extinguished, the guests delivered themselves up to a hateful promiscuousness, it is difficult not to admit that he produced strange follies in that direction. A certain Marcellinus, who came to Rome under Anicet, adored the portraits of Jesus Christ, Pythagoras, Plato and Aristotle, offering them worship. Prodicus and his disciples, named also Adamites, pretended to renew the joys of the earthly Paradise by some practices far removed from the primitive innocence. Their church called itself Paradise; they heated it, and attended it naked. Notwithstanding this they called themselves continent, and made the pretension of living in a perfect virginity. In name of a sort of divine and natural law all these sects, Prodicians, Eutychites, and Adamites, denied the force of the established laws, which they qualified by arbitrary rules and pretended laws.

The numerous conversions of Pagans which had taken place created these kinds of scandals. They entered the church, drawn by a certain odour of moral purity; but they did not become saints for all that. A painter of some talent, named Hermogenes, thus became a Christian, but without renouncing the freedom of his pencil or his taste for women, or his recollections of Greek philosophy, which became amalgamated, good and evil alike, with Christian dogma. He admitted a primary matter, serving as a substratum to all God's works, and the cause of the defects inherent in creation. They imputed several oddities, and Tertullian, with like rigorists, treated him with an extreme brutality.

The heresies of which we are speaking were all Hellenic. It was the Greek philosophy, especially that of Plato, which was the origin of it. Markos, whose disciples were called Markosians, left, on the other hand, the school of Basilides; the formulas upon the tetrade which he pretended were revealed to him by a heavenly woman, who was none other than Sige herself, would have been inoffensive had they not been joined to magic, thaumaturgical prestiges, philtres and arts capable of seducing women. He invented special sacraments, rites, anointings, and specially a sort of mass for his own use, which might have been imposing enough, had he not mixed with them sleight of hand passes analogous to the miracles of St. Januarius. He pretended by virtue of a certain formula to really change the water into blood in the chalice. By means of a powder, he gave the water a reddish colour. He caused the consecration to be made by a woman over a little chalice; then he turned the water of the smaller chalice into a large one which he held, pronouncing over it these words: "May the infinite and ineffable grace which is above all things fill thy internal being, and increase in thee its knowledge; shedding the grain of mustard seed upon good soil." The liquid was then increased, no doubt the result of some chemical reaction, and overflowed in a great stream. The poor woman was stupefied, and everyone was struck with wonder.

The church of Markos was not only a nest of impostors; it passed also for a school of debauched and secret infamies. Perhaps this character was exaggerated, because in the Markosian cult the women acted as priests, and offered the Eucharist. Many Christian ladies they said allowed themselves to be bewitched; they put themselves under the direction of the sophist, and only came out bathed in tears. Markos flattered their vanity, holding towards them a language of equivocal mysticism, trampling over their timidity, teaching them to prophesy, and imposing on them. Then, when they were fatigued and ruined, they returned to the church, confessed their faults, and vowed themselves to penitence; weeping and groaning over the misfortune which had happened to them. The epidemic of Markos desolated principally the churches of Asia. The kind of connection which existed between Asia and Lyons brought this dangerous man to the banks of the Rhone. We shall see him make many dupes there; some frightful scandals celebrate his arrival in that church of saints.

Colarbasus, according to certain accounts, came very near Markos, but we do not know if we have here the name of a real person. It is explained by Col arba Qol arba, a Semitic expression for the Markosian tetrade. The secret of those bizarre enigmas will probably always escape us.

CHAPTER VIII

ORIENTAL SYNCRETISM--THE OPHITES--FUTURE APPARITION OF MANICHÆISM

We should exceed our limits if we followed the history of those chimeras of the 3rd century. In the Greek and Latin world Gnosticism had been a fashion, it disappeared just as such with equal rapidity. Matters proceeded differently in the East. Gnosticism commenced a second life, much more brilliant and comprehensive than the first, through the eclecticism of Bardisanus, much more durable by Manichaeism. Already, since the 2nd century, the opponents of Alexandria were veritable dualists, attributing the origin of good and evil to two different gods. Manichæism shall go further; three hundred and fifty years before Mahommet, the genius of Persia realises already that which the genius of Arabia shall realise more powerfully, a religion which aspires to become universal, and to replace the work of Jesus, represented as imperfect or corrupted by his disciples.

The intense confusion of ideas which reigned in the East led to a general syncretism of the strangest of these. Some little mystical sects from Egypt, Syria, Phrygia, Babylonia, profiting by apparent resemblances, pretended to be joined to the body of the Church, and sometimes were received. All the religions of antiquity appeared to have revived again to anticipate Jesus and to adopt him as one of their pupils. The cosmogonies of Assyria, Phoenicia, and Egypt, the doctrines of the mysteries of Adonis, Osiris, and Isis, of the great goddess of Phrygia, made an invasion into the Church, and continued what might be called the Oriental branch--scarcely Christian--of Gnosticism, inasmuch as Jehovah, the God of the Jews, was identified with Assyro-Phoenician Ialdebaoth, "the Son of Chaos." At other times the old Assyrian IAΩ, which offers with Jehovah some strange traces of family connection, was brought into fashion, and approached with its quasi-homonymism in such a way that it was difficult to distinguish between the shadow and the reality.

The Ophialatros sects, so numerous in antiquity, lent themselves peculiarly to these senseless associations. Under the name of Nahassians, or Ophites, certain Pagan serpent-worshippers grouped themselves, whom it suited for a certain time to take the name of Christians. It is from Assyria that there comes the form of this bizarre Church; but Egypt, Phrygia, Phoenicia, and the Orphic mysteries have their share in it. Like Alexander of Abonoticos, preacher of his serpent-god Glycon, the Ophites had certain tamed serpents (agatho-demons) which they kept in cages. At the moment of celebrating the mysteries they opened the door to the little god and called upon him. The serpent came out, mounted on the table where the loaves were, and coiled himself round them. The Eucharist appeared then to the sectaries a perfect sacrifice. They broke the bread, distributed it, worshipped the agatho-demon, and offered through him, they said, a hymn of praise to the Heavenly Father. They sometimes identified their little animals with the Christ or with the serpent which taught men the knowledge of good and evil.

The theories of the Ophites upon the Adamas, considered as an Æon, and upon the cosmic egg, recall the cosmogonies of Philo of Byblos, and the symbols common to all the mysteries of the East. Their rites were more analogous to the mysteries of the Great Goddess of Phrygia than to the pure assemblies of the believers in Jesus. What was most singular about it was that they had their Christian literature, their gospels, and their apocryphal traditions, connecting them with James. They used principally the gospel of the Egyptians, and that of Thomas. Their Christology was that of all the Gnostics. Jesus Christ was according to their view composed of two persons, Jesus and Christ--Jesus the son of Mary, the most righteous, wisest, and purest of men, who was crucified; Christ, the heavenly Æon, who came to unite himself to Jesus, quitted him before the passion, sent from Heaven a virtue which made Jesus to rise, with a spiritual body, in which he lived eighteen months, giving to a small number of chosen disciples a higher instruction.

Upon these hidden borders of Christianity the most varied dogmas blended themselves together. The tolerance of the Gnostics and proselytism opened so wide the gates of the Church that everything passed through them. Some religions which had nothing in common with Christianity, and some Babylonian cults, perhaps some branches of Buddhism, were classed and numbered by the heresiologies among Christian sects. Such were the Baptists or Sabians, afterwards known under the name of Mendaites, the Perates, the adherents of a cosmogony half Phoenician, half Assyrian; a perfect balderdash, more worthy of Byblos, of Maboug, or Babylon, than the Church of Christ; and especially the Sethians, a sect in reality Assyrian, and which flourished also in Egypt. It was connected by some punsters with the patriarch Seth, the supposed father of a vast literature, and sometimes identified with Jesus Christ himself. The Sethians arbitrarily combined Orphism, Neo-Phoenicianism, and the ancient Semitic cosmogonies, and found the whole of this in the Bible. They said that the genealogies of Genesis included sublime views, which vulgar minds had looked upon as simple family records.

A certain Justin about this same time, in a work entitled Baruch, transformed Judaism into a mythology, and left scarcely any position to Jesus. Some exuberant imaginations, nourished by innumerable cosmogonies, and strangely placed in the severe régime of the Hebrew and gospel literature, could not accommodate themselves to so much simplicity. They inflated, if I may venture to say so, the historical records, legendary, or evhemeristic of the Bible in order to connect them with the genius of the Greek and Oriental fables to which they were accustomed.

It will thus be seen that the whole mythological world of Greece and the East was introduced surreptitiously into the religion of Jesus. Intelligent men of the Greco-Oriental world felt indeed that one and the same spirit animated all the religious creations of humanity. They commenced by comprehending Buddhism. Although it was then far from the time when the life of Buddha had become the life of a holy Christian, they spoke of him with nothing but respect.

The Babylonian Manichæism, which represented in the third century a continuation of Gnosticism, is strongly impregnated with Buddhism. But the attempt to introduce all this pantheistic mythology into the framework of a Semitic religion was condemned in advance. Philo, the Jew, the epistles to the Colossians and the Ephesians, the pseudo-Johannine writings, had been under this conviction as long as it was possible. The Gnostics marked the true sense of every word by pretending that they were Christians.

The essence of the work of Jesus was the improvement of the soul. Now these empty speculations embraced everything in the world except good sense and good morals. Even by holding as calumnies what has been said of their promiscuous intercourse and licentious habits, one cannot doubt that the sects of which we speak had had in common an evil tendency to moral indifference, and a dangerous quietism, a world of generosity, which led them to proclaim the uselessness of martyrdom. Their obstinate Docetism, their system of attributing the two Testaments to two different gods, their opposition to marriage, their denial of the resurrection and the final judgment, closed to them the gates of a church. There the rule of the leaders was always a kind of moderation and opposition to excess. Ecclesiastical discipline, represented by the episcopate, was the rock against which those disorderly attempts all came to be broken.

We should be afraid by speaking longer of such sects to have the appearance of taking too seriously what they did not take so themselves. What were they but Phibionites, Barbelonites, or Borborians, the stratiotics or soldiers, the Levitics or Codists? The fathers of the Church are unanimous in throwing upon all these heresies a ridicule which they doubtless deserved, and a hatred which perhaps they did not. There was in the whole of them more of charlatanism than wickedness.

With their Hebrew words often taken in an opposite sense, their magic formulas, and later on their amulets and their Abracadabras, the Gnostics of the lower type merited only to be despised.

But this contempt ought not to be poured out upon those great men who sought in that powerful narcotic the repose or the stupefication of their thoughts. Valentinus was in his own way a genius; Carpocrates and his son, Epiphanes, were brilliant writers, spoiled by utopia and paradox; but sometimes astonishingly profound. Gnosticism had a considerable part in the work of the Christian propaganda. Often it was the transition by which people passed from Paganism to Christianity. The proselytes thus gained became nearly always orthodox; they never returned to Paganism.

It is especially Egypt which preserves from these strange rites an ineffaceable impression. Egypt had not had any Judeo-Christianity. A remarkable fact is the difference between the Coptic literature and the other Christian literature of the East, while the greater number of Judeo-Christians are found in Syriac, Arabic, Ethiopic, Armenian; Coptic only shows a Gnostic background without anything further. Egypt also passes without the intermediary of the Pagan illumination to the Christian light. Alexandria was almost entirely converted by the Gnostics. Clement of Alexandria was what one would call a moderate Gnostic. He quotes with respect Heracleon as a doctor, claiming authority from many points of view. He uses in good sense the word Gnostic, and regards it as synonymous with Christian. He is far in any case from entertaining against the new ideas the hatred of Irenæus, of Tertullian, or the author of the Philosophumena. We may say that Clement of Alexandria and Origen introduced into Christian science that which the too bold attempt of Heracleon and Basilides had of acceptability.

Mixed intimately with all the intellectual movement, the gnosis had a decisive influence upon the turn which speculative philosophy took in the third century in that city, then become the centre of the human intellect. The consequence of these disputes without end was the constitution of a sort of Christian academy, a true school of sacred letters and exegesis, which Pantænus, Clement, and Origen soon made famous. Alexandria became every day more and more the capital of Christian theology.

The effect of the gnosis upon the Pagan school of Alexandria was not less. Ammonius Saccas, born of Christian parents, and Plotinus, his disciple, were both impregnated with it. The most open minds, such as Numenius of Apamea, entered by this path into the knowledge of Jewish and Christian doctrines, up till then so rare in the heart of the Pagan world. The Alexandrian philosophy of the third, fourth, and fifth centuries is full of what may be called the Gnostic spirit, and it linked to the Arabian philosophy a germ of mysticism which that should develop still more. Judaism on its side shall yield to similar influences. The Cabbala is nothing else than the Gnosticism of the Jews. The sephiroth are the perfections of Valentinus. Monotheism, to create itself a mythology, has only one process, and that is to give life to the attributes which it is accustomed to range around the throne of the Eternal.

The world, wearied of an effete polytheism, demanded in the East, and especially in Judæa, some divine names less used than those of the current mythology. These Oriental names had more weight than the Greek names, and a singular reason was given for their theurgic superiority; it is that the Divinity having been invoked by the Orientals at a more ancient period than by the Greeks, the names of the Oriental theology answered better than the Greek names to the nature of the gods, and pleased them more. The names of Abraham, Isaac, Jacob, and Solomon passed in Egypt for talismans of the first potency. Amulets answering to this unruly syncretism covered the whole world. The words IAω, AΔωNAI, CΛBAωΘ, εΛωAI and the Hebraic formulas in Greek characters were mixed up with some Egyptian symbols and with the sacramental ΛBPACAΞ, equivalent to the number 365. All this is much more Judeo-Pagan than Christian, and Gnosticism in Christianity representing the aversion to Jehovah pushed even to blasphemy; it is entirely inexact to connect with Gnosticism these monuments of absurdity. They were the effect of the general turn which the superstition of the time had taken, and we believe that at the period we have arrived at, Christians of all sects remained indifferent to these little talismans. It is from the conversion en masse of the Pagans, in the fourth and fifth centuries, that the amulets were introduced into the Church, and that some words and symbols decidedly Christian are begun to be met with there.

Orthodoxy was, therefore, ungrateful not to recognise the services which these undisciplined sects had rendered her. In dogma they provoked nothing but reaction, but their position was more considerable in Christian literature and liturgical institutions. They borrowed nearly always a good deal from those whom they anathematised. The first Christianity, quite Jewish still, was very simple, it was the Gnostics who made a religion of it. The sacraments were to a large extent their creation; their anointings, especially at the deathbeds of the sick, produced a deep impression. The holy chrism confirmation (at first an integral part of baptism), the attribution of a supernatural power to the sign of the Cross, and many other elements of Christian mysticism came from them. A young and active party, the Gnostics wrote much and launched boldly into apocrypha. Their books, assailed with discredit at first, finished by entering into the orthodox family. The Church soon accepted what it had at first inveighed against. A multitude of superstitions, festivals, and symbols of Gnostic origin thus became the superstitions, festivals, and symbols of Catholicism. Mary the mother of Jesus, in particular, with whom the Orthodox Church had little concerned itself, owed to these innovators the first development of her almost divine position. The apocryphal gospels are fully half at least the work of Gnostics. Now the apocryphal gospels have been the source of a great number of festivals, and have furnished the most cherished subjects for Christian art. The first Christian image, the first portraits of Christ, were Gnostic. The strictly orthodox Church would have remained iconoclastic if heresy had not penetrated it, or rather had not demanded from her, for the necessities of the times, more than one concession to Pagan weaknesses.

Moving from time to time from genius to folly, Gnosticism defies all absolute judgments on it. Hegel and Swedenborg, Schelling and Cagliostro, elbow each other there. The apparent frivolity of some of its theologians should not repel us. Every law which is not the pure expression of positive science must submit to the caprices of fashion. So Hegel's formula, which in his time had been the most lofty view in the world, causes us to smile now. Such a phraseology in which to sum up the universe one day shall appear clumsy or weak. To all who make shipwreck in the sea of the infinite, indulgence must be given. Good sense, which appears at first sight irreconcilable with the chimeras of the Gnostics, was not so wanting in them as we might imagine. They did not fight against civil society; they did not seek for martyrdom; and they held excess of zeal in aversion. They had high wisdom, tolerance, and sometimes (can it be believed?) even discreet scepticism. Like all religious forms, Gnosticism softened, consoled, and excited the mind. Here are the terms in which a Valentinian epitaph, found on the Latin Way, tries to sound the abyss of death:--

"Desirous to see the light of the Father, companion of my blood, of my bed, O my wise one, perfumed in the sacred bath, with the incorruptible and pure myrrh of the Christ, thou hast hastened to go and contemplate the divine faces of the Æons, the great angel of the grand council, the true Son, hurried as thou wast from sleeping in the nuptial couch, into the bosom of the Æons.

"This death is not the lot of ordinary human beings. She is dead, and she sees and really may see the light incorruptible. To the eyes of the living she is living; those who believe her dead are really dead. Earth, what shall be said of thy wonders in presence of this new kind of manes! What shall be said of thy fear!"

CHAPTER IX

THE RESULT OE MARCIONISM--APELLES

Excellent for producing consolation and individual edification, Gnosticism was very weak as a church. There could not be drawn from it either Presbytery or Episcopacy; ideas so ill-ordered produced only dogmatism. Marcion alone succeeded in raising a compact edifice upon this fleeting basis. He had a Marcionite church strongly organised. Certainly the church was stained by some grave faults which brought it under the ban of the Church of Christ. It is not without reason that all the founders of Episcopacy shew by one common sentiment aversion to Marcion. Metaphysics did not regulate those minds enough to prevent them from cherishing a pure theological hatred. But time is a good judge. Marcionism continued. It was, like Arianism, one of the grand fractions of Christianity, and not, like so many other sects, a bizarre and passing meteor.

Marcion, while remaining quite faithful to certain principles which to him constituted the essence of Christianity, changed more than once in his theology.

He does not appear to have imposed on his disciples any very distinct creed. After his death the internal dissensions of his sect were extreme. Potitus and Basilicus remained faithful to dualism; Synerôs held three natures, without it being known rightly how he expressed it; Apelles inclined decidedly to monachism. He had at first been personally a disciple of Marcion; but he was gifted with too independent a spirit to remain a scholar; he broke with his master, and quitted his church. These ruptures, outside the Catholic Church, were accidents occurring every day. The enemies of Apelles tried to cause it to be believed that he had been expelled, and that the cause of his excommunication was a freedom of morals which contrasted with the severity of his master. There was much said about a virgin, Philumena, whose seductions had influenced all his wanderings, and who had played to him the rôle of a Priscilla or Maximilla. Nothing is more doubtful. Rhodon, his orthodox adversary, who knew him, represents him as an old man venerable by the ascetic rule of his life. Rhodon speaks of Philumena, and represents her as a virgin "possessed," whose inspirations Apelles really looked on as divine. Such accidents of credulity befel the most austere doctors, especially Tertullian.

The symbolic language of the Gnostic doctrines led to grave misunderstandings, and often gave place to grave mistakes on the part of the orthodox, interested in calumniating such dangerous enemies. It was not with impunity that Simon the Magician played on the allegory of Helena-Ennoia. Marcion was perhaps the victim of a mistake of the same order. Apelles' somewhat variable philosophic imagination might also cause it to be said that, pursuing an inconstant love, he quitted the truth to run after perilous adventures. We may be allowed to suppose that he gave as a framework to his teaching the revelations of a symbolic personage whom he called Philumena (the beloved Truth). It is certain, at least, that the words attributed by Rhodon to our doctor are those of an honest man, of a sincere friend of the truth. After having quitted Marcion's school, Apelles went to Alexandria, and attempted a sort of eclecticism among the confused ideas that passed before him, and then returned to Rome. He did not cease to retouch during his whole life his master's theology, and it appears that he finished by becoming weary of metaphysical theories which, according to our ideas, drew him from the true philosophy.

The two grand errors of Marcion, as of the greater portion of the first Gnostics, were dualism and docetism. By the first, he gave in advance a hand to Manichaeism, by the second to Islam. The Marcionite doctors and Gnostics of the latter part of the second century generally attempted to extenuate these two errors. The last Basilidians arrived by this at a pure Pantheism. The author of the pseudo-Clementine romance, in spite of his bizarre theology, is a Deist. Hermogenes awkwardly flounders about among insoluble questions raised by the doctrine of the Incarnation. Apelles, whose ideas sometimes much resemble those of the pretended Clement, seeks to escape from the subtleties of the gnosis by maintaining with energy the principles of what may be called the theology of good sense.

The absolute unity of God is the fundamental dogma of Apelles. God is perfect goodness; the world does not sufficiently reflect this goodness, and the world cannot be His work. The true world created by God is a higher world, peopled by angels. The chief of these angels is the Glorious Angel, a sort of demiurge or created Logos, creator in his turn of the visible world; that is but defective imitation of the higher world. Apelles shunned thus the dualism of Marcion and placed himself in an intermediary situation between Catholicism and the gnosis. He corrected really the system of Marcion, and gave to this system a certain consequence; but he fell into many other difficulties. Human souls, according to Apelles, made part of the higher creation from which they had fallen by concupiscence. To bring them back to Him, God has sent His Christ into the lower creation. Christ has come thus to improve the defective and tyrannical work of the demiurge. Apelles re-entered here in the classical doctrine of Marcionism and Gnosticism, according to which the essential work of the Christ has been to destroy the worship of the demiurge, that is to say, Judaism. The Old Testament and the New appear to him two enemies. The God of the Jews, like the God of the Catholics (in the eyes of Apelles, these last were Judaisers), is a perverse God, author of sin and of the flesh. Jewish history is the history of evil; the prophets themselves are inspired with the evil spirit. The God of good had not revealed Himself before Jesus. Apelles admitted that Jesus had a heavenly elementary body, beyond the ordinary physical laws, although endowed with a complete reality.

With different renewals, Apelles appeared to have felt that this doctrine of the radical opposition of the two Testaments had something too absolute about it, and, as his was not a stubborn mind, he came little by little from that to ideas which St. Paul would perhaps not have repelled. At certain times, the Old Testament appeared to him rather incoherent and contradictory than decidedly bad; so that the work of Christ would have been to make the discernment of good and evil, conformably to this word so often quoted by the Gnostics: "Be ye good trapezites." So, as Marcion had written his Antithesis to show the incompatibility of the two Testaments, Apelles wrote his Syllogisms, a vast compilation of weak passages from the Pentateuch, destined especially to show the variableness of the ancient legislator and his small amount of philosophy. Apelles exhibited there a very subtle criticism, reminding us occasionally of that of the unbelievers of the eighteenth century. The difficulties which the first chapters of Genesis present, when mythical explanations were excluded, were heightened with much sagacity. His book was considered as a refutation of the Bible and repelled as blasphemous.

Possessed of a mind too just for the sectarian world in which he was engaged, Apelles was condemned always to change. To the end of his life he was tormented about the Scriptures. Even his fundamental idea of the divine unity wavered before him, and he arrived, without doubting, at perfect wisdom, that is to say, at a disgust for systems and at good sense. Rhodon, his adversary, has given us a conversation which he had with him at Rome about 180. "The old Apelles," he says, "conferring with us, we showed him that he was deceived in many things, so that he was led to say that it was not necessary to examine matters of religion so much, that each one might remain in his own belief, and that those were saved who trusted in the Crucified, provided they were found good men. He confessed that the most obscure point to him was that which concerned God. He admitted, like us, but a sole principle. . . . Where is the proof of all that,' I asked of him, and how is it that you are at liberty to assert that there is but a sole principle?' He confessed to me then that the prophecies could teach us nothing true, since they contradicted and reversed themselves; that this assertion, There is but one principle,' was rather with him the result of instinct than of a positive knowledge. Having asked him, upon his oath, to tell the truth, he swore to me that he spoke sincerely; that he did not know how there was but one God unbegotten, but that he believed it. As to me, I reproached him with laughter for giving himself the title of master,' without being able to adduce any proof in favour of his doctrine."

Poor Rhodon! It was the heretic Apelles who, on that day, gave him a lesson in good taste, tact, and true Christianity. The pupil of Marcion was really cured, since to a clumsy gnosis he preferred Faith, the secret instinct of the truth, the love of the good, trust in the Crucified.

What gave a certain force to ideas like those of Apelles is that they were only, in many points of view, a return to St. Paul. It was not doubtful that St. Paul, had he risen again at the point in Christianity at which we have arrived, would have found that Catholicism made too many concessions to the Old Testament. He would have protested and maintained that they were returning to Judaism, which was called the new wine in old bottles, and that they suppressed the difference between the Gospel and the Law.

The teaching of Apelles did not go outside Rome, and barely lasted till after his death. Tertullian, nevertheless, felt himself obliged to refute it. A certain Lucan or Lucian made, like Apelles, a distinct sect in the Marcionite church. It seems that he admitted, like Synerôs, three principles, one good, the second bad, and the third just. The strictly just principle was represented by the demiurge or creator. In his hatred against this last, Lucian forbade marriage. By his blasphemies against the creation he appeared to others to approach Cerdo.

Severus appears to have been a later Gnostic more than a Marcionite. Prepon, the Assyrian, denied the birth of Christ, and maintained that in the fifteenth year of the reign of Tiberius Jesus descended from heaven in the figure of a completely formed man.

Marcionism, like Gnosticism, was in the second generation. These two sects had not after this time any celebrated doctor. All the grand fancies hatched under Hadrian vanished like dreams. The shipwrecked from these little adventurous churches hung on greedily to the borders of the Catholic Church, and re-entered it. The Church writers had the advantage over them that those who do not search and do not doubt have over the crowd. Irenaeus, Philip of Gortyne, Modestus, Melito, Rhodon,

Theophilus of Antioch, Bardesanes, Tertullian, set themselves as a task to unmask what they called the infernal tricks of Marcion, and they did not restrain their language from any violence.

Although struck with death, the church of Marcion remained indeed a long time a distinct community beside the Catholic Church. During several centuries there were in all the provinces of the East some Christian communities who were honoured by bearing the name of Marcion, and wrote this name on the front of their "synagogues." These churches show successions of bishops quite comparable to that in which the Catholic Church glories. They had martyrs, virgins, everything that constituted sainthood. The faithful led an austere life, braved death, wore the monastic sackcloth, imposed on themselves strict fasts, and abstained from everything which had had life in it. "There are some hornets who imitate the swarms of bees," the orthodox said. "These wolves clothe themselves with the skin of the sheep they kill," said others. Like the Montanists, the Marcionites fabricated false apostolic writings and false psalms. It is needless to say that this heretical literature has entirely perished.

In the fourth and fifth centuries the sect, lively still, was fought against with energy, as with an actual flail, by John Chrysostom, St. Basil, St. Epiphanes, Theodoret, the Armenian Eznig, the Syrian Boud, the Periodoute. But the exaggerations ruined it. A general horror of the works of the Creator carried the Marcionites to the most absurd abstinences. They were in many points of view pure encratites; they forbade wine even in the mysteries. It was said to them that to be consistent they should allow themselves to die of hunger. They looked on baptism as a means of justification, and permitted women to officiate in the churches. Badly protected against superstition, they fell into magic and astrology. They became confounded gradually with the Manichæans.

CHAPTER X

TATIAN HERETICAL--THE ENCRATITES

What shows that the order of ideas which filled the minds of Marcion, Apelles, and Lucan came from the theological situation by a kind of necessity is that we see the faithful from all parts turning from the same side without their antecedents being possibly foreseen. Such was in special the fate which was reserved for the disciple of the tolerant Justin, for the apologist who had twenty times risked his life for his faith--Tatian. At a date which cannot be precisely fixed, Tatian, who at bottom was always an Assyrian at heart, and who much preferred the East to Rome, returned to Adiabene, where the number of Jews and Christians was considerable. There his doctrine altered more and more. Cut off from all the churches he remained in his own country what he was already in Italy--a sort of solitary Christian, not belonging to any one sect, although approaching the Montanists in asceticism, and some Marcionites by his doctrine and exegesis. His ardour for work was prodigious; his burning brain would not allow him to rest; the Bible, which he read without ceasing, inspired him with the most contradictory ideas; he wrote on this subject books without end.

After having been, in his apology, the fanatical admirer of the Hebrews against the Greeks, he fell into the opposite extreme. The exaggeration of the ideas of St. Paul, which had led Marcion to inveigh against the Jewish Bible, led Tatian to sacrifice entirely the Old Testament to the New. Like Apelles and the greatest number of the Gnostics, Tatian admitted a Creator God subordinate to the Supreme God. In the act of creation, by pronouncing the words "Let light be!" the Creator, according to him, proceeded, not by command, but by way of prayer. The Law was the work of the Creator God, only the Gospel was the work of the Supreme God. An exaggerated demand for moral perfection caused Tatian, after having repelled the Hellenic antiquity as impure, to repel likewise the Biblical antiquity. Hence an exegesis and a criticism little different from that of the Marcionites. His Problems, like the Antitheses of Marcion and the Syllogisms of Apelles, had doubtless for their object to prove the inconsequences of the ancient law and the superiority of the new. He presented there, with very lucid good sense, the objections which could be made against the Bible, by placing himself on the ground of reason. The rationalistic exegesis of modern times finds its ancestors in the school of Apelles and Tatian. Notwithstanding its injustice to the Law and the Prophets, this school was certainly, in exegesis, more sensible than the orthodox doctors with their entirely arbitrary allegorical and typical explanations.

The idea which governed Tatian's mind in the composition of his celebrated Diatessaron could not be worthy in the opinion of the orthodox. The discordance of the gospels shocked him. Desirous above all to meet the objections of reason, he sought at the same time to do what would be most for edification. Everything in the life of Jesus which according to him brought the God too near the man was mercilessly sacrificed. However convenient was this attempt at the fusion of the gospels, it was denounced, and the copies of the Diatessaron were violently destroyed. The principal adversary of Tatian in this last period of his life was his old pupil Rhodon. Taking up one by one the Problems of Tatian, this presumptuous exegete set himself to reply to all the objections his master had raised. He also wrote a commentary on the work of six days. No doubt if we had the work which Rhodon composed upon so many delicate questions, we should see that it was less wise than that of Apelles or Tatian; those prudently confessed that they did not know how to solve them.

The faith of Tatian varied like his exegesis. Gnosticism, half conquered in the West, flourished in the East still. Combining together Valentinus, Saturninus, and Marcion (the disciple of St. Justin), forgetful of his master, fell into the dreams which he had probably refuted at Rome. He became a heresiarch. Full of horror on the matter, Tatian could not bear the idea that Christ should have had the least contact with it. The sexual relations of man and woman are sinful. In the Diatessaron, Jesus had no earthly genealogy. Like some apocryphal gospel, Tatian would have said: "In the reign of Tiberius, the Word of God was born at Nazareth." He went so far logically as to maintain that the flesh of Christ was only an apparition. The use of flesh and wine classed a man in his eyes among the impure. In the celebration of the mysteries, he wished to be served with nothing but water. He passed thus as the head of those numerous sects of encratites or abstinents, forbidding marriage, wine and flesh, who arose in all places, and pretended to draw this from the rigorous sequence of Christian principles. From Mesopotamia these ideas spread to Antioch, Cilicia of Pisidia, through all Asia Minor, to Rome and all

France. Asia Minor, especially Galatia, remained the centre. The same tendencies appeared in many places at the same time. Had not Paganism, on its side, the maceration of the cynics? A collection of false ideas, much spread, led men to believe that, evil arising from concupiscence, the return to virtue implied the renunciation of the most lawful desires.

The distinction between precepts and counsels remained still undecided. The Church was looked on as an assembly of saints waiting in prayer and in ecstasy the new heaven and new earth; nothing would be too perfect for it. The institutions of the religious life shall solve one day all these difficulties. The convent shall realise the perfect Christian life, a gift which the world has not to bestow. Tatian was not a heretic, except that he wished to put upon all as an obligation what St. Paul had presented as best.

Tatian presents, we may see, some likeness to Apelles. Like him, he changed much, and never ceased modifying his rule of faith; like him, he attacked the Jewish Bible resolutely and made himself the free exegete of it. He nearly approached some Protestants of the sixteenth century, particularly Calvin. He was in any case one of the most deeply Christian men of his century, and, if he fell, it was like Tertullian by excess of severity. We could rank among his disciples that Julius Cassian, who wrote many books of Exegetica, maintaining, by arguments analogous to those of the Discourse against the Greeks, that the philosophy of the Hebrews was much more ancient than that of the Greeks, pushed Docetism to such excess that he was looked on as the head of that heresy, and associated with it a horror of works of the flesh, which led him to a sort of nihilism destructive of humanity. This advent of the kingdom of God appeared to him like the suppression of the sexes and modesty. A certain Severus followed a still freer fancy, repelling the Acts of the Apostles, insulting Paul, and taking up the old myth of Gnosticism. From shipwreck to shipwreck, he went over nearly all the chimeras of the archonites, continuators of the follies of Markos. From his name the Encratites were called Severians.

All the aberrations of the mendicant orders of the middle ages existed at this time. There had been, from the first centuries, saccophores or sack-carrying brothers; apostles, pretending to reproduce the life of the Apostles; angelics, cathares or pure ones, apotactites or renouncers, who refused communion and salvation to all those who were married and possessed any property. Not being guarded by authority, these sects fell into the apocryphal literature. The Gospel of the Egyptians, the Acts of St. Andrew, of St. John, and St. Thomas were their favourite books. The orthodox pretended that their chastity was only apparent, since they drew women into their sect by every means, and were continually with them. They formed a sort of community in which the two sexes lived together, the women serving the men and following them in their travels by the title of companions. This kind of life was far from softening them, for they furnished in the struggles of martyrdom some athletes who put the executioners to shame.

The ardour for the faith was such that it was against the excess of sanctity that it was necessary to take measures; it was the abuse of zeal which needed to be guarded against. Some words which implied nothing but what was praiseworthy, such as "abstinent," "apostolic," became the marks of heresy. Christianity had created such an ideal of indifference that it recoiled before its own work, and said to the faithful: "Do not take me so very seriously, or you will destroy me!" They were afraid of the fire they had lit. The love of the two sexes had been so terribly abused by the most irreproachable teachers that the Christians, who wished to go to the end of their principles, came to hold it as sinful, and to banish it utterly. By force of frugality they blamed the creation of God, and left useless nearly all His gifts. Persecution produced, and up to a certain point excused, these unhealthy aspirations. Let us think of the hardness of the times, of that preparation for martyrdom which filled up the life of the Christian, and made out of it a kind of fascination analogous to that of gladiators. Boasting the efficacy of fasting and asceticism Tertullian says: "Behold how they endure prison, hunger, thirst, privations, and distresses; see how the martyr knows how to come forth from the concealment into which he has entered, not to meet there unknown pains; not finding there anything but the macerations of every day--certain of conquering in the fight, because he has killed the flesh, and because in him the torments have no point to seize. His dried epidermis will be like a cuirass to him, the iron nails will slip there as over a thick horn. Such shall be he who, by fasting, has often seen death near him, and has been emptied of his blood--a heavy and inconvenient burden from which the impatient soul longs to escape."

CHAPTER XI

THE GREAT BISHOPS OF GREECE AND ASIA--MELITO

Alongside of moral excesses, the result of a badly regulated feeling, and of an exuberant production of legends, children of the Oriental fancy, there fortunately was the Episcopate. It was especially in the purely Greek portions of the Church that this fine institution flourished. Opposed to all aberrations, classic in a way and moderate in its tendencies, more busied about the humble path of simple believers than the transcendant pretensions of ascetics and speculators, the Episcopate became more and more the Church itself, and saved the work of Jesus from the inevitable shipwreck it would have suffered in the hands of Gnostics, Montanists, and even of Judaisers. What doubled the power of the Episcopate was that this sort of federal oligarchy had a centre; that centre was Rome. Anicet had seen, during the ten or twelve years of his presidency, nearly every movement of Christianity concentrate itself around him. His successor, Soter (probably a converted Jew, who translated his name Jesus into Greek), saw this movement increase still more. The vast correspondence which had for so long been established between Rome and the Churches assumed a larger scope than ever. A central tribunal of controversies had gradually become established.

Greece and Asia continued to be, with Rome, the theatre of the principal incidents of Christian growth. Corinth possessed in its Dionysius one of the most respected men of the age. The charity of this bishop was not confined even to the Church. From all directions he was consulted, and his letters carried nearly as much authority as sacred writings. These were called "Catholic," because they were written not to individuals, but to churches in a body. Seven of these epistles were collected, and venerated as at least equal to the letters of the Roman Clement. They were addressed to the believers of Lacedemon, Athens, Nicomedia, Cnosse, Gortyne, and other churches of Crete, Amastris, and other churches of the West. Soter, according to the custom of the Church of Rome, having sent to the Church at Corinth some alms, accompanied by a letter full of pious instructions, Dionysius thanked him for this kindness.

"It is to-day the Sabbath," he wrote, "and we have seen your letter, and we preserve it to read again, when we desire to listen to salutary advices, as we do with those letters which Clement has already written. By your exhortation you have drawn tighter the bond between the two plantations,' the one by the hand of Peter, the other by that of Paul--I mean the Church of Rome and that of Corinth. These two apostles, indeed, came into our Corinth, and taught us in common, then sailed together towards Italy, to teach there in concert and to suffer martyrdom about the same time."

The Church of Corinth yielded to the tendency of all the churches; it wished, like the Church of Rome, to have as its founders the two apostles whose union was held as the basis of Christianity. It pretended that Peter and Paul, after having passed to Corinth at the most brilliant point in their apostolic life, went together to Italy. The little agreement which prevailed concerning the history of the apostles made such suppositions as these possible, although contrary to all likelihood and all truth.

The writings of Dionysius passed as masterpieces of literary talent and zeal. He fought energetically with Marcion. In a letter to a pious sister named Chrysophora, he traced with a masterly hand the duties of the life consecrated to God. He was no less opposed to the grosser exaggerations of Montanism. In his letter to the Amastrians, he instructed them at length on marriage and virginity, and commanded them to receive joyfully all those who would repent, whether they had fallen into heresy or had committed any other sin. Palma, bishop of Amastris, fully accepted the right which Dionysius assumed to instruct the faithful. Dionysius did not find resistance to this to his taste in the case of his admonition to the bishop of Cnosse, Pinytus, an enthusiastic rigorist. Dionysius had begged him to consider the weakness of certain persons, and not to impose on the faithful generally the too heavy burden of chastity. Pinytus, who possessed eloquence, and passed for one of the lights of the Church, replied by declaring his great esteem and respect for Dionysius; but, in his turn, he counselled him to give his people more solid nourishment and stronger instruction, lest, always feeding them with the milk of toleration, they should insensibly grow old without having ever left in mind the weakness of childhood. Pinytus's letter was much admired, and considered a model of episcopal ardour. It was confessed that the vigour of zeal, when it expresses itself with charity, has rights equal to those of prudence and sweetness.

Dionysius was much opposed to the speculations of the sects. A friend to peace and unity, he repelled everything which tended to division. Heresies had in him a determined adversary. His authority was such that the heretics, "the apostles of the devil," as he calls them, falsified his letters, and "sowed them with tares," adding or cutting out what they pleased. "What should surprise one," said Dionysius, "if certain people have the audacity to falsify the Scriptures of the Lord, since they have dared to lay hands on the writings which have not the same sacred character?"

The Church of Athens, always characterised by a sort of frivolous lightness, was far from having a basis as assured as that of Corinth. Things took place there which did not happen elsewhere. The bishop Publius had bravely suffered martyrdom; then there had been a nearly general apostasy, a sort of abandonment of religion. A certain Quadratus, different doubtless from the apologist, reconstituted the Church, and there was something like an awakening of the faith. Dionysius wrote to this inconstant Church, not without some bitterness, trying to lead it back to the purity of belief and the severity of evangelical life. The Church of Athens, like that of Corinth, had its legend. It was connected with that Dionysius called the Areopagite, who is spoken of in the Acts, and it had made him the first bishop of Athens, so much had the episcopate become already the form without which one could not conceive of the existence of a Christian community.

Crete, we have seen, had churches very flourishing, pious, benevolent, and generous. The Gnostic heresies, and especially Marcionism, beset them without impairing them. Philip, bishop of Gortyne, wrote a fine work against Marcion, and was one of the most respected bishops of the time of Marcus-Aurelius.

Proconsular Asia continued to be the first province in Christian movement. The great struggle, the great persecutions, the great martyrs were there. Nearly all the bishops of the considerable towns were saintly men, eloquent, fairly sensible, having received a good Hellenic education, and, if one may say so, of very skilful religious politics. The bishops were multiplied; but many important families had a sort of claim on the episcopate in the small towns. Polycrates of Ephesus, who, during thirty years, shall defend so energetically against the bishop of Rome the traditions of the churches of Asia, was the eighth bishop of his family. The bishops of the large cities had a primacy over the others; they were the presidents of the provincial assemblies of bishops. The archbishop began to appear, although the word, if one had dared to use it, would have been repelled with horror.

Melito, bishop of Sardis, had, in the midst of those eminent pastors, a sort of uncontested superiority. It was unanimously agreed that he had the gift of prophecy, and it was believed that he was guided in everything by the light of the Holy Spirit. His writings followed each other year by year, in the midst of the universal admiration. His criticism was that of the time; at least, he was careful that his faith should be reasonable and consistent with itself. In many points of view he recalls Origen, but he had not to instruct him the facilities which were presented to the latter by the schools of Alexandria, Cesarea, and Tyre.

The considerable anxiety which the Christians of St. Paul possessed to study the Old Testament, and the weakness of Judaism in the regions of Asia at a distance from Ephesus, made it difficult to procure in that country distinct ideas as to the Biblical books. Their number and order were not exactly known. Melito, impelled by his own curiosity and, as it appeared, at the instance of a certain Onesimus, made a journey into Palestine to inform himself as to the true state of the canon. He brought back a catalogue of books received universally; it was purely and simply the Jewish canon, composed of twenty-five books, to the exclusion of Esther. The apocrypha, such as the book of Enoch, the apocalypse of Esdras, Judith, Tobit, &c., which were not received by the Jews, were equally excluded from the list of Melito. Without being a Hebraiser, Melito became the careful commentator of these sacred writings. At the entreaty of Onesimus, he reunited in six books the passages of the Pentateuch and the Prophets which related to Jesus Christ, and the other articles of the Christian faith. He worked upon the Greek versions, which he compared with the greatest possible diligence.

The exegesis of the Orientals was familiar to him; he discussed it point by point. Like the author of what is called the Epistle of Barnabas, he seems to have had a marked tendency towards allegorical and mystical explanations, and it is not impossible that his lost work, entitled The Key, was already one of these repertories of figurative explanations, by which it was sought to remove the anthropomorphising from the biblical text, and to substitute for meanings too simple meanings more lofty.

Among the scriptures of the New Testament, Melito only seems to have commented on the Apocalypse. He liked its sombre pictures; for we see that he himself announces that the final conflagration is at hand, that after the deluge of wind and the deluge of water shall come the deluge of fire which shall consume the earth, idols, and idolaters; the righteous only shall be saved, as they were formerly in the Ark. These strange beliefs did not prevent Melito from being, in his way, a cultured man. Familiar with the study of philosophy, he sought, in a series of works which unfortunately have been nearly all lost to us, to explain by rational psychology the mysteries of Christian dogma. He wrote besides some treatises where the preoccupation of Montanism seems to rule his thought, without its being possible to say whether he was its adversary or partly favourable to it. Such were the book on the Rule of life and the prophets, on the Church, on the Day of the Sabbath, on the Obedience which the senses owe to the Faith, on the Soul and the Body, or on Understanding, on Baptism, on the Creation and the Birth of Christ, on Hospitality, on Prophecy, on the Devil and the Apocalypse of John, on the Incarnate God, on the Incarnation of Christ, against Marcion. We can believe that there also was a book of prophecies which he composed.

Melito passed indeed for a prophet; but it is not certain that his prophecies formed a separate work. Admitting the prolongation of the gift of prophecy up to his time, he could not repulse à priori the Montanists of Phrygia. His life, besides, resembled theirs in a sort of asceticism. Only he did not recognise the revelations of the saints of Pepuza, otherwise certainly orthodoxy would have cast him from her arms.

One of these treatises, that which he entitled On the Truth, seems to have come down to us. The scoffs of monotheism against idolatry are full of bitterness, and hatred of idols has never been expressed with more force. Truth, according to the author, reveals itself to man, and, if he cannot see it, it is his fault. To deceive himself with the multitude is no excuse; error is multiplied only more fatally. God is an unchangeable, uncreated being; to confound Him with such or such an element is a crime, "especially now that the revelation of the truth has been spread through all the world." The Sibyl had already said, "Idols are only the images of dead kings, who cause themselves to be worshipped." People considered a discovered fragment of Philo of Byblos, exposing to us the old Phoenician Evemerism of Sanchoniathon, that curious page where Melito, taking up handfuls of the most singular and bizarre fables of Greek and Syrian mythology, seeks to prove to us that the gods are personages quite real, who have been deified because of the service they have rendered to certain countries, or the terror they have inspired. The worship of the Cæsars seemed to him the continuation of this practice.

"Do we not see still in our days," says he, "the images of the Cæsars and their family more respected than those of the ancient gods, and those gods themselves paying homage to Cæsar as to a god greater than themselves? and truly, if death were the punishment for despisers of the gods, they would say that it was because they deprived the Treasury of a revenue. It is the same in those countries where the worshippers in certain temples pay a fixed sum to the Treasury. The great misfortune of the world is that those who adore inanimate gods, and of that number is the greatest number of the wise, whether by love of lucre or love of vainglory, or by the taste for power, not only adore them, but, besides, constrain simple minds to adore them also.

"Such a prince might perhaps say, I am not free to do good. Being head, I am obliged to conform myself to the will of the majority.' He who speaks so is to be laughed at. Why should the sovereign not have the initiative in everything that is good? Why should he not compel the people who are under him to act rightly, to know God according to the truth? and why should he not present in himself an example of all good actions? Who more properly? It is an absurd thing that a prince should conduct himself wrongly, and nevertheless be a judge, condemning those who commit evil deeds. As for myself, I think that a State can never be so well governed as when the sovereign, knowing and fearing the true God, judges everything as a man who knows he shall be in his turn judged before God, and when his subjects, on their side fearing God, should be careful not to give offence to their sovereign, as he is to them. Thus, thanks to the knowledge and the fear of God, all evil could be suppressed by the State.

"If the sovereign, in fact, does not act unjustly towards his subjects, or they towards him, it is clear that the whole country will live in peace, and the greatest good will result; for necessarily the name of God will be praised among them all. The first duty of the sovereign, and that which is most pleasing to God, is therefore to free from error the people who are under him. All evils indeed proceed from error, and the grand error is not to know God, and to adore in His stead that which is not God."

We see how Melito is far removed from the dangerous principles which ruled at the end of the fourth century, and made the Christian empire. The sovereign erected into a protector of the truth, employing all means to make truth triumph, that is the ideal which was dreamt of. We shall find the same ideas in the apology addressed to Marcus-Aurelius. The dogmatic intolerance, the idea that it is culpable and displeasing to God to be ignorant of certain dogmas, is frankly avowed. Melito admits of no excuse for idolatry. And those who say that the honour rendered to idols in connection with the persons they represent, and those who content themselves with saying "It is the worship of our fathers," are equally to blame.

"Ah, what! are those to whom our fathers have left poverty forbidden to become rich? Are those whose parents have not instructed them condemned to remain ignorant of what their fathers did not know? Are the sons of the blind not to see, and the sons of the lame not to walk? . . . . Before imitating thy father, see if he has been in a good path. If he has been in a bad one, take the good, so that thy children may follow thee in their turn. Weep over thy father, who is following the path of evil, perhaps thy sorrow may save him yet. As to thy children, say to them: There is but one God, father of all, who had no beginning, who has not been created, and who makes all things subsist by His own will.'"

We shall soon see the part which Melito took in the controversy as to Easter, and the kind of way which so many distinguished minds took to present some apologetic writings to Marcus-Aurelius. His tomb is shown at Sardis as one of the just and the most certain to rise at the call of heaven. His name remained much respected among the Catholics, who considered him one of the first authorities of his age. His eloquence especially was boasted of, and the remains of him we have are, indeed, quite brilliant. A theology like his, where Jesus is at once God and man, was a protest against Marcion, and ought at the same time to please the adversaries of Artemon and Theodotus "the currier." He knew the Gospel called St. John's, and identified Christos with the Logos, putting him in the second rank behind the one God, before and above all. His treatise where Christ is presented as a created being might surprise; but no doubt it was little read, and this offensive title was changed in good time. In the fourth century, when orthodoxy had become more suspicious, these writings, so much admired two hundred years before, were no longer copied. Many passages doubtless appeared little conformed to the creed of Nicea. Melito's fortune was that of Papias, and of so many other doctors of the second century, true founders, the first fathers in reality, and who had no other fault than not having divined beforehand what one day would be revealed by the councils.

Claudius Apollinaris, or Apollinarus, maintained the fame of the Church of Hierapolis, and, like Melito, joined literary culture and philosophy with sanctity. His style passed as excellent, and his doctrine for the purest. By his distance from Judeo-Christianity and his taste for the Gospel of John, he belonged to the party of movement rather than to that of tradition. As this was the movement which triumphed, his adversaries were behind from that time. We see him, nearly at the same period as Melito, presenting an apology to Marcus-Aurelius. He wrote five books addressed to the Pagans, two against the Jews, two on the Truth, and one on Piety, without mentioning many other works which did not obtain a great publicity, but were much esteemed by all who read them. Apollinaris fought energetically with Montanism, and was perhaps the bishop who contributed most to save the Church from the dangers into which those preachers had made her run. Towards the excesses of the Encratites also he was very severe. An astonishing mixture of good sense and literature, of fanaticism and moderation, characterised those extraordinary men, true ancestors of the lettered bishop, clever politicians, always having the appearance of hearing nothing but the inspiration of heaven, opposed to the violent while quite violent themselves. Thanks to the mendacious softness of a liberal language, these anticipative Dupanloups proved that the most refined worldly calculations do not exclude the most odd illuminism, and that with perfect honesty they could unite in their person all the appearance of reasonable men and all the rapture of enthusiasts.

Miltiades, like Apollinaris, the great adversary of the Montanists, was also a fertile writer. He composed two books against the Pagans, two books against the Jews, not forgetting an apology addressed to the Roman authorities. Musanus fought with the Encratites, the disciples of Tatian. Modestus set himself especially to unveil the tricks and errors of Marcion. Polycrates, who, later on, was to preside in a manner over the Church of Asia, already shone by his writings. A crowd of books were produced on all sides. Never perhaps has Christianity written more than during the second century in Asia. Literary culture was widely spread in this province; the art of writing was very common, and Christianity profited by this. The literature of the fathers of the Church began. The following centuries never surpassed these first essays of Christian eloquence; but from the orthodox point of view, the books of these fathers of the second century presented rather a stumbling block. The reading of them became suspected; they were copied less and less, and thus nearly all these fine writings disappeared, to give place to the classical writers, after the council of Nicea, writers more correct as to doctrine, but, in general, less original than those of the second century.

A certain Papirius, whose episcopal seat is unknown, was extremely esteemed. Thraseas, bishop of Eumenia, in the region of the high Meander, had the most envied glory, that of martyrdom. He probably suffered at Smyrna, since it is there that his tomb is honoured. Sagaris, bishop of Laodicea, on the Lycus, had the same honour under the pro-consulate of L. Sergius Paullus about the year 165. Laodicea preserved most preciously his remains. His name remained so much the more fixed in the remembrance of the churches, as his death was the occasion of an important episode connecting itself with one of the gravest questions of the period.

CHAPTER XII

THE QUESTION OF EASTER

Chance decreed that the execution of Sagaris coincided nearly with the festival of Easter. Now the fixing of that festival gave place to difficulties without end. Deprived of its pastor, the Church of Laodicea fell into unsolvable controversies. These controversies belonged to the very essence of the development of Christianity and could not be avoided. By force of a reciprocal charity, a veil had been thrown over the deep difference between the two Christianities--on one side, the Christianity which appeared like a sequence of Judaism; on the other side, the Christianity which appeared like the destruction of Judaism. But the reality was less flexible than the spirit. The day of Easter was among the Christian churches a cause of much discord. They could not fast, they could not pray the same day. The one class was still in tears while the other was singing songs of triumph. Even the churches which no question of principles separated were embarrassed. The Passover cycle was so badly fixed that some neighbouring churches, like those of Alexandria and Palestine, wrote that in the spring they celebrated the feast the same day and in full sympathy.

What could be more shocking indeed than to see such a Church plunged in grief, attenuated by fasting, while just such another was already floating in the joys of the Resurrection? The fasts which preceded Easter, and which gave Lent its origin, were also practised with the greatest diversities.

It was Asia which was most agitated by these controversies. We have already seen the question treated of, ten or twelve years back, between Polycarp and Anicet. Nearly all the Christian churches, having the Church of Rome at their head, had misplaced the Passover, observing that festival on the Sunday which came before the fourteenth Nisan, and identifying it with the festival of the Resurrection. Asia had not followed the movement; on this point, if one may so speak, it had remained behind. The majority of the bishops of Asia, faithful to the tradition of the old Gospels, and appealing especially to Matthew, would have it that Jesus, before dying, had eaten the Passover with His disciples on the fourteenth of Nisan; they celebrated this festival on the same day as the Jews, on whichever day of the week it fell. They advanced in favour of their opinion the Gospel, the authority of their predecessors, the prescriptions of the law, the canon of the faith and especially the authority of the apostles John and Philip, who had lived among them, without looking for a single contradiction from John. It is more than probable indeed that the apostle John celebrated Easter all his life on the fourteenth Nisan; but in the Gospel which is attributed to him, he appears to point to quite another doctrine, treats disdainfully the ancient Jewish Passover festival, and makes Jesus die the same day as that on which they ate the lamb, as if to indicate thus the substitution of a new Paschal lamb for the old.

Polycarpus, we have seen, followed the tradition of John and Philip. It was so with Thraseas, Sagaris, Papirius, and Melito. The Montanists were also doubtless of the same opinion. But the opinion of the Universal Church became each day more imperious and embarrassing for these determined persons. Apollinaris of Hierapolis was, as it would appear, converted to the Roman practice. He repelled the Easter of the fourteenth Nisan as a remnant of Judaism, and advanced to maintain his opinion the Gospel of John. Melito, seeing the embarrassment of the faithful of Laodicea, deprived of their pastor, wrote for them his work on Easter, in which he maintains the tradition of the fourteenth Nisan. Apollinaris preserves a moderation which was not always imitated. The universal opinion of Asia remained faithful to the Judaising tradition; the controversy of Laodicea and the manifestation of Apollinaris had not any immediate consequences. The remote parts of Syria, and with greater reason the Judeo-Christians and Ebionites, remained equally faithful to the Jewish observance. As to the rest of the Christian world, carried away by the example of the Church of Rome, it adopted the anti-Jewish usage. Even the churches of Gaul of Asiatic origin, which at first had doubtless celebrated Easter on the fourteenth Nisan, conformed themselves speedily to the universal calendar, which was the truly Christian calendar. The remembrance of the Resurrection replaced all at once that of the exodus from Egypt, as the exodus from Egypt had replaced the purely naturalistic meaning of the ancient Semitic paskh, the Spring festival.

About the year 196 the question came up more freshly than ever. The churches of Asia persisted in their old usage. Rome, always ardent for unity, wished to compel them. On the invitation of the Pope Victor, assemblies of bishops were held; a vast correspondence was exchanged. Eusebius had in his hands the synodal epistle of the council of Palestine, presided over by Theophilus of Cesarea and Narcissus of Jerusalem, the letter of the Synod of Rome, countersigned by Victor, the letters of the bishops of the West, over whom Palma presided as being the oldest, the letter from the churches of France, of which Irenæus was bishop, and finally those of the churches of Osrhoêne, without speaking of individual letters from many bishops, notably from Bachylles of Corinth. They were found unanimous for the translation of Easter to Sunday. But the bishops of Asia, strong in the tradition of the two apostles and of so many illustrious men, would not yield. Old Polycrates, bishop of Ephesus, wrote in their name a letter bitter enough to Victor and to the Church of Rome.

"It is we who are faithful to tradition, without adding anything to it, without giving up anything. It is in Asia that these great foundation men repose, who will arise on the day of the Lord's appearing, in that day when He shall come from heaven with glory to raise all the saints: Philip, he who was one of the twelve apostles, who is buried at Hierapolis, also his two daughters who grow old in virginity, not to speak of another daughter who observed during her life the rule of the Holy Spirit, and who reposes at Ephesus; then John, he whose head reclined on the bosom of the Lord, who was pontiff carrying thepetalon, and martyr, and doctor, who also is interred at Ephesus; then Polycarpus, he who was bishop and martyr at Smyrna; then Thraseas, at once bishop and martyr of Eumenia, who is buried at Smyrna. Why speak of Sagaris, bishop and martyr, who is buried at Laodicea, of the blessed Papirius, and of Melito, the holy eunuch, who observed in everything the rule of the Holy Spirit, and rests at Sardis, waiting the heavenly call which shall make him rise among the dead? All these men celebrated Easter on the fourteenth day, according to the Gospel, without innovation of any kind, following the rule of the faith. And I also, I have done so likewise, I, Polycrates, the least of you all, agreeably to the tradition of my relatives, of whom some have been my teachers (for there have been seven bishops in my family: I am the eighth); and all my revered relatives observed the day when the people began to purge out the leaven. I then, my brethren, who reckon sixty-five years in the Lord, who have conversed with the brethren from the whole world, who have read from one end to the other the Holy Scripture, I shall not lose my head, whatever they may do to terrify me. Greater people than I have said: It is better to obey God rather than man.' I could quote the bishops here present, whom, upon your demand, I have convoked; if I wrote their names the list would be long. All having come to see me, poor wretch as I am, have given their adhesion to my letter, knowing well that it is not for nothing that I carry white hairs, and being assured that all I do I do in the Lord Jesus."

What proves that the Papacy was already born, and well born, is the incredible design which the somewhat bitter terms of this letter inspired in Victor. He pretended to excommunicate, to separate from the Church universal, the most illustrious, because it would not yield its traditions before the Roman discipline. He published a decree in virtue of which the churches of Asia were placed under the ban of Christian communion. But the other bishops were opposed to this violent measure, and recalled Victor to charity. Irenæus of Lyons, in particular, who, by necessity of the society in which he found himself placed, had accepted for himself and for the Gallic churches the Western custom, could not endure the thought that the mother churches of Asia, to which he felt himself bound by the bowels of his love, should be separated from the body of the Church universal. He energetically dissuaded Victor from excommunicating churches which held by the tradition of their fathers, and recalled the examples of his most tolerant predecessors.

"Yes, the ancients who presided before Soter in the Church which thou now leadest, we speak of Pius, Hyginus, Telesophorus, Xystus, did not observe the Jewish Passover, and did not permit any around them to observe it; but, while not observing it, they did not preserve the less peace with the members of churches who did observe it, when those came to them; although this observance, in the midst of people who did not observe it, rendered the contrast more striking. Never was any one repelled for this reason; on the contrary, the elders who have preceded thee, who, I repeat, did not observe, sent the Eucharist to the ancients of the Church who observed it. And when the blessed Polycarp came to Rome under Anicet, both of them gave each other first the kiss of peace; they had between them some small matters of difficulty: as to this point they did not make it the subject of a discussion. For neither did Anicet seek to persuade Polycarpus to abandon a practice which he had always kept and which he held from his association with John, the disciple of the Lord, and with the other apostles, nor did Polycarp try to persuade Anicet, he saying that he would keep the customs of the ancients who had gone before him. In this state of things they communicated with each other, and in the Church Anicet yielded to Polycarp the eucharistic consecration, to do him honour, and they separated from each other in perfect peace; and it was evident that the observants, as well as the nonobservants, each on their own side, were in accord with the Church universal."

This act of rare good sense, which opened so gloriously the annals of the Gallican Church, kept the schism of the East and West from taking place from the second century. Irenæus wrote on all hands to the bishops, and the question remained open in the churches of Asia. Naturally, Rome continued its propaganda against the Easter of the 14th Nisan. A Roman priest, Blastus, who sought to establish the Asiatic custom at Rome, was excommunicated. Irenæus disputed with him; the usage was not forbidden by apocryphal documents. The Roman practice gained day by day.

The question was not determined except by the Council of Nicæa. From thenceforth it was considered heretical to follow the tradition of John, Philip, Polycarp, and Melito. It happened as it had happened so many times. The defenders of the ancient tradition found themselves by their fidelity put outside the Church, and were no more than heretics, the quartodecimans.

The Jewish calendar presented some difficulties, and in the countries where there were no Jews they would have been embarrassed to determine the 14th Nisan. They declared that the Sunday of the Resurrection should be the Sunday which corresponds to or succeeds the first full moon after the spring equinox. The Friday preceding became naturally the memorial day of the Passion; the Thursday that of the institution of the Supper. Holy Week thus was established according to the tradition of the ancient gospels, not after the Gospel called St. John's. Pentecost, become the festival of the Holy Spirit, fell on the seventh Sunday after Easter, and the cycle of the movable feasts of the Christian year was held to be fixed uniformly for all the Churches until the Gregorian reform.

The practice which caused this debate had more importance than the debate itself. In connection with this difference, indeed, the Church was led to a clearer idea of its organisation. And first, it was plain that the laity were nothing. Only the bishops intervened in the question, circulating an opinion. The bishops were gathered together in provincial synods, presided over by the bishop of the capital of the province (the archbishop of the future), sometimes by the oldest. The synodal assembly met by a letter which was sent to the other churches. It was, therefore, like a rudiment of federal organisation, an attempt to resolve questions by means of provincial assemblies, presided over by the bishops and corresponding to them. It was attempted later, in parts of this great ecclesiastical struggle, to find precedents for the question of presiding at synods and the hierarchy of the churches. Among all the churches, that of Rome appeared to have a special right to the initiative. This initiative was exercised especially in view of bringing the churches into unity, even at the risk of the gravest schisms. The bishop of Rome claimed for himself the exorbitant right of driving from the Church every fraction which maintained its own traditions. From the year 196 this exaggerated desire for unity necessarily led to the schisms which took place later on. But a great bishop, animated by the true spirit of Jesus, prevailed on the pope at this time. Irenaeus protested, undertook a mission of peace, and succeeded in correcting the harm which Romish ambition had done. The infallibility of the bishop of Rome was still far from being believed in; for Eusebius declares that he read the letters in which the bishops forcibly blamed Victor's conduct.

CHAPTER XIII

LAST RECRUDESCENCE OF MILLENARIANISM AND PROPHETISM--THE MONTANISTS

The great day, in spite of the affirmations of Jesus and of prophets inspired by him, refused to come. The Christ was slow in showing himself; the ardent piety of the first days, which had for its mainspring the belief in this approaching appearance, had grown cold among many. It was on such a world as this, in the very bosom of that Roman society, so corrupted but so preoccupied by reform and progress, that people dreamed of founding the Kingdom of God. Christian morals, from the moment they aspired to be those of a complete society, began to relax themselves in many points from their primitive severity. Men did not become more Christian, as in the first ages, under the force of a strong personal impression; many were born Christians. The contrast became each day less decided between the Church and the surrounding world. It was inevitable that some rigorists should be found who would sink into the mire of the most dangerous worldliness, and that there should arise a party of pietists to fight with the general coldness, to continue the supernatural gifts of the Apostolic Church, and to prepare humanity, by a redoubling of austerities, with proofs of the last days.

Already we have seen the pious author of the Hermas weeping over the decay of his time, and calling by his vows for a reform which should make the Church a convent of holy men and women.

There was, in fact, something rather inconsistent in the kind of quietude in which the orthodox Church slumbered, in that tranquil morality to which the work of Jesus was more and more reduced. People neglected the very precise predictions of the founder as to the end of the present world and on the Messianic reign which should follow. The speedy appearance in the clouds was nearly forgotten. The desire for martyrdom, the taste for celibacy, results of such a belief, grew weak. People accepted relations with an impure world, condemned soon to end; they temporised with persecution and sought to escape from it by the price of money. It was inevitable that the ideas which formed the basis of budding Christianity should reappear from time to time, in the midst of this general depression, in the shape of what was severe and terrifying. Fanaticism, which softened good orthodox judgment, made some kinds of eruption, like a slumbering volcano.

The most remarkable of these very natural returns to the apostolic spirit was that which was produced in Phrygia, under Marcus-Aurelius. It was something quite analogous to what we have seen in our time in England and America among the Irvingites and the Latter Day Saints. Some simple and enthusiastic minds believe themselves called to renew the prodigies of individual inspiration, beyond those already heavy chains of the Church and the episcopate. A doctrine for a long time spread through Asia Minor, that of a Paraclete who should come to complete the work of Jesus, or, to speak more correctly, to take up the teaching of Jesus, to establish it in truth, to purge out the alterations which the apostles and bishops had introduced into it; such a doctrine, I say, opened the door to all innovations. The Church of the saints was conceived of as always progressive and as destined to run through successive degrees of perfection. Prophetism passed for the most natural thing in the world. The Sibyllists, the prophets of every kind, ran through the streets, and in spite of their gross artifices found credence and acceptance.

Some little towns of the poorest districts of Phrygia, Brûlée, Tymium, and Pepuza, whose site even is unknown, were the theatre of this late enthusiasm. Phrygia was one of the countries of antiquity the most carried away by religious dreams. The Phrygians were generally looked on as silly and simple. Christianity had among them, from its origin, a mystic and ascetic character. Already in the Epistle to the Colossians Paul fights with errors, where the precursory signs of Gnosticism and the excesses of a badly understood asceticism seemed to be mixed up. Nearly everywhere else Christianity was a religion of the large cities; here, as in Syria or beyond the Jordan, it was a religion of clowns and countrymen. A certain Montanus, of the town of Ardaban, in Mysia, on the confines of Phrygia, contrived to give to these pious follies a contagious character which they did not possess till then.

Doubtless imitation of the Jewish prophets, and of those who had produced the new law at the beginning of the apostolic age, was the principal element of this re-birth of prophetism. There was mixed with it also perhaps an orgiastic or corybantic element, peculiar to the country, and entirely outside the regulated habits of ecclesiastical prophecy, already subjected to a tradition. All this credulous world was of the Phrygian race, and spoke Phrygian. In the most orthodox parts of Christendom, besides, the miraculous passed for quite a simple thing. Revelation was not closed; it was the life of the Church. The spiritual gifts, the apostolic charismas, were continued in many communities; they were cited in proof of the truth. They quoted Agabas, Judas, Silas, the daughters of Philip, Ammias of Philadelphia, and Quadratus, as having been favoured by the prophetic spirit. They declared from the first that the prophetic charisma would remain in the Church by an uninterrupted succession until the coming of Christ. The belief in a Paraclete, conceivedly as a source of permanent inspiration for the faithful, kept up these ideas. Who cannot see how full of dangers such a belief was? Thus the spirit of wisdom which directed the Church tended more and more to subordinate the exercise of its supernatural gifts to the authority of the presbyterate. The bishops were credited with the discernment of spirits, the right to approve some and to exorcise others. This time it was a prophetism quite popular which arose without the permission of the clergy, and sought to govern the Church outside of the hierarchy. The question of ecclesiastical authority and of individual inspiration, which fills up all the history of the Church, especially since the sixteenth century, took up its position from that time with distinctness. Between the believer and God is there or is there not an intermediary? Montanus said no, without hesitation. "Man, said the Paraclete, in an oracle of Montanus, is the lyre, and I fly like the bow; man sleeps, and I awake."

Montanus justified no doubt by some superiority this pretension of being the elect of the Spirit. We willingly credit his adversaries when they tell us that he was a believer of recent date; we even admit that the desire of the primacy was no stranger to his singularities. As to the debauches and the shameful end they say he had, they were the ordinary calumnies which were never wanting under the pen of orthodox writers when the blackening of dissentients was concerned. The admiration which he excited in Phrygia was extraordinary. Some of his disciples pretended to have learned more from his books than from the law, the prophets, and the reunited evangelists. It was believed that he had received the fulness of the Paraclete; sometimes they took him for the Paraclete himself, that is to say, for this Messiah, in some things superior to Jesus, whom the churches of Asia Minor believed to have been promised by Jesus himself. They went so far as to say, "The Paraclete has revealed the greatest things by Montanus, as Christ by the Gospel." The law and the prophets were considered as the infancy of religion; the Gospel was its youth; the coming of the Paraclete was considered to be the sign of its maturity.

Montanus, like all the prophets of the new alliance, was full of curses against the age and against the Roman empire. Even the seer of 69 was surpassed. Neither hatred of the world nor the desire of seeing Pagan society destroyed had yet been expressed with such a distinct fury. The only theme of the Phrygian prophets was the approaching judgment of God, the punishment of persecutors, the destruction of the profane world, the reign of the thousand years and its joys. Martyrdom was praised as the highest perfection; to die in one's bed seemed unworthy of a Christian. The Encratites, condemning sexual connection, recognised in it importance from the natural point of view; Montanus did not even take the trouble to forbid an act become absolutely insignificant, from the moment that its humanness came to an end.

The gate was thus opened to the debauch, at the same time as it closed to the pleasantest duties. By the side of Montanus appeared two women, the one called sometimes Prisca, sometimes Priscilla, sometimes Quintilla, and the other Maximilla. These two women, who, from what appeared, had all quitted the state of marriage to embrace the prophetic career, entered into their position with an extreme boldness and a complete misunderstanding of the hierarchy. In spite of the wise prohibitions of Paul against women taking part in the prophetic and ecstatic exercises of the Church, Priscilla and Maximilla did not draw back before the brilliancy of a public ministry. It seems that individual inspiration had had, this time as usual, licence and boldness. Priscilla had some features which made her like St. Catharine of Sienna and Maria Alacoque. One day, at Pepuza, she slept and saw Christ come towards her, clothed in a shining robe and having the appearance of a woman. Christ was asleep by her side, and, in this mysterious embracing, inoculated her with all wisdom. He revealed to her especially the sacredness of the town of Pepuza. This privileged spot was the site where the heavenly Jerusalem, in descending from heaven, would be placed. Maximilla preached in the same way, announcing fearful wars, catastrophes, and persecutions. She survived Priscilla, and died maintaining that after her there would be no other prophesy till the end of time.

It was not only prophecy, it was all the functions of the clergy, which this bizarre Christianity claimed to belong to women. The Presbyterate, the Episcopate, the charge of the Church in all degrees devolved on them. To justify this pretension they instanced Miriam, the sister of Moses, the four daughters of Philip, and even Eve, for whom they pleaded extenuating circumstances, and of whom they made a saint. What was strange in the worship of the sect was the ceremony of the weepers or virgin lampadophores, who recalled in many points of view the Protestant "revivals" of America. Seven virgins, bearing torches and clothed in white, entered the church, uttering penitential groans, pouring forth torrents of tears and deploring by expressive gestures the wretchedness of human life. Then began the scenes of illuminism. In the midst of the people the virgins were seized with enthusiasm, preached, prophesied, and fell into ecstasies. The audience sobbed and went forth penetrated by compunction.

The influence these women exercised over the crowds, and even over a portion of the clergy, was extraordinary. They went so far as to prefer the prophetesses of Pepuza to the apostles, and even to Christ. The most moderate saw in them those prophets foretold by Jesus as coming to finish his work. All Asia Minor was troubled. From neighbouring countries people came to see these ecstatic phenomena, and to give an opinion on the new prophetism. The feeling was so much the greater that no one rejected à priori the possibility of prophecy. The only question was whether it was real. The most distant churches, those of Lyons and Vienne, wrote to Asia to be informed on the subject. Many bishops, especially Ælius Publius Julius of Debeltus, and Sotas of Anchiale in Thrace, came forward as witnesses. All Christendom was set in motion by these miracles, which appeared to bring back the Christianity of a hundred and thirty years before, in the days of its first appearance.

The greater number of the bishops, Apollinaris of Hierapolis, Zoticus of Comane, Julian of Apamia, Miltiades the famous ecclesiastical writer, a certain Aurelius of Cyrene, described as "martyr" by his life, and the two bishops of Thrace, refused to look seriously upon the enlightened of Pepuza. Nearly all of them declared individual prophesying to be subversive of the Church, and treated Priscilla as "possessed." Some orthodox bishops, in particular Sotas of Anchiale and Zoticus of Comane, wished even to exorcise her; but the Phrygians would not allow it. Some notables, moreover, such as Themison, Theodotus, Alcibiades, and Proclus, yielded to the general enthusiasm and betook themselves to prophesying in their turn. Theodotus, especially, was the chief of the sect after Montanus and his principal zealot. As to the simple people they were all enchanted. The dark oracles of the prophetesses were carried away and commented on. A real Church formed itself around them. All the gifts of the apostolic age, especially the gift of tongues and the ecstasies, renewed themselves. They allowed themselves to go too easily into this dangerous reasoning: "Why should that which had a place not have place still? The present generation is not more disinherited than the others. The Paraclete, representing Christ, is he not an external source of revelation?" Innumerable little books spread these chimeras to a distance. Good people who read these found them finer than the Bible. The new exercises appeared to them superior to the charismas of the Apostles, and many dared to say that something greater than Jesus had appeared. All Phrygia became nearly mad; ordinary ecclesiastical life was as if suspended.

A life of lofty asceticism was the consequence of this burning faith in the approaching advent of God to the earth. The prayers of the saints at Phrygia were unceasing. They wore from affectation a sad air, and they were very bigoted. Their habit of holding the index finger against the nose while in prayer, to give themselves a contrite appearance, obtained for them the nickname of "nose-pegs" (in Phrygian tascodrugites). Fasts, austerities, rigorous xerophagy, abstinence from wine, absolute reprobation of marriage, such was the morale which logically imposed itself on these pious people in retreat in the hope of the last day. Even for the Supper they only used, like certain Ebionites, bread and water, cheese and salt. Austere disciplines are always contagious in crowds incapable of high spirituality; for they bring certain salvation at a good price, and they are easy for simple people (who have only good intentions) to practise. On all sides these habits spread about; they penetrated even into Gaul with the Asiatics, who numbered so many adherents in the valley of the Rhone. One of the Lyons martyrs in 177 showed himself attached to them even in prison, and it required either good Gallic sense or, as one may believe, a direct revelation from God, to make him renounce them.

What was most troublesome, indeed, in the excesses of zeal of these ardent ascetics was that they showed themselves intractable against all those who did not share their affectations. They spoke only of the general falling away. Like the flagellants of the middle ages, they found in their exterior practices a principle of foolish pride and rebellion against the clergy. They dared to say that, since Jesus, at least since the Apostles, the Church had lost its time, and that it only required a little time to sanctify humanity and to prepare it for the Messianic reign. The Church of the whole world, according to them, was no better than Pagan society. It sought to form within the general church a spiritual church, a nucleus of saints, of which Pepuza should be the centre. These elect ones showed themselves supercilious towards the simple believers. Themison declared that the Catholic Church had lost all its glory, and obeyed Satan. A church of saints, that was their ideal, very little different from that of the pseudo-Hermas. He who is not a saint does not belong to the Church. The Church, they said, is the totality of saints, not the number of bishops.

Nothing was further, it may be seen, from the idea of Catholicity, whose tendency was prevalent and whose essence consisted in opening the doors to all. The Catholics took the Church as it was, with its imperfections; one could not, according to them, be a sinner without ceasing to be a Christian. As to the Montanists, these two terms were irreconcilable. The Church should be as chaste as a virgin; the sinner is excluded from it by his very sin, and loses from that time all hope of re-entering it. The absolution of the Church is of no value. Holy things ought to be administered by the saints. The bishops have no privilege in what concerns spiritual gifts. Only the prophets, organs of the Spirit, can assure that God forgives.

Thanks to the extraordinary manifestations of an external and barely discreet pietism, Pepuza and Tynium became indeed a kind of holy towns. They were called Jerusalem, and the sectaries wished them to be the centre of the world. People came there from all directions, and many maintained that, conformably to the prediction of Priscilla, the ideal Sion was already created. Was not ecstasy the provisional realisation of the kingdom of God, begun by Jesus? Women quitted their husbands, as if at the end of human affairs. Every day they believed they should see the clouds open and the New Jerusalem appear in the blue heavens.

The orthodox, and especially the clergy, sought naturally to prove that the attraction which drew these Puritans to eternal things did not detach them altogether from the world. The sect had a central treasury for their propaganda. Collectors went out in all directions to seek offerings. The preachers received a salary; the prophetesses, in return for interviews they gave or audiences they vouchsafed, received money, dresses, and handsome presents. We can see what a handle this would give against the pretended saints. They had their confession and their martyrs, and this was what annoyed the orthodox most; for these would have desired that martyrdom should be considered the criterion of the true Church. Thus they spread slanders to lessen the merits of those sectarian martyrs. Themison having been arrested escaped, this being followed up by the payment of money. One Alexander was also imprisoned, and the orthodox had no peace till he was represented as a thief who perfectly deserved his lot, and had a judicial sentence against him in the archives of the province of Asia.

CHAPTER XIV

RESISTANCE OF THE ORTHODOX CHURCH

The struggle lasted more than half a century; but the victory was never doubtful. The Phrygians, as they were called, had but one fault; it was grave; it was to do what the apostles did; and that when, for a hundred years back, the freedom of the charisms had been nothing but an inconvenience. The Church was already too strongly constituted for the undisciplined character of the Phrygians to do her real harm. While admiring the saints who produced this grand school of asceticism, the immense majority of the faithful refused to leave their pastors to follow wandering masters. Montanus, Priscilla, and Maximilla died without leaving any successors. What assured the triumph of the orthodox Church was the talent of its polemics. Apollinaris of Hierapolis led all who were not blinded by fanaticism. Miltiades developed the theory that "a prophet ought not to speak in ecstasy of a book which was held to be one of the bases of Christian theology." Serapion of Antioch collected, about 195, the evidences which condemned the innovators. Clement of Alexandria betook himself to refute them.

The most complete among the works which kept up the controversy was that of a certain Apollonius, unknown elsewhere, who wrote forty years after the appearance of Montanus (that is to say between 200 and 400). It is by extracts from this that Eusebius has preserved to us what we know of the origins of the sect. Another bishop, whose name has not been preserved to us, composed a kind of history of this singular movement, fifteen years after the death of Maximilla, under the Severuses. To the same literature probably belongs the writing of which the fragment known under the name of the Canon of Muratori makes a part, directed at the same time, it would appear, against the Gnostic dreams. The Montanists, indeed, could not look for less than to have admitted to the body of the New Testament the prophecies of Montanus, Priscilla, and Maximilla. The conference which took place about 210 between Proclus, become the chief of the sect, and the Roman priest Caïus, turned on this point. Generally, the Church of Rome, up to Zephyrin, held very strongly against these innovations.

Animosity was great on both sides; they excommunicated each other reciprocally. When the confessors of the two parties were drawn together by martyrdom, they separated from each other, and would have nothing in common. The orthodox redoubled calumnies and sophistries to prove that the Montanist martyrs (and no church had more) were all miscreants or impostors, and especially to establish that the authors of this sect had perished miserably, by suicide, as madmen, out of their minds, having become the dupes or the prey of the devil.

The infatuation of certain towns in Asia Minor for these pious follies knew no bounds. The Church of Ancyra, at a special moment, was quite drawn with its elders towards the dangerous novelties. It needed the close reasoning of the nameless bishop and of Zoticus of Otre to open their eyes, and even their conversion was not lasting. Ancyra, in the fourth century, continued to be the scene of the same aberrations. The Church of Thyatira was attacked in a still deeper manner. Phrygianism had established its stronghold there, and for a long time this old church was considered lost to Christendom. The councils of Iconium and of Synnade, about 231, realised the evil without being able to cure it. The extreme credulity of these honest populations of the centre of Asia Minor, Phrygians, Galatians, &c., had been the cause of their prompt conversion to Christianity, and now this credulity placed them at the mercy of all illusions. Phrygian became nearly synonymous with heretic. About 235, a new prophetess rose from the fields of Cappadocia, going with naked feet among the mountains, announcing the end of the world, administering the sacraments and desiring to draw her disciples to Jerusalem. Under Decius, the Montanists furnished a considerable contingent to martyrdom.

We shall see the perplexity of conscience which the sectaries of Phrygia will cause to the confessors of Lyons, in the very height of their struggle. Divided between admiration for so much holiness and the astonishment which these oddities caused to their right minds, our heroic and sensible compatriots tried in vain to stifle the discussion. For a moment even the Church of Rome was surprised. Bishop Zephyrin had already almost recognised the prophecies of Montanus, Priscilla, and Maximilla, when an ardent Asian, a confessor of the faith, Epigones, called Praxeas, who knew the sectaries better than the elders at Rome, unveiled the weaknesses of the pretended prophets, and showed the pope that he could not approve of these dreams without giving the lie to his predecessors who had condemned them.

The debate complicated the question of penitence and reconciliation. The bishops claimed the right to absolve, and used it with a freedom which offended the Puritans. The illuminated pretended that they alone could replace the soul into favour with God, and they showed themselves as very severe. Every mortal sin (homicide, idolatry, blasphemy, adultery, fornication) shut, according to them, the avenue to repentance. If these extraordinary principles had remained confined in the remote provinces of Catacecaumena, the evil would have been a small matter. Unfortunately, the little sect of Phrygia served as the nucleus to a considerable party, who presented some real dangers, since it was capable of drawing away from the orthodox Church its most illustrious apologist, Tertullian.

This party, which dreamed of an immaculate Church, and only obtained a strict conventicle, succeeded, in spite of its very exaggerations, in recruiting from the Church all the austere and excessive. It had so much of the logic of Christianity. We have already seen the same thing happen in the case of the Encratites and Tatian. With its unnatural abstinences, its disesteem of marriage, its condemnation of second marriage, Montanism was nothing else than a consequent millenarianism, and millenarianism was Christianity itself. "Who would mix up," said Tertullian, "cares of nurselings with the last judgment? It will be beautiful to see flowing bosoms, the nauseas of an accouched woman, and squalling brats mingled with the appearance of the Judge and the sounds of the trumpet. Oh! good, wise women--the executioners of the Antichrist!" The enthusiasts related how, during forty years, they had seen every morning, hanging in the sky in Judea, a city which vanished when one drew near it. They invoked, to prove the reality of this vision, the evidence of the Pagans, and each one imagined the delights he should enjoy in this heavenly dwelling as compensation for the sacrifices he had made here below.

Africa especially, by its ardour and harshness, fell into this snare. Montanists, Novatianists, Donatists, innumerable are the different names under which was produced the spirit of undiscipline, the unhealthy ardour of the martyr, hatred to the Episcopate, millenarian dreams, which always were classic ground to the Berber races. These rigorists who revolted against being called a sect, but who in every church gave themselves out as the elect, as Christian souls worthy of that name, these Puritans, implacable towards those who wished to repent, became the worst scourge of Christianity. Tertullian treats the general church as a cave of adulterers and prostitutes. The bishops, not having either the gift of prophecy nor of miracles, would, in the eyes of the enthusiasts, be lower than pneumatics. It is by them, and not by the official hierarchy, that the transmission of the sacramental graces, the movement of the Church and progress are accomplished. The true Christian, only living in prospect of the last judgment and of martyrdom, passes his life in contemplation. Not only should he not flee from persecution, but he is commanded to seek it. He must prepare without ceasing for martyrdom as for a necessary complement of the Christian life. The natural end of the Christian is to die in torture. An unbridled credulousness, a faith to the uttermost in the spiritualistic charismas, made of Montanism one of the most extraordinary types of fanaticism which the history of humanity records.

What it has of weight about it is that this frightful dream seduced the imagination of the only man of grand literary talent whom the Church had counted in its bosom for three centuries. An incorrect writer, but with a strong energy, an ardent sophist, wielding by turns irony, blame, the lowest triviality, the plaything of an ardent conviction even in his most manifest contradictions, Tertullian found means to give some chefs d'oeuvres to the half-dead Latin tongue, by applying to this wild idea an eloquence which had hitherto remained unknown to the ascetic bigots of Phrygia.

The victory of the Episcopate was, in these circumstances, the victory of leniency and humanity. With rare good sense the general church looked on the exaggerated abstinences as a sort of partial anathema cast on the creation and as an injury to the work of God. The question of the admission of women to ecclesiastical functions and to the administration of the sacraments, a question that certain precedents of the apostolic history left undecided, were determined for ever. The bold pretence of the sectaries of Phrygia to insert some new prophecies into the biblical canon led the Church to declare, more distinctly than she had ever done before, the New Bible closed for ever. Finally the rash seeking for martyrdom became a sort of offence, and alongside the legend which exalted the true martyr there was the legend intended to show that he was culpable who anticipated penalties, and infringed without being compelled the laws of his country.

The flock of believers, necessarily of average virtue, followed the pastors. Mediocrity founded authority. Catholicity began. For it the future! The principle of a kind of Christian yoguism is suppressed for a time. There was here the first victory of the Episcopate, and perhaps the most important; for it was obtained over a sincere piety. The ecstasies, the prophecy, the speaking with tongues had texts and history for them. But they had become a danger; the Episcopate put them in good order; it suppressed all these manifestations of individual faith. How far are we from the time so much admired by the author of the Acts? Already in the bosom of Christianity existed this party of moderate good sense, who have always gained in the struggles of Church history. The hierarchical authority, at its origin, was strong enough to quell the enthusiasm of the undisciplined, to put the laity into guardianship, and to cause this principle to triumph, that the bishops alone are concerned in theology and are the sole judges of revelations. It was, indeed, the death of Christianity, by the destruction of the Episcopate, which these good fools of Phrygia devised. If individual inspiration, the doctrine of individual revelation and of its change as to permanence had been carried, Christianity would have perished in little conventicles of epileptics! Those puerile macerations which could not be suitable for the wide world would have arrested the propaganda. All the faithful, having the same right to the priesthood, to spiritual gifts, and power to administer the sacraments, would have fallen into a complete anarchy. The charisma would have abolished the sacrament; the sacrament gained the day, and the foundation-stone of Catholicism was irrevocably established.

In fact, the triumph of the ecclesiastical hierarchy was complete. Under Callixtus (217-222) moderate maxims prevailed in the Church of Rome, to the great scandal of the rigorists, who revenged themselves by atrocious calumnies. The council of Iconium closed the debate for the Church without bringing back the wanderers. The sect died, but very slowly; it continued up to the fourth century in the condition of Christian democracy, especially in Asia Minor, under the names of Phrygians, Phrygasts, Cataphryges, Pepuzians, Tascodrugites, Quintellians, Priscillians, and Artotyrites. They called themselves the pure ones or spiritualists. For some centuries Phrygia and Galatia were devoured by certain pietistic and Gnostic heresies, dreaming of clouds and angels and Æons. Pepuza was destroyed; we do not know in what circumstances or at what date, but the district remained sacred. This desert became a place of pilgrimage. The initiated gathered from all Asia Minor and celebrated there secret worship, as to which popular rumour had fine scope for exercise. They affirmed positively that it was there the celestial vision was to be revealed. They remained there for days and nights in a mystic waiting, and at the end of that time they saw Christ personally coming to respond to the ardour which consumed them.

CHAPTER XV

COMPLETE TRIUMPH OF THE EPISCOPATE--RESULTS ON MONTANISM

Thus, thanks to the Episcopate, reputed representative of the tradition of the twelve apostles, the Church wrought out, without weakening herself, the most difficult of transformations. She passed from the conventual state, if I may say so, to the laic condition--from the condition of a little chapel of visionaries to the state of the Church opened to all, and, consequently, exposed to imperfections. What seemed destined never to be anything but a dream of fanatics had become a durable religion. To become a Christian, whatever Hermas and the Montanists said, one doesn't need to be a saint. Obedience to ecclesiastical authority is now what makes the Christian, much more than spiritual gifts. These spiritual gifts shall be even suspected henceforth, and shall frequently expose the most favoured by grace to become heretics. Schism is the ecclesiastical crime par excellence. For dogma, again, the Christian Church possessed already a centre of orthodoxy which called heresy everything that leaves the received type; it had also an average morality which could be that of all the world, and not draw people forcibly, as that of the abstinents did, to the end of the world. In repulsing the Gnostics the Church had repulsed the refinements of dogma; in rejecting the Montanists it rejected the refinements of holiness. The excesses of those who dreamed of a spiritual church, a transcendant perfection, struck against common sense and the established Church. The masses, already considerable, who entered the Church and constituted the majority, brought down the moral temperature to the lowest possible level. In politics the question was in the same position. The exaggerations of the Montanists, their furious declamations against the Roman Empire, their hatred against Pagan society, could not be the act of everyone. The empire of Marcus-Aurelius was very different from that of Nero. With him there had been no reconciliation to hope for; with the former, one might expect it. The Church and Marcus-Aurelius pursued, in many points of view, the same end. It is clear that the bishops would have abandoned to the secular arm all the saints of Phrygia, if such a sacrifice had been the price of the alliance which would have put into their hands the spiritual direction of the world.

Charismas, indeed, and other supernatural exercises, excellent for maintaining the fervour of little congregations of the illuminated, became impracticable in the large churches. Extreme severity as to the rules of penitence was an absurdity and a meaningless thing, if one aspired to nothing else than a conventicle of so-called pure ones. A people is never made up of the spotless, and the simple believer needed to be admitted to repentance more than once. It was therefore admitted that one might be a member of the Church without being either a hero or an ascetic; it was sufficient for this that one was submissive to his bishop. The saints implored; the struggle between individual holiness and that of the hierarchy is not finished yet, but the middle view shall gain; it will be possible to sin without ceasing to be a Christian. The hierarchy shall prefer even the sinner who employs the ordinary means of reconciliation to the proud ascetic who justifies himself, or who believes that he has no need of justification.

It never will be given to either of these two principles to annihilate the other. Alongside the Church of all there will be the Church of the saints; alongside of the age there will be the convent; alongside the simple believer there will be the "religious." The kingdom of God, such as Jesus has preached it, being impossible in the world as it is, and the world being determined not to change, what must be done then, if not to found little kingdoms of God, a kind of islets in an irremediably perverse ocean, where the application of the Gospel is made to the letter, and where that distinction between precepts and some counsels which serve, in the worldly Church, as a valve to escape from impossibilities? The religious life is one in some sort logically necessary in Christianity. A grand organism finds it the means of developing all that exists in its bosom in germ. The ideal of perfection which lies at the base of the Galilean preaching of Jesus, and which some true disciples always will determinedly maintain, cannot exist in the world; it is needful, therefore, to create, that this idea may be realisable, some enclosed worlds, monasteries, where poverty, self-denial and reciprocal correction, obedience and chastity should be rigorously practised. The Gospel is really rather the Enchiridion of a convent than a code of morality; it is the essential rule of all monastic order; the perfect Christian is a monk; the monk is consequently a Christian; the convent is the place where the Gospel, always Utopian elsewhere, becomes a reality. The code which claims to teach the imitation of Jesus Christ is a book for the cloister. Satisfied to know that the morality preached by Jesus is practised somewhere, the laity will console itself with its mundane connections, and will easily become used to believe that such lofty maxims are not made for it. Buddhism has resolved the question in another way. Every one is a monk there a part of his life. Christianity is content if it has some part in the places where true Christianity is practised; the Buddhist is content provided that at one point of his life he has been a perfect Buddhist.

Montanism was an exaggeration; it could not but perish. But, like all exaggerations, it left deep traces. The Roman Christian was in part its work. Its two great enthusiasms, chastity and martyrdom, remained the two fundamental elements of Christian literature. It was Montanism which invented this strange association of ideas, created the martyr Virgin, and, introducing the female charm into the most gloomy accounts of sufferings, inaugurated that bizarre literature from which Christian imagination to the beginning of the fourth century could not release itself. The Montanist Acts of St. Perpetua and the martyrs of Africa, breathing forth their faith in charisms, full of an extreme rigorism and a burning ardour, impregnated with a strong savour of slave love, mixing the finished images of a skilful æsthetic with the most fanatical dreams, opened the series of these works of austere voluptuousness. The search for martyrdom became a fever impossible to govern. The circumcellious, running through the country in mad bands seeking death, forcing people to martyr them, making this access of gloomy hysteria become an epidemic.

Chastity in marriage remained one of the bases in the interest of Roman Christians. Now there was there another Montanist idea. Like the false Hermas, the Montanists stirred unceasingly the dangerous ember which they might well have allowed to sleep with its concealed fires, but that it was imprudent to extinguish it violently. The precautions they took in this matter evidence a certain preoccupation, more lascivious at bottom than the liberty of the man of the world; in any case these precautions are such as aggravate the evil, or at least betray it, bringing it to life. An excessive tenderness in regard to temptation we must gather from this exaggerated apprehension of beauty, from those interdicts against the toilette of women and especially on dressing their hair, which are found in every page of the Montanist writings. The woman who, by the most innocent turn given to her hair, seeks to please and conveys the conviction that she is pretty, becomes, in the speech of these bitter sectaries, as culpable as she who excites to lewdness. The demon of the hair will be charged with her punishment. Aversion to marriage came from motives which must be sought for there. The pretended chastity of the Encratites was often only an unconscious deception.

A romance which was certainly of Montanist origin, since we find in it arguments to prove that women have the right to instruct and to administer the sacraments, turns entirely on this rather dangerous ambiguity. We speak of Thécla. However rough and provoking is the romance of the saints Nerea and Achilea, nothing could be more voluptuously chaste; marriage has never been treated with a more naïve immodesty. Let one read in Gregory of Tours the delicious legend of the "Two Lovers of Auvergne," in the Acts of John the piquant story of "Drusiana," in the Acts of Thomas the tale of "The Betrothed Spouses of India," in St. Ambrose the story of the Virgin of Antioch with the adulterer; and then one can understand how the ages which nourished such recitals can, without merit, be described as having renounced profane love. One of the mysteries most profoundly held by the founders of Christianity is that chastity is a pleasure, and that modesty is one of the forms of love. The people who are afraid of women are generally those who love them most. How often may it be said with justice to the ascetic: Fallit te incautum pietas tua. In certain portions of the Christian community there was seen appearing, at different times, the idea that women ought never to be seen, that the life which befits them is a life of seclusion, according to the habit which has prevailed in the Mussulman East. It is easy to see to what a degree, if such a thought had prevailed, the character of the Church would have been changed. What, in fact, distinguishes the church from the mosque and even from the synagogue is, that the woman enters freely there and on the same footing as the man, although separated or even veiled. It appears as if their Christianity would have been, as Islamism was later on, a religion for men, from which the woman is almost altogether excluded. The Catholic Church took care not to commit this fault. Women had the functions of the diaconate in the Church, and were engaged in it with man in subordinate but frequent affairs. Baptism, the eucharistic communion, and works of charity took them apart from the customs of the East. Here again the Catholic Church formed the medium among the exaggerations of the different sects with a rare sense of tact.

Thus is explained that singular mixture of timid modesty and soft abandon which characterise moral sentiment in the primitive churches. Away with the vile suspicions of vulgar debauches, incapable of understanding such innocence! Everything was pure in these holy freedoms; but it was necessary also to be pure to be able to enjoy it. Legend shows us the Pagans jealous of the privilege which the priest has of perceiving one moment in baptismal nudity her who, by the holy immersion, becomes his spiritual sister. What should be said of the "holy kiss" which was the ambrosia of these chaste generations, of that kiss which, like the consolamentum of the Cathares, was a sacrament of strength and love, and whose remembrance, mingled with the most solemn impressions of the Eucharistic act, was sufficient for days to fill the soul with a kind of perfume? Why was the Church so beloved, that to re-enter it when they had left it men went anticipating death? Because it was a school of infinite joys. Jesus was really in the midst of his own. More than a hundred years after his death, he was still the master of learned pleasures, the initiator into transcendant secrets.

CHAPTER XVI

MARCUS-AURELIUS AMONG THE QUADES--THE BOOK OF THOUGHTS

Too little concerned about what passed in the rest of the world, the government of Marcus-Aurelius seemed to exist only for home progress. The only great organised empire which touched the Roman frontier, that of the Parthians, yielded before the legions. Lucius Verus and Aridius Cassius conquered some provinces which Trajan had only shortly occupied: Armenia, Mesopotamia, and Adiabene. The real danger was beyond the Rhine and the Danube. There lived in a threatening obscurity some energetic people, for the most part Germans in race, whom the Romans scarcely knew save by the handsome and faithful body-guard (the Swiss of that age), which certain emperors loved to keep, or by the superb gladiators who, unveiling all at once in the amphitheatre the beauty of their naked forms, called forth the intense admiration of the audience.

To conquer step by step this impenetrable world, to make the limits of civilisation extend league after league: to establish itself strongly in Bohemia, in the central quadrilateral of Europe, where there might still be a considerable nucleus of Celtic Boïans; from thence to advance like the backwoodsman of America to destroy tree after tree of the Hercynian forest, to substitute colonies for these tribes without association with the soil, to fix and civilise those peoples full of a future, to cause the empire to be benefited by their rare qualities, their solidity, their corporeal force, their energy; to extend the true frontiers of the empire, on one side to the Oder or the Vistula, on the other to the Pruth or the Dneister, and to give thus to the Latin portion of the empire a decided preponderance, which should prevent the schism of the Greek or Oriental portion; instead of building that fatal Constantinople, to place the second capital at Bâle or Constance, and to secure thus for the great good of the empire to the Celto-German peoples, the political beginning which they might conquer later on upon the ruins of the empire--this would have been the programme of the enlightened Romans, if they had been better informed as to the state of Europe and Asia, geography and comparative ethnography.

The badly-arranged expedition of Varus (year 10 of J. C.) and the eternal breach it left in the number of the legions were like a fan which turned Roman thought from the great Germany. Tacitus alone saw the importance of this region as the equilibrium of the world. But the state of division in which the Germanic tribes were, lulled to sleep the disquietude which sagacious minds ought to have felt. Indeed, while those people, more concerned with local independence than centralisation, did not form a military aggregation, they gave little cause for fear. But their confederations were very great. Men knew what result that had which was formed in the third century on the right bank of the Rhone under the name of France. About the year 166, a powerful league was formed in Bohemia, Moravia and the north of the present Hungary. The names of a multitude of nations, which were later on to fill the world, were heard for the first time. The great advance of the barbarians commenced; the Germans, up till now unassailable, attacked. The banks of the Danube were burst in the region of Austria and Hungary, towards Presbourg, Comorn and Gran. All the German and Slav peoples, from France to the Danube, Marcomans, Quades, Narisques, Hermunduri, Suevi, Sarmatians, Victovales, Roxolans, Bastarnes, Costoboques, Alaris, Pencins, Vandals and Jazyges, assembled with one accord to force the frontier and inundate the empire. Pressure came from the farthest point. Reinforced by some septentrional barbarians, probably the Goths, the whole Slav and Germanic mass appeared in motion; these barbarians, with their wives and children, wished to be received into the empire, seeking for some land and money, offering in return their arms for any kind of military service. It was a veritable human cataclysm. The line of the Danube was broken. The Vandals and Marcomans established themselves in Pannonia; Dacia was trampled over by twenty peoples; the Costoboques advanced as far as Greece; Rhetia and Norica were overrun; the Marcomans crossed the Julian Alps, took up their position before Aquiba, pillaging everything up to Pavia. Before this fearful shock the Roman army yielded; the number of captives taken by the barbarians was enormous; the alarm was great in Italy; it was declared that, since the tithe of the Carthaginian wars, Rome had never had to meet such a furious attack.

It is a well-authenticated truth that the philosophical progress of the laws does not correspond always to a progress in the power of the State. War is a brutal thing; it has brutal desires; often it thus happens that moral and social improvements bring with them military weakness. The army is a remnant of barbarism, which the man of progress preserves as a necessary evil; and it is rarely that one does with success what is done as a last shift. Antoninus had already a strong dislike to the use of arms; under his reign the manners of the field were much softened. One cannot deny that the Roman army had not lost, under Marcus-Aurelius, a part of its discipline and vigour. Recruiting had become difficult; the replacing and enrolment of the barbarians had entirely changed the character of the legion; doubtless Christianity had already drained the best of the State's strength. When one thinks that by the side of this decrepitude there were acting bands of men without country, engaged in the working of the ground, not caring but to kill, seeking nothing but war, should this be even against their own relatives, it was clear that a great substitution of races would ensue. Civilised humanity had not as yet so subdued evil as to be able to abandon itself to the dream of progress through peace and morality.

Marcus-Aurelius, before this colossal assault of the whole barbarian world, was truly admirable. He did not like war, and never engaged in it but against his desire; but when he did it, he did it thoroughly; he made a great captain through duty. A terrific pestilence was joined to the war. Thus tried, Roman society appealed to all its traditions and rites; and there was, as is common in the time of such a scourge, a reaction in favour of the national religion. Marcus-Aurelius lent himself to this. We see the good emperor presiding himself in his quality as grand pontiff at the sacrifices, taking the blade of a javelin in the temple of Mars, plunging it into the blood, and throwing it towards the direction of heaven in which the enemy was. Everybody was armed, slaves, gladiators, bandits, diogmites (police agents); some German troops were levied against the Germans; money was coined out of precious objects in the imperial property, to save the establishment of new taxes.

The life of Marcus-Aurelius was henceforth almost entirely passed in the region of the Danube at Carnoute, near Vienna, or at Vienna itself upon the banks of the Gran in Hungary, sometimes at Sirmium. His ennui was tremendous; but he knew how to conquer it. Those tasteless campaigns against the Quades and the Marcomans were very well conducted; the disgust he felt for them did not prevent him from putting into them the most conscientious application. The army loved him, and did its duty thoroughly. Moderate even towards his enemies, he preferred a plan of campaign long but sure to dashing blows; he delivered Pannonia completely, repulsed all the barbarians on the left bank of the Danube, made even great points beyond that river, and prudently practised the tactics, which have been abused at a later day, of opposing barbarians to barbarians.

Paternal and philosophic towards these hordes of half-savages, he was determined, out of respect to himself, to preserve towards them considerations which they could not understand, in the same way as a gentleman who, by force of his own personal dignity, behaves towards Red-skins as to well-educated people. He preached artlessly to them of reason and justice, and he finished by inspiring them with respect. Perhaps, but for the revolt of Aridius Cassius, he would have succeeded in making a province of Marcomania (Bohemia), another of Sarmatia (Galicia), and so have saved the future. He admitted the German soldiers to his legions on a large scale; he gave lands in Dacia, Pannonia, and Media, in Roman Germany, to those who wished to work, but maintained very firmly the military boundary, established a rigorous police on the Danube, and did not allow the prestige of the empire to suffer a single time from the concessions which policy and humanity drew from him.

It was in the course of one of these expeditions that, encamped on the banks of the Gran, in the midst of the monotonous plains of Hungary, he wrote the finest pages of the exquisite work which has revealed his whole soul. What cost Marcus-Aurelius most in these distant wars was his being deprived of the ordinary society of learned men and philosophers. Nearly all had drawn back before the fatigues, and remained at Rome. Occupied the whole day in military exercises, he passed the evenings in his tent alone with himself. There he disembarrassed himself of all the constraint which his duties imposed on him; he made his examination of his conscience, and thought of the nobleness of the struggle he so valiantly maintained. Sceptical as to war, even while he made it, and diving into the contemplation of universal vanity, he doubts the lawfulness of his own victories: "The spider is proud when it seizes a fly," he wrote; "another is proud when he takes a leveret; a third when he takes a pilchard; another when he takes a wild boar; and another still when he takes some Sarmatians. Looked at from real principles they are brigands." The Conversations of Epictetes, by Arrien, was the favourite book of the emperor; he read these with delight, and, without intending it, he was led to imitate them. Such was the origin of these detached thoughts, forming twelve books, which were collected after his death under the title of On the subject of Himself.

It is probable that for a good while Marcus kept a journal special to his mental condition. He wrote there in Greek the maxims to which he betook himself for strength, reminiscences of his favourite authors, passages from the moralists who struck him most, the principles which during the day had sustained him, sometimes reproaches which his scrupulous conscience thought should be addressed to himself.

"We seek for solitary retreats, rustic cottages, the sea shore, mountains; like others, thou lovest to dream of all this. What childishness, since every hour thou art allowed to retire into thine own soul! No part of man has a more peaceful retreat, especially if it possesses in itself some of those things whose contemplation suffices to bring it calmness. Learn then to enjoy this retreat, and renew thy strength there. Have there these short fundamental maxims, which will at once bring serenity to thy soul, and send thee back in a condition to support with resignation the world to which thou must needs return."

During the gloomy winters of the north this consolation became still more necessary. He was more than fifty; old age came on him pre-maturely. One evening all the images of his pious youth came back to his memory, and he passed some delightful hours in reckoning what he owed to each of the good beings who had surrounded him.

"Examples from my ancestor Verus; sweetness of manner, and unalterable patience.

"Qualities which have been taken from my father--the remembrance he has left me--modesty and a manly character.

" Souvenir of my mother: her piety, her kindness; purity of soul, which went so far as to abstain, not only from doing evil, but even from conceiving the thought of it; a frugal life, and what resembles so little the luxury of the rich."

Then there appeared to him in his turn Diognetes, who inspired him with the taste for philosophy, rendering the pallet so pleasant in his eyes, its coverlet consisting of a simple skin and the apparatus of Hellenic discipline; Junius Rusticus, who taught him to shun all affectation of elegance in style, and lent him the Conversations of Epictetes; Apollonius of Chalcis, who realised the stoic ideal of extreme firmness and perfect sweetness; Sextus of Cheroneus, so grave and so good; Alexander of Cotia, who showed such refined politeness; Fronton, "who taught him what there was of envy, duplicity and hypocrisy in a tyrant, and what hardness there may be in the heart of a patrician;" his brother, Severus, who caused him to know Thrasea Helvidius; Cato; Brutus, who gave him the idea of what a free State is, where the rule is the natural equality of the citizens and the equality of their laws, of a monarchy which respects before all the liberty of the citizens; and, dominating all the others with his pure greatness, Antoninus, his father by adoption, whose portrait he traces for us with a reduplication of gratitude and love.

"I thank the gods," he says in closing, "for having given me good ancestors, good parents, a good sister, good teachers, and in my household, in my neighbours, in my friends, people nearly all moved by kindness. Never do I allow myself to act with any want of respect towards them; by my natural disposition, I might have on some occasion committed an irreverence; but the goodness of the gods has not permitted that to arise. I owe likewise to the gods my having preserved pure the flower of my youth; having not having been made a man of before the age, of having even delayed that; having been educated under the law of a prince and a father, who separated my mind from all the smoke of pride, and made me understand that it is possible--while living in a palace, surrounded by guards, by splendid dresses, by torches and statues --that a prince can compress his life within the limits of that of a simple citizen, without showing with all that less nobleness or strength when he is to act as emperor and treat of State affairs. They have vouchsafed to me likewise to meet a brother whose manners were a continual exhortation to watch over myself, at the same time that his deference and attachment made the joy of my heart. . . . . If I have had the good fortune to raise those who have guided my education to the honours they seemed to desire; if I have known Apollonius, Rusticus, Maximus; if often there has been presented to me, surrounded with so much light, the image of a life conformed to nature (I remained on this side of that goal it is true--but it is my own fault); if anybody has resisted till this hour the rough life I lead; if I have not touched either Benedicta nor Theodotus; if, in spite of my frequent anger against Rusticus, I have never passed the bounds, nor done anything I have had cause to repent of; if my mother, who died young, was able to pass near me her last years; if, every time I have wished to come to the help of some poor or afflicted person, I have never had to say that gold or silver were wanting; if I myself have not needed to receive anything from anyone; if fate has given me a wife so complaisant and so guileless; if I have found so many people capable of educating my children; if, at the outset of my passion for philosophy, I did not become the prey of some sophist;--it is to the gods I owe it all. Yes; such good things cannot but be the effect which the help of the gods and a happy fortune have rendered me."

This divine candour breathes through every page. Never has one written more simply for himself, for the sale end of emptying his heart, with no other witness than God. Not a shadow of system here! Marcus-Aurelius, to speak properly, has no philosophy; although he owes nearly everything to Stoicism, transformed by the Roman mind, he is of no school. According to our taste he has too little curiosity, for he does not know all that a contemporary of Ptolemy and Gallien could learn; he has on the system of the world some opinions which were not on a level with the loftiest science of his time. But his moral thought, thus set free from every tie to any system, gains by that a peculiar elevation. The author of the book of The Imitation himself, although much drawn away from the quarrels of the schools, does not reach so far; for his manner of feeling is essentially Christian; putting away Christian dogmas, his book loses more than a part of its charm. The work of Marcus-Aurelius, not having any dogmatic basis, shall eternally preserve its freshness. Everyone, from the atheist, or he who believes himself to be such, to the man most absorbed in the special belief of each cult, can find there some edifying truths. It is the most purely human book there is. He does not trench upon any controverted question. In theology, Marcus-

Aurelius floats between pure Deism, Polytheism understood in a physical sense after the manner of the Stoics, and a sort of cosmic Pantheism. He does not hold more to the one hypothesis than the other, and he uses indifferently three vocabularies, the Deistic, Polytheistic, and Pantheistic. His considerations have always two faces, according as God and the soul have or have not reality. "To quit the society of men has nothing very terrible, if there are gods; and if there are no gods, or if they are not occupied with human things, what is the use of living in a world empty of gods and empty of providence; But certainly there are gods, and they have human affairs at heart."

It is the dilemma we feel every hour; for if it is materialism the most complete which is right, we who have believed in the true and the good shall be no more duped than others. If idealism is right, we shall have been the true sages, and we shall have been in the only position which we ought to have taken, that is to say, without any interested hope, without having reckoned on any remuneration.

Marcus-Aurelius is not therefore a freethinker; he is even scarcely a philosopher, in the special sense of the word. Like Jesus, he has no speculative philosophy; his theology is entirely contradictory; he has no fixed idea on the soul and immortality. How profoundly moral was he without the beliefs which are regarded to-day as the foundations of morality! How eminently religious was he without having professed any of the dogmas of what is called natural religion! It is that which it is useful to seek for here.

The doubts which, from the point of view of speculative reason, soar over the truths of natural religion, are not, as Kant has admirably shown, accidental doubts, susceptible of being removed, belonging, as has sometimes been imagined, to certain conditions of the human mind. These doubts are inherent in the very nature of the truths, and one can say without paradox that, if they were removed, the truths which they attack would disappear at the same blow. Let us suppose, indeed, a direct proof, positive, evident to all, of future reward and punishment, where should be the merit of doing good? Only fools would they be who, in the gaiety of their heart, would run to their own damnation. A multitude of base souls would lay their salvation cards on the table; they would in some sense "force the hand" of the Deity. Who would see in such a system either morality or religion? In moral and religious matters, it is indispensable to believe without demonstration; certainty is not concerned, but faith. See what a certain Deism forgets, with its habits of intemperate affirmation. It forgets that too precise beliefs upon human destiny take away all moral merit. For our part, if men would set forth a peremptory argument of this sort, we should do as St. Louis did, when they spoke to him about the miraculous wafer; we should refuse to go to look! What need have we of these vulgar proofs, which have no application except in the gross order of facts, and which would annoy our freedom? We should fear to be likened to those speculators on virtue or those timorous vulgarians, who import into the things of the soul the gross egotism of practical life. In the first days which followed the establishment of the belief in the resurrection of Jesus, this sentiment was produced in the most touching way. The true friends of the heart, the tender one loved better to believe without proof than to see him. "Blessed are those who have not seen and yet have believed!" became the "word" of the situation. Charming word! Eternal symbol of tender and generous idealism, which is horrified to touch with its hands what should not be seen except with the heart!

Our good Marcus-Aurelius, on this point as on all others, anticipated the ages. Never does he care to put himself in sympathy with himself as to God and as to the soul. As if he had read the Kritik of Pure Reason, he sees well enough that, since the infinite is in question, no formula is absolute, and that in such a matter there is no chance of having perceived the truth once in one's life if it has been much disproved. He separates widely moral beauty from all received theology; he does not allow the right of resting any metaphysical opinion on the first cause. Never was the intimate union with the hidden God pushed to more unheard-of refinements.

"Offer to the government of God him who is in himself a manly being, ripe in age, a friend of the public good, a Roman, an emperor, a soldier at his post, waiting the signal of the trumpet, a man ready to quit life without regret. There are some grains of incense destined for the same altar; the one falls sooner, the other later into the fire; but the difference is nothing. Man ought to live according to nature during the few days which are given to him on earth, and, when the moment of his withdrawal is come, to submit himself with sweetness, as an olive which, in falling, blesses the tree which has produced it, and renders thanks to the branch which bore it. All that is arranged for thee arrange for me, O cosmos. Nothing is to me premature or late of what in thy view comes in season. I take my fruit of what thy seasons bring, O Nature! From thee comes everything: in thee is everything: towards thee goes everything.

> City of Cecrops, how I love thee!'
> said the poet; why not say:
> City of Jupiter, how I love thee!'

"O man! thou hast been a citizen in a great city; what does it matter whether it has been three or five years? What is conformable to the laws is not unjust to any one. What, then, is very vexatious in being sent from the city not by a tyrant, not by an unjust judge, but by that nature itself which brought thee into it? It is as if a comedian were dismissed from the theatre by the same manager who has engaged him. But,' thou wilt say, I have not played out the five acts; I have only played three.' You answer rightly; but in life three acts are sufficient to make up the whole piece. He who scores up the end is he who after having been the cause of the combination of the elements is now the cause of their dissolution; thou art nothing in the one or other of these facts.

"Go therefore content; for he who dismisses thee is without wrath."

Do we say that he is not revolted sometimes by the strange lot which is pleased to leave man alone face to face, with his eternal wants of devotion, sacrifice, heroism, and nature, with his transcendent immorality, its supreme disdain for virtue? No. Once, with less absurdity, the colossal injustice of death strikes him. But soon his temperament, completely mortified, reveals and calms itself.

"How is it that the gods who have ordered all things so well and with so much love for man should have neglected a single point, viz., that men of approved virtue, who have had during their lifetime a sort of fellowship with the Deity, who are beloved by him because of their pious actions and sacrifices, should not revive after death, but are blotted out for ever? Since the matter is so, learn that, if it ought to have been otherwise, it would have been so; for if that had been just it would have been possible; if that had been agreeable to nature, nature would have carried it out. Therefore, from this which is not so, strengthen thyself by this consideration, that it was necessary that it should not be so. Thou seest for thyself that how to make such a search is to dispute with God as to his right. Now we should not dispute thus against the gods, if they were not sovereignly good and just; and if they are so, they have not allowed anything to take place in the ordering of the world which is contrary to justice or reason."

Ah, this is too much resignation, dear master! If it were truly thus we have the right to complain. To say, that if this world has not its counterpart, the man who is sacrificed for good or for the truth should quit contentedly and absolve the gods, is too guileless! No, he has a right to blaspheme them! For indeed, why should they so abuse his credulity? Why have put in him those deceptive instincts, of which he has been the honest dupe? Why this premium given to the frivolous or wicked man? Is it then not he who is not deceived who is the prudent man? . . . . But then cursed be the gods who placed their preferences so badly! I wish the future were an enigma; but if there be no future this world is a frightful ambuscade. Remark, indeed, that our desire is not that of the gross vulgarian. What we wish is not to see the punishment of the guilty, nor to touch the interests of our virtue. What we desire has nothing egotistical in it; it is simply to be, to remain in connection with the light, to continue our thought begun, to know more of it, to enjoy one day that truth which we seek with so much labour, to see the triumph of the good we have loved. Nothing more legitimate. The worthy emperor, besides, felt this well. "What! The light of a lamp shines up to the moment when it is extinguished, and loses nothing of its brightness; and truth, justice, temperance, which are in thee, shall go out with thee!" All his life was passed in this noble hesitation. If he sinned, it was from too much piety. Less resigned, he would have been more just; for surely, to demand that he should be a close and sympathetic spectator with struggles for the good and true, that would not have been to ask too much.

It is possible also, that if his philosophy had been less exclusively moral, if it had implied a more curious study of history and the universe, it would have escaped certain excesses of rigour. Like the ascetic Christians, Marcus-Aurelius sometimes pushed this renunciation even to dryness and subtilty. This calm which never leaves him, we feel, is obtained by an immense effort. Certainly, evil had never any attraction for him; he had not to fight with any passion: "Let them do and say what they will," he writes, "I must be a good man, as the emerald might say, Let them do or say what they like, I must be an emerald and keep my colour.'" But to keep himself always on the icy summit of Stoicism, it was needful that he should do cruel violence to nature and cut out more than one noble part of it. That perpetual repetition of the same reasonings, those thousand images under which he sought to represent the vanity of everything, those often artless proofs of universal frivolity, evidence the combats which he had to fight to extinguish in him all desire. Sometimes the result of it is something bitter and gloomy; the reading of Marcus-Aurelius fortifies, but does not comfort; it leaves in the soul a void, at once delicious and cruel, which one would not exchange for full satisfaction. Humility, renunciation, severity over self have never been pushed further. Glory, that last illusion of great souls, is reduced to nothing. He can do good without disquieting himself, if no one knows of it. It is clear that history will speak of him; but how unworthily will it speak? Absolute mortification, when it was reached, had extinguished self-love within him to the last shred. One might even say that this excess of virtue has injured him. Historians have taken him at his word. Few great reigns have been worse treated by the historiographer. Marius Maximus and Dion Cassius speak of Marcus with affection but without talent; their works, besides, do not reach us but in scraps, and we do not know the life of the illustrious sovereign except by the mediocre biography of Jules Capitolin, written a hundred years after his death, thanks to the admiration which the emperor Diocletian had devoted to him.

Joseph Ernest Renan

Fortunately the little casket which enclosed the thoughts by the banks of the Gran and the philosophy of Carmoute was saved. It came forth from this incomparable book, in which Epictetes was surpassed, this manual of resigned life, this Gospel for those who do not believe in the supernatural, which could not have been better understood than it may in our days. A veritable eternal Gospel, the book of the Thoughts will never grow old; for it affirms no dogma. The Gospel has aged in some portions; science does not permit any longer the admission of the artless conception of the supernatural which makes its basis. The supernatural is not in the Thoughts, except a little insignificant spot which does not mar the marvellous beauty of the whole. Science may destroy God and the soul, while the book of the Thoughts remains young yet in life and truth. The religion of Marcus-Aurelius, as was occasionally that of Jesus, is the absolute religion--that which results from the simple fact of a high moral conscience placed face to face with the universe. It is neither of one race nor of one country. No revolution, no advance, no discovery, can change it.

CHAPTER XVII

THE LEGIO FULMINATA--APOLOGIES OF APOLLINARIS, MILTIADES, AND MELITO

An incident of the campaign against the Quades put Marcus-Aurelius and the Christians face to face in some sort, and caused, at least among the latter, a lively prepossession. The Romans were engaged in the interior of the country; the heats of summer had succeeded a long winter without transition. The Quades found a means of cutting off the invaders' supplies of water. The army was devoured by thirst, worn out by fatigues, shut in an enclosed spot, where the barbarians attacked it with every advantage. The Romans replied feebly to the blows of the enemy, and one would have feared a disaster, when all at once a terrible storm took place. A tremendous rain fell on the Romans and refreshed them. It was claimed, on the contrary, that the thunder and hail were turned against the Quades and frightened them, so that a part of them threw themselves in desperation into the ranks of the Romans.

Everybody believed it was a miracle. Jupiter had plainly pronounced for the Latin race. Most people attributed the prodigy to the prayers of Marcus-Aurelius. They made pictures, in which were seen the pious emperor supplicating the gods and saying, "Jupiter, I raise towards thee that hand which has never caused bloodshed." The Antonine column is consecrated to this event. Jupiter Pluvius is shown there under the figure of a winged old man, whose hair, beard, and arms allow torrents of water to escape from them, which the Romans are receiving in their helmets and bucklers, while the barbarians are struck and overturned by the lightning. Some believed in the intervention of an Egyptian magician, named Arnonphix, who followed the army, and whose incantations, it was supposed, had made the gods intervene, especially the aerial Hermes.

The legion which had received this mark of heavenly favour took, at least used it for a time, the name of Fulminata. Such an epithet had nothing new about it. Every place touched by lightning was sacred among the Romans; the legion whose encampments had been struck by the celestial bolts came to be looked on as having received a sort of baptism of fire. Fulminata became for it a title of honour. One legion, the twelfth, which, after the siege of Jerusalem, in which it took part, was stationed at Melitene, near the Euphrates, in little Armenia, bore this title from the time of Augustus, without doubt because of some physical accident which made this to he substituted for the surname Antigua which it had borne till then.

There were some Christians around Marcus-Aurelius; there were probably some in the legion engaged against the Quades. This prodigy, admitted by all, excited them. A good miracle could not but be the work of the true God. What a triumph, what an argument to make persecution cease, if the emperor could be persuaded that this miracle came from the believers! For some days after the incident occurred a version of it circulated, according to which the storm favourable to the Romans was the result of the prayers of the Christians. It was while kneeling, according to the custom of the Church, that the pious soldiers had obtained from heaven this mark of protection, which flattered from two points of view the Christian pretensions; first, by showing what might come from heaven at the request of a handful of believers; and also by showing that the God of the Christians had some favour for the Roman Empire. Let the empire cease to persecute the saints, and they would see what favour they would obtain from heaven. God, to become the protector of the empire against the barbarians, waited for only one thing, and that was that the empire should cease to show itself pitiless towards a chosen people who were in the world as the leaven of all good.

This manner of representing the facts was very quickly accepted, and went the round of the churches. To each process to each opponent they had this reply to make to the authorities: "We have saved you." This reply gained a new force when, at the end of the campaign, Marcus-Aurelius received his seventh imperial salutation, and the column, which may be seen to-day in Rome, was raised, by order of the Senate and the people, bearing among its reliefs the representation of the miracle. Occasion was even taken to fabricate an official letter from Marcus-Aurelius to the Senate, in which he forbade the persecution of the Christians, and made their denunciation punishable by death. Not only is the fact of such a letter inadmissible, but it is very probable that Marcus-Aurelius did not know of the claim which the Christians had raised as to being the authors of the miracle. In certain countries, in Egypt for example, the Christian fable does not appear to have been known. Otherwise it did nothing but add to the dangerous reputation for magic which began to attach itself to the Christians.

The legion of the Danube, if it for a while took the name of Fulminata, did not keep it officially. As the twelfth legion resident at Melitene was always designated by this title, and as moreover the legion of Melitene shone soon by its Christian ardour, it wrought confusion, and we might suppose it was this last legion which, transported out of all likelihood from the Euphrates to the Danube, obtained the miracle and received the name of Fulminata; it would need to be forgotten that the legion had borne the name two centuries before.

What is in any case certain is that the conduct of Marcus-Aurelius towards the Christians was in no way modified. It has been supposed that the revolt of Avidius Cassius, supported by the sympathy of all Syria, especially Antioch, inclined the emperor against the numerous Christians in these places. This is not very probable. The revolt of Avidius took place in 172, and the breaking out of persecution is specially observable about 176. The Christians held themselves apart from all politics; moreover, as to Avidius, his pardon came from the loving heart of Marcus-Aurelius. The number of the martyrs meanwhile only increased; in three or four years the persecution reached the highest degree of fury which it had known before Decius. In Africa, Vigellius Saturinus drew the sword, and God knows when it was put back into the scabbard. Sardinia was filled with the transported, who were recalled under Commodus by the influence of Marcia. Byzantine saw some horrors. Nearly the whole community was arrested, put to the torture, led to death. Byzantine having been ravaged some years after by Septimus Severus (in 196), the governor, Cæcilius Capella, cried out "What a splendid day for the Christians!"

It was still graver in Asia. Asia was the province in which Christianity had affected social order most deeply. Thus, the proconsuls of Asia were those who, of all provincial governors, were the most bitter in the persecution. Without the emperor having issued new edicts, they alleged certain instructions which obliged them to proceed with severity. They applied without mercy a law which, according to its interpretation, might be atrocious or inoffensive. These repeated punishments were a bloody contradiction to an age of humanity. The fanatics, whose gloomy dreams these violences confirmed, did not protest; often they rejoiced. But the moderate bishops dreamed of the possibility of obtaining from the emperor the end of such injustices. Marcus-Aurelius received all the requests, and was supposed to have read them. His reputation as a philosopher and as a Hellenist suggested to those who felt any facility for writing in Greek to address themselves thus to him. The incident of the war of the Quades offered a way of putting the question more clearly than could have been done by Aristides, Quadratus, or St. Justin.

There was produced a series of new apologies, composed by some bishops and writers of Asia, which unfortunately have not been preserved. Claudius Apollinaris, bishop of Hierapolis, shone in the first rank in this campaign. The miracle of Jupiter Pluvius had had so much publicity that Apollinaris dared to recall it to the emperor, connecting the divine intervention with the prayers of the Christians. Miltiades addressed himself also to the Roman authorities, doubtless to the proconsuls of Asia, to defend "his philosophy" against the unjust reproaches which had been addressed to him. Those who could read his apology had not sufficient eulogium for the talent and knowledge he displayed.

Much the most remarkable work which this literary movement produced was the Apology of Melito. The author addressed himself to Marcus-Aurelius in the tongue which the emperor loved: "What has never been seen, the race of pious men in Asia is persecuted and hunted in Asia, in the name of new edicts. Some imprudent sycophants, greedy of the spoils of others, making a pretext of the existing legislation, exercise their brigandage before all, watching night and day, to have them seized, people who have done no harm. . . . If all this is executed by thine order, it is well; for a just prince cannot order any unjust thing; willingly then should we accept such a death as the fate we have deserved. We only address to thee one request; it is that, after having examined thyself the case of those whom they represent to thee as seditious, thou wouldest judge if they deserve death, or if they are not rather worthy to live in peace under the protection of the law. But if this new edict and these measures which are not allowed against the most barbarous enemies do not come from thee, we implore thee, as earnestly as we can, not to abandon us henceforth to such a public brigandage."

We have already seen Melito make in the empire the most singular advances, in the case where he wished to become the protector of the truth. In the Apology these advances were still more accentuated. Melito sets himself to show that Christianity contents itself with the common law, and that it has something in it to make it dear to the heart of a true Roman.

"Yes, it is true our philosophy first took birth among the barbarians; but the moment it commenced to flourish among the peoples of thy State, having coincided with the great reign of Augustus, thy ancestor, that was a happy augury for the empire. It is from that moment, in fact, that is dated the colossal development of that brilliant Roman power of which thou art, and wilt be with thy son, the applauded inheritor of our vows, provided thou wilt well protect this philosophy which has in some sense been the foster-sister of the empire, since it was born with its founder, and since thy ancestors have honoured it as the equal of other cults. And what proves that our doctrine has been destined to flourish parallel to the progress of your glorious empire, is that from its appearance everything has succeeded with you to a wonderful degree. Nero and Domitian only, deceived by some calumniators, have shown themselves malevolent to our religion; and these calumnies, as ordinarily happens, were accepted at once without examination. But their error has been corrected by thy pious parents, who, in frequent rescripts, repressed the zeal of those who wished to enter into ways of severity against us. Thus, Hadrian, thy ancestor, wrote of it on various occasions, and especially to the proconsul Fundanus, governor of Asia. And thy father, at the period in which thou wast associated with him in the administration, wrote to the cities to do nothing new as to us, especially to the Lariseans, the Thessalonians, the Athenians, and all the Greeks. As to thee, who hast not for us the same sentiments, with a still more elevated degree of philanthropy and philosophy, we are sure that thou wilt do what we ask."

The system of the apologists, so warmly maintained by Tertullian, according to whom the good emperors have favoured Christianity and the bad emperors have persecuted it, was already completely begun. Born together, Christianity and Rome had grown greater together, prospered together. Their interests, their sufferings, their fortune, their future, all were in common. The apologists are advocates, and the advocates of all causes are like each other. They have arguments for all occasions and for all tastes. A hundred and fifty years would roll away before these gentle and moderately sincere invitations should be listened to. But the simple fact that they were presented under Marcus-Aurelius to the mind of one of the most enlightened leaders of the Church is a prognostic of the future. Christianity and the empire were reconciled; they were made for each other. The shade of Melito might tremble with joy when the empire shall become Christian, and the emperor shall take in hand the cause "of the truth."

Thus the Church took already more than one step towards the empire. Through politeness no doubt, but also by a consequence quite just from its principle, Melito did not admit that an emperor can make an unjust order. It might be easily believed that certain emperors had not been absolutely hostile to Christianity; people liked to tell how Tiberius had proposed in the Senate to put Jesus into the rank of the gods; it was the Senate who would not have it. The decided preference which Christianity shall show for power, when it can hope for favour, may be imagined by anticipation. They betook themselves to show, against all the facts, that Hadrian and Antoninus had sought to repair the evil caused by Nero and Domitian. Tertullian and his generation will say the same thing of Marcus-Aurelius. Tertullian shall doubt, it is true, if one can at the same time be Cæsar and a Christian; but that incompatibility a century after his time shall strike no one, and Constantine shall charge himself with proving that Melito of Sardis was a very sagacious man the day when he pointed out so well, 132 years in advance, through proconsular persecutions, the possibility of a Christian empire.

A voyage to Greece, to Asia and the East, which the emperor made at that time, did not change his ideas. He went smiling, but without any internal irony, through this world of sophists of Athens and Smyrna, listened to all the celebrated professors, founded a great number of new chairs at Athens, saw especially Herod Atticus, Ælius Aristides, and Hadrian of Tyre. At Eleusis he entered alone into the most secret parts of the temple. In Palestine the remnants of the Jewish and Samaritan peoples, plunged into distress by the last revolts, received him with acclamations, and doubtless with complaints. A fetid odour of misery reigned throughout all the land. These unruly crowds from which a stench came forth put his patience to the proof. Once, pushed into a corner, he cried, "O Marcomans, O Quades, O Sarmatians, I have found people at last who are more beastly than you!"

Philosophy, according to Marcus-Aurelius, had all disappeared, except the Roman. He had against Jewish and Syrian piety instinctive prejudices. The Christians, nevertheless, were very near him. His nephew, Ummidius Quadratus, had in his household a eunuch named Hyacinthus, who was an elder of the Church of Rome. To this eunuch was confided the care of a young girl named Marcia, of ravishing beauty, whom Ummidius made his concubine. Later, in 183, Ummidius having been put to death, in connection with the conspiracy of Lucillus, Commodus found this pearl among his spoils. He appropriated her. Eclectos, the attendant, followed the fate of his mistress. By yielding to the caprices of Commodus, sometimes by knowing how to command them, Marcia exercised over him a boundless power. It is not probable that she was baptized, but the eunuch, Hyacinthus, had inspired her with a tender sentiment for the faith. He continued to be near her, and he drew greater favours from her, in particular for the confessors condemned to the mines. Later on, pushed to the point by the monster, Marcia was at the head of the plot which took the empire from Commodus. Eclectos was still found at her side at that time. By a singular coincidence, Christianity was mixed up very closely in the final tragedy of the Antonine house, as a hundred years before it was by a Christian medium that the plot was arranged which put an end to the tyranny of the last of the Flavii.

CHAPTER XVIII

THE GNOSTICS AND THE MONTANISTS AT LYONS

For nearly twenty years the Asiatic colony of Lyons and Vienne, notwithstanding more than one internal trial, prospered in all the works of Christ. Thanks to her, the evangelical preaching already lit up the valley of the Saône. The Church of Autun especially was, in many points of view, a daughter of the Graeco-Asiatic Church of Lyons. Greek had been for a long time the language of mysteries, and held there during some centuries a certain liturgical importance. Then there appeared, in a sort of matinal and uncertain penumbra, Tourners, Chalon, Dijon, Langres, whose apostles and martyrs were connected with the Greek colony of Lyons, and not with the great Latin evangelisation of Gaul in the third and fourth centuries.

Thus, from Smyrna even to the inaccessible parts of Gaul, there stretched a ridge of strong Christian activity. The Lugduno-Viennese community was connected by an active correspondence with the mother churches of Asia and Phrygia. The facilities offered by the navigation of the Rhone served for the speedy importation of all novelties; such a Gospel of recent manufacture, such a system newly drawn by Alexandrinian subtlety, such a charisma set in fashion by the sectaries of Asia Minor were known at Lyons or at Vienne nearly the next day after their appearance. The lively imagination of the inhabitants was a more powerful vehicle still. An exalted mysticism, a delicacy of nerves approaching hysteria, a warmth of heart capable of making all sacrifices, but susceptible also of being led in all directions, were the character of this Gallo-Grecian Christianity. The venerable Pothin, more than ninety years of age, had the most difficult task of governing these souls, more ardent than submissive, and who sought in their submission even something else than the austere charm of accomplished duty.

Irenæus had become the right hand of Pothin, his coadjutor, if one might express it so, his designated successor. An abundant writer and a finished controversialist, he began, on his arrival at Lyons, to write in Greek against all the different Christian tendencies, in particular against Blastus, who wished to return to Judaism, and against Florin, who admitted with the Gnostics a god of good and a god of evil. The teachings of Valentinus, by their breadth and philosophical appearance, gained many adherents among the Lyonese population. Irenæus made himself a kind of speciality in combating them. No orthodox polemic, before him, had at this point comprehended the depth of the Gnosis and its anti-Christian character.

Valentine was a fine kind of spirit, who certainly never would have succeeded either in replacing the Catholic Church nor seizing the direction of it. Gnosticism reached the Rhone in the person of a doctor much more dangerous. I mean Markus, who seduced women by the strange manner in which he celebrated the Eucharist, and by the audacity with which he made them believe that they had the gift of prophecy. His style of administering the sacraments brought with it the most dangerous familiarities. Feigning to be the dispenser of the grace, he persuaded women that he was in the secret of their guardian angels, that they were destined to an eminent rank in his church, and ordered them to prepare a mystical union with him. "From me and through me,' he said to them, "thou wilt receive the grace. Place thyself as a betrothed receives her fiancé, that thou mayest be what I am and I what you are. Prepare thy bed to receive the seed of light. Behold the grace is descending on thee. Open thy mouth and prophesy." "But I have never prophesied, and I don't know how to prophesy." He redoubled his invocation, terrifying and stupefying his victim. "Open thy mouth, I tell thee, and speak: everything thou utterest will be prophecy." The heart of the initiated beat hard; the waiting, the embarrassment, the idea that perhaps she was about to prophesy made her lose her head; she raved at hazard. It was represented to her afterwards that she had spoken full and sublime sense. The unfortunate one, from that moment, was lost. She thanked Markos for the gift he had communicated, asked what she could do in return, and, recognising that the giving up of all her goods in his favour was a small matter, she offered herself to him if he would condescend to accept her. Often the best and most distinguished were thus surprised; for on all sides already there was a talk of penitents vowed to mourning for the rest of their life, who, after having received from the seducer the prophetic communion and initiation, recoiled in horror, and came to the orthodox asking pardon and forgetfulness.

Such a man was particularly dangerous at Lyons. The mystic and impassioned character of the Lyonese, their somewhat material piety, their taste for the bizarre and for sensible emotions, exposed them to all sorts of falls. What goes on to-day in the feminine public in the towns in the South of France on the arrival of a fashionable preacher took place then. The new fashion in preaching was much liked. The richest ladies, those who were distinguished by a beautiful border of purple on their robes, were the most curious and the most imprudent. The Christians thus seduced were not slow to be disabused. Their conscience burned them: their life henceforth was blasted. Some confessed their sin in public and re-entered the Church; others, out of shame, did not dare to do this, and remained in the most false position, neither in nor out. Others, falling into despair, went far away from the Church, and concealed themselves "with the fruit they had drawn from their connection with the sons of Gnosis," adds Irenæus maliciously.

The ravages which this gloomy seducer made in souls was terrible. People spoke of philtres, of poisons. The penitents confessed that he had completely exhausted them, that they had loved him with a love superhuman and fatal, which imposed itself on them. They told above all of the abominable conduct of Markos towards a deacon of Asia, who received him into his house with a thorough Christian affection. The deacon had a wife of rare beauty. She allowed herself to be won over by this dangerous guest, and lost the purity of the faith at the same time as the honour of her body. From that time Markos took her everywhere about with him, to the great scandal of the churches. The good brothers had pity on her, and spoke to her with sadness to lead her back: they succeeded not without difficulty. She was converted, confessed her faults and misfortunes, and passed the rest of her life in a perpetual confession and penitence, telling in humility everything she had suffered by the magician.

What was worse than this was that Markos made some pupils, like him, great corrupters of women, giving themselves the title of "perfect," claiming transcendent knowledge, pretending that "they alone had drunk the fulness of the Gnosis of the ineffable Virtue," and that this knowledge raised them high above all power, so that they could do freely what they wished. It was claimed that the mode of their initiation was most abominable. They dressed up a cabinet like a nuptial couch; then, with a solemnity of doubtful mysticism and some cabalistic words, they feigned to proceed to their spiritual nuptials, copied from those of the superior syziges. Thanks to their rites and the use of certain invocations to Sophia, the Markosians believed they could obtain a sort of invisibility which made them escape, in their nuptial chapels, the eyes of the Sovereign Judge. Like all the Gnostics, they abused the anointings with oil and balm; they made up all sorts of sacraments, apolytroses or redemptions, replacing even baptism. Their extreme unction over the dying had something touching in it, and has alone remained in use.

Pothin and Irenæus energetically resisted these perverse guides. Irenæus threw into the struggle the idea of his great work, Against Heresies, a vast arsenal of arguments against all the varieties of Gnosticism. His correct and moderate judgment, the philosophical basis which he gave to Christianity, his clear and purely deistic ideas on the relations between God and man, his intellectual mediocrity itself, preserved him from the aberrations of an intemperate speculation. The fall of his friends Blastus and Florinus was an example to him. He saw salvation only in the middle path represented by the universal Church. The authority and catholicity of that Church appeared to him the unique criterion of truth.

Gnosticism in fact disappeared from Gaul, both by the violent antipathy which it inspired among the orthodox, and by a gentle transformation which allowed nothing of its theories to remain but an inoffensive mysticism. A marble of the third century found at Autun preserves to us a little poem presenting, like the eighth book of the Sibylline oracles, the acrostic ΙΧΘΥΣ. The pious Valentinians and the orthodox could both equally enjoy the singular style of this strange piece.

"O divine race of the heavenly ΙΧΘΥΣ, receive with a heart full of respect immortal life among mortals; rejuvenate thy soul among the divine waters, by the eternal waves of the Sophia which gives its treasures. Receive sweet nourishment like the honey of the Saviour of the holy; eat in thy hunger and drink in thy thirst; thou holdest ΙΧΘΥΣ in the palms of thy hands."

Montanism, like Gnosticism, visited the Rhone Valley and obtained great successes. Even during the life of Montanus, Priscilla and Maximilla the Lyonese heard with admiration of their prophesies and supernatural gifts. Coming forth from a world closely bordering on Montanism, the Church of Lyons could not remain indifferent to a movement which carried away Phrygia and troubled all Asia Minor. The terrible oracles of the new prophets, the pious practices of the saints at Pepuza, their brilliant charismas, this return of the supernatural phenomena of the apostolic age--such were the tidings which came one by one after each other from Asia, and which struck with stupor the whole Christian world, and they could not but move them peculiarly. It was almost themselves they beheld in these ascetics. Their Vettius Epagathuses, were they not called so because of their austerities, the most famous nazirs? The majority found it easy to believe that the fountain of God's gifts had not been dried up. Many distinguished members of the Lyonese Church, and a certain Alexander, a physician by profession, who had lived in Gaul for many years, came from that country. This Alexander, who astonished everybody by his love of God and his boldness and preaching, appeared favoured with all the apostolic graces.

The Lyonese, at a distance, give us therefore the impression of belonging with many relationships to the pietistic circle of Asia Minor. They sought for martyrdom, they had visions, practised charismas, enjoyed communications with the Holy Spirit or Paraclete, looking on the Church as a virgin. An ardent millenarianism, a constant expectation of anti-Christ and the end of the world were in some sort the common ground from which these great enthusiasts drew their vigour. But a touching docility, joined to rare practical good sense, made the majority of the faithful suspicious of the evil spirit who was hidden frequently under these proud peculiarities.

Sometimes, indeed, certain bizarre results came from Phrygia, evidencing a Christian effervescence which no reason could guide. A certain Alcibiades, who came from this country to settle in Lyons, astonished the Church by his exaggerated macerations. He practised all the austerities of the saints of Pepuza, absolute poverty, excessive abstinences. Nearly the whole creation he repelled as impure, and people asked how he could live while refusing the most evident necessaries of life. The pious Lyonese saw in this at first nothing save what was praiseworthy; but the arbitrary manner in which the Phrygian understood things disquieted them. Alcibiades had sometimes the appearance of a madman. He seemed, like Tatian and many others, to condemn in principle an entire class of God's creatures, and he offended many brethren by the manner in which he guided his kind of life in the outset. It was still worse when, arrested with the others, he determined to continue his abstinences. A heavenly revelation was required to restore him to reason, as we shall soon see.

Irenæus, so firm on the question of Marcionism and Gnosticism, was, in regard to Montanism, much more undecided. The holiness of the Phrygian ascetics could not but affect him; but he saw too plainly into Christian theology not to perceive the danger of the new doctrines as to prophecy and the Paraclete. He does not mention the Montanists among the heretics with whom he fights. He energetically blames certain subversive pretensions, without once naming their authors, and the precautions which he took show that he did not wish to put the Phrygian pietists in the same rank as the schismatic sects. A man of order and hierarchy beyond everything, he ended, it would seem, by seeing in them false prophets; but he hesitated for a long time before arriving at this severe opinion. All the Lyonese were in the same perplexity as he. In their embarrassment they thought of consulting Eleutherus, who a short time back had succeeded Soter in the Roman see. Already the Bishop of Rome was the authority from whom the solution of difficult cases was demanded, who counselled the various churches, and was the centre of concord and unity.

CHAPTER XIX

THE MARTYRS OF LYONS

Lyons and Vienne were counted among the most brilliant centres in the Church of Christ, when a frightful storm fell upon these young churches and put "in evidence" the gifts of force and faith which they contained in their bosom.

It was the seventeenth year of the reign of Marcus-Aurelius; the emperor had not changed, but opinions annoyed him. The scourges which desolated, the dangers which menaced the empire, were considered as having for their cause the impiety of the Christians. On all sides the people adjured the authorities to maintain the national worship, and to punish the despisers of the gods. Unhappily the authorities yielded. The two or three last years of the reign of Marcus-Aurelius were saddened by spectacles quite unworthy of such a perfect sovereign.

At Lyons popular clamour grew into rage. Lyons was the centre of that great cult of Rome and of Augustus, which was the cement of Gallic unity and the mark of its communion with the empire. Around the celebrated altar situated at the confluence of the Rhone and the Saone was grouped a federal town composed of permanent delegates from sixty peoples of Gaul, a town rich and powerful, strongly attached to the religion which was its raison d'être. Every year on the first of August, the great day of the Gallic fairs, and the anniversary of the consecration of the altar, deputies from the whole of Gaul met together there. It was this they called the Concilium Galliaruin, an assembly without great political weight, but of high social and religious importance. Fetes were celebrated, which consisted in contests of Greek and Latin eloquence, and in bloody games.

All these institutions gave much strength to the national cult. The Christians who did not practise this worship appeared atheists and impious. The fables universally admitted concerning them were repeated and empoisoned. They practised, it was said, certain festivals of Thyeste, certain incests in the fashion of OEdipus. No absurdity was too great; there were alleged against them enormities impossible to describe, crimes which had never existed. In all ages secret societies which affect mystery have provoked such suspicions. Let us add that the disorders of certain Gnostics, especially the Markosians, might give such an appearance; and that was not one of the smallest reasons for which the orthodox disliked those sectaries who compromised them in public opinion.

Before going as far as punishments, malevolence expressed itself in quarrels and vexations every day. This cursed people, to whom were attributed all misfortunes, were put in quarantine. .It was forbidden to Christians to appear at the baths, in the forum, or to show themselves in public or even in private houses. If one of them happened to be seen, wild clamours arose, he was beaten, pulled about, struck by blows of stone, and he was forced to barricade himself in. Vettius Epagathus alone by his social position escaped these insults, but his credit was not sufficient to preserve from the popular fury his co-religionists.

The authority did intervene only as slowly as it could, and partly to put an end to these intolerable disorders. One day, nearly all the people known as Christians were arrested, led to the forum by the tribune, and by the duumvirs of the city interrogated before the people. All Confessed themselves Christians. The imperial legate pro prætore was absent; the criminated, while waiting for him, were subjected to the sufferings of a rude prison.

The imperial legate having arrived, the case began. The preliminary "question" was applied with extreme cruelty. The young and noble Vettius Epagathus, who had till now escaped the severities which his co-religionists had suffered, could not bear this. He presented himself at the tribunal, and demanded to defend the accused, and at least to show that they did not deserve the accusation of atheism and impiety. A frightful cry arose. That people of the lower regions, Phrygians and Asiatics, should be given to certain perverse superstitions, that appeared simple enough; but that a man of consideration, an inhabitant of the "high town," a noble of the country, should become an advocate of such follies, that appeared altogether unbearable. The imperial legate repulsed roughly the just request of Vettius. "And thou also, art thou a Christian?" he asked of him. "I am," replied Vettius, with a distinct voice. They did not arrest him nevertheless; doubtless in that town, where the condition of persons was very different, some immunity sheltered him.

The interrogation was long and cruel. Those who had not been arrested, and who continued in the town to be the butt of the most cruel treatments, did not quit the confessors; by paying they obtained leave to serve them and to encourage them. The great misery of the accused was not the punishment, it was the fear that some, less well prepared than others for these terrible struggles, would allow themselves to deny Christ. The trial in fact proved too strong for about a dozen of the unfortunates who renounced their faith with their lips. The grief which these acts of weakness caused the prisoners and the brethren who surrounded them was great. What consoled them was that the arrests continued daily; other believers more worthy of martyrdom filled up the blanks which apostasy had left in the ranks of the elect phalanx. Persecution reached soon to the Church of Vienne, which it appears then had been scattered at first. The élite of the two churches, nearly all the founders of Gallo-Grecian Christianity found themselves together in the prisons of Lyons, ready for the assault which was about to be made upon them. Irenaeus did not suffer arrest; he was one of those who surrounded the confessors, who witnessed all the particulars of their struggle, and it is perhaps to him that we owe the account of them. Old Pothin, on the contrary, was soon, if not at the very beginning, among his faithful followers; he followed day by day their sufferings, and, almost dying as he was, he did not cease to instruct and encourage them.

According to custom in the great criminal investigations the slaves were arrested at the same time as their masters; now many of these slaves were Pagans. The tortures which they saw inflicted on their masters frightened them; the soldiers of the officium whispered to them what it was necessary for them to say in order to escape the torture. They declared that the infanticides, repasts of human flesh, were realities, as well as that the monstrous stories which they told concerning Christian immorality had not been exaggerated.

The indignation of the public was then at its height. Up till then the believers who had remained free had found some communication with their relations, their neighbours, and their friends; now everybody showed nothing but contempt for them. It was resolved to push the art of torture to its last refinements, to obtain from the faithful the avowal of the crimes which would place Christianity among the monstrosities for ever cursed and forgotten.

The executioners actually surpassed themselves, but they could not subdue the heroism of the victims. The exaltation and joy of suffering together put them into a state of "quasi-anæsthesis." They imagined themselves but as a divine water flowing from the side of Jesus. Publicity sustained them. What glory to confess before all people, his Word and his Faith. This became a pledge and very few yielded. It is proved that self-love often suffices to sustain an apparent heroism when publicity is added to it. The Pagan actors submitted, without flinching, to the most cruel punishments. The gladiators made a good figure before approaching death, not to confess to weakness under the eyes of an assembled crowd; what otherwise was vanity, brought into the heart of a little group of men and women imprisoned together, became a pious intoxication and a sensible joy. The idea that Christ suffered in them filled them with pride, and of poor weak creatures made a kind of supernatural beings.

The deacon Sanctus, of Vienne, shone among the most courageous. As the Pagans knew him to be the depository of the secrets of the Church, they sought to draw from him some word which should give a ground to the infamous accusations against the community. They did not succeed in making him tell his name, nor the name of his people, nor the name of the town from which he came, nor whether he was bond or free. To everything they asked of him he replied in Latin Christianus sum. There was in that his name, his country, his race, his all. The Pagans could draw from his mouth no other avowal than that. This obstinacy only redoubled the fury of the legate and the torturers. Having expended all their means without conquering him, they took the idea that they would apply the copper-plates at a white heat upon the most sensitive organs. Sanctus during this time remained inflexible, never leaving his obstinate confession Christianus sum. His body was nothing but a sore, a mass bloody, torn, convulsed, contracted, presenting no longer a human appearance. The faithful triumphed, saying that Christ knew how to make his own people insensible, and put himself in their place when they were in torture, that he might suffer in their stead. What was most terrible was that some days after they re-commenced the torture of Sanctus. The state of the confessor was such that when they touched his hand they made him leap with pain. The executioners took one after the other the inflamed sores, they renewed each one of his wounds, they repeated upon each of his organs the frightful experiences of the first day; they hoped to conquer him or to see him die in torments, so that the others might be terrified. It was not so, however; Sanctus resisted so well that his companions believed in a miracle, and pretended that this second torture, having upon him the effect of a cure, had straightened his limbs again and given back to his body the human appearance which it had lost.

Maturus, who was only a neophyte, behaved himself like a valiant soldier of Christ. As to the slave, Blandina, she showed that a revolution was accomplished. Blandina belonged to a Christian lady, who, doubtless, had her initiated in the faith of Christ. The feeling of her low social position only excited her to equal her masters. The true emancipation of the slave, the emancipation through heroism, was mainly her work. The Pagan slave was supposed to be bad and immoral. What could be a better manner of rehabilitating them, and allowing them to show themselves capable of the same virtues and the same sacrifices as the free man? How could one treat with disdain those women they saw in the amphitheatre even more sublime than their mistresses? The good Lyonese slave had been told that the judgments of God are the reverse of human appearances, that God is often pleased to choose the most humble, the most uncomely, the most despised, and confound that which appears most beautiful and strong. Penetrated by a sense of her own position she called for the torturers and longed to suffer. She was little, weak in body, so much so that the faithful feared she should not be able to resist the torments. Her mistress especially, who was of the number of the accused, feared that this weak and delicate being would not be capable of affirming her faith. Blandina had prodigious energy and boldness. She exhausted the brigades of executioners who exercised themselves on her from morning to night; the conquered torturers confessed that they had no more punishment for her, and declared that they could not understand how she could still breathe with a body so dislocated and transpierced; they declared that only one of the tortures they had applied to her ought to have been sufficient to make her die. The blessed one, like a generous athlete, gained new strength in the act of confessing Christ. It was for her a strengthener and an anaesthetic to say, "I am a Christian, nothing evil is done among us." Scarcely had she uttered these words when she appeared to recover all her vigour, presenting herself refreshed for new struggles. This heroic resistance irritated the Roman authorities; to the tortures of "the question" they added that of lying in a prison which was made the most horrible that could be. They put the confessors into obscure and unbearable holes, they put their feet in the stocks, stretching them out to the fifth hole, they spared them none of the cruelties which the jailers had to cause their victims to suffer. Many died asphyxiated in the dungeons. Those who had been tortured resisted amazingly. Their sores were so frightful that people could not understand how they survived. Entirely occupied in encouraging the others, they appeared to be themselves animated by a divine strength. They were like veteran athletes hardened to everything. On the contrary, the last arrested, who had not yet suffered "the question," nearly all died shortly after their imprisonment. They might be compared to novices half-trained, whose bodies, little accustomed to tortures, could not support the trial of the dungeon. Martyrdom would appear more and more as a kind of gymnastics, or school of gladiators, in which a long preparation was necessary, and a sort of preliminary asceticism.

Although isolated from the rest of the world, the pious confessors lived in the life of the universal Church with a singular intensity. Par from feeling separated from their brethren they were interested in everything which occupied Catholicism. The appearance of Montanism was the great matter of the period. People spoke only of the prophecies of Montanus, Theodotus, and of Alcibiades. The Lyonese interested themselves in these all the more that they shared in many of the Phrygian ideas, and that many of them, such as Alexander the physician, Alcibiades the ascetic, were at least the admirers and partly the votaries of the movement begun at Pepuza. The report of the dissensions which these novelties excited reached even them. They had no other subject, and they occupied the intervals between one torture and another in discussing these phenomena, which, without doubt, they would have desired to find true. Strong in the authority which the title of "prisoner of Jesus Christ" gave to the confessors, they wrote upon this delicate subject many letters full of tolerance and charity. It was admitted that the prisoners of the faith had, in their last days, a sort of mission to settle the differences of the churches, and to solve the questions that were in suspense; they attributed to them, in this point of view, a state of grace and a special privilege.

The majority of the letters written by the confessors were addressed to the churches of Asia and Phrygia, with whom the faithful Lyonese had many spiritual ties; one of these was addressed to Pope Eleutherus, and it was conveyed by Irenæus. The martyrs made thus the warmest eulogium on this young priest.

"We wish thee joy in God for everything, Father Eleutherus. We have charged to carry these letters our brother and companion Irenæus, and we pray thee to receive him in great honour, imitator as he is of the Testament of Christ. If we believed that the position of the people is what it ought to be by their deserts, we should have recommended him to thee as a priest of our Church, a title which he really possesses."

Irenæus did not leave at once; one may suppose that Pothin's death, which soon followed, prevented him from setting out immediately. The letters of the martyrs were sent to their addresses later on, with the epistle which contained the recital of their heroic struggles. The old Bishop Pothin had spent his life; age and prison sapped it; only the desire of martyrdom sustained him. He breathed with difficulty on the day on which he was to appear before the tribunal; he had scarcely enough breath left to confess Christ worthily. We can see indeed, from the respect by which the faithful surrounded him, that he was their religious chief--a great curiosity attached itself to him in passing from the prison to the tribunal; the authorities of the town followed him; the squad of soldiers who surrounded him with difficulty drew him from the press; the most diverse cries were heard. As the Christians were sometimes called the disciples of Pothin, sometimes the disciples of Christos, many demanded if it was the old man who was Christos. The legate put the question to him: "Who is the God of the Christians?" "Thou should'st know that if thou wert worthy," replied Pothin. They drew him about brutally; they struck him blows; without regard to his great age, those who were near him buffeted him with their fists and feet; those who were at a distance from him threw at him whatever came to their hands; everyone would have been believed guilty of the crime of impiety if he had not done what he could to cover him with insults; they believed that they would revenge thus the injury done to their gods. They put the old man back into prison half dead. At the end of two days he yielded up his last sigh. What made a strange contrast, and rendered the situation tragical in the highest degree, was the attitude of those whom the force of torture had conquered, and who had denied Christ. They had not been released for that; the fact that they had been Christians implied the avowal of crimes for which they were persecuted even after their apostasy. They were not separated from their brethren who remained faithful, and all the aggravations of the prison rule by which the confessors suffered were applied to them. But how different was their condition! Not only did the renegades find that they had drawn no advantage from an act which had been painful to them; but their position was in some sort worse than that of the faithful. Those indeed were only persecuted for bearing the name of Christians, without formulating any special crime against them; the others were, by their own avowal, under accusations of homicide and monstrous prevarication. Thus their look was pitiable. The joy of martyrdom, the hope of promised blessedness, the love of Christ, the Spirit sent from the Father, made everything light to the confessors. The apostates, on the contrary, appeared to be torn by remorse. It was especially in going from the prison to the tribunal that one could see the difference. The confessors advanced with a calm and radiant air; a sort of sweet majesty and grace shone upon their faces. Their chains appeared to be the ornament of brides adorned in all their finery; the Christians believed they could feel around them what they called the perfume of Christ; some pretended indeed that an exquisite odour was exhaled from their bodies. Very different were the poor renegades. Ashamed, and with their heads lowered, without grace and without dignity, they marched like common criminals; the Pagans even treated them as dastards and ignoble murderers convicted by their own speech; the fine name of Christian, which rendered so proud those who paid for it with their life, belonged to them no longer. This difference of gait made the strongest impression. Thus the Christians were often seen to make their confession as soon as possible, so that they might deprive themselves of all possibility of recalling it.

Pardon was sometimes indulgent to those unfortunates who expiated so dearly a moment of surprise. A poor Syrian woman of fragile frame, originally from Byblos, in Phoenicia, had denied the name of Christ. She was again put to the question; they hoped to draw from her weakness and her timidity an avowal of the secret monstrosities with which they reproached the Christians. She came to herself again somewhat upon the wooden horse, and, as if awakening from a profound sleep, she denied energetically all the calumnious assertions. "How can you think," she said, "that people to whom it is forbidden to eat the blood of beasts should eat children?" From that moment she avowed herself a Christian, and followed the fate of other martyrs.

The day of glory at length came for a portion of these veteran combatants who founded by their faith the faith of the future. The legate gave expressly one of those hideous fetes, consisting in exhibitions of punishments and in fights with beasts which, in spite of the most humane of emperors, were more in vogue than ever. These horrible spectacles were put down for fixed dates; but it was not rare for extraordinary executions to take place, when they had beasts to exhibit to the people as well as unfortunates to deliver to them.

The festival was probably given in the amphitheatre of Lyons, that is to say, of the colony which was ranged under the roof of Fouriviers. This amphitheatre was, as it appears, situated at the base of a hill, near the present Place de Jean, near the cathedral. The Rue Tramassac marks nearly the grand axis. One could believe that it had been made five years previously. An exasperated crowd covered the benches and called for the Christians with loud cries. Maturus, Sanctus, Blandina, and Attalus were chosen for that day. They were quite nude; there had not been that day any of those spectacles by gladiators whose variety had such an attraction for the people.

Maturus and Sanctus traversed anew in the amphitheatre the whole series of punishments as if they had never before suffered anything. Men compared them to athletes, who, after having conquered in many separate combats, were reserved for a last struggle which carried with it the final crown. The instruments of these tortures were arranged for the distance of a spina, and transformed the arena into a representation of hell. Nothing was spared the victims. They began, according to custom, by a hideous procession, in which the condemned, filing naked before the squad of soldiers, received each one dreadful blow on the back. Then they let loose the beasts. It was the most terrible moment of the day. The beasts did not devour the victims all at once; they bit them, they drew them about, their fangs were stuck into the naked flesh, in which they left bloody traces. At these moments the spectators became mad with delight. The summons crossed the seats of the amphitheatre. What in fact made the interest of the ancient spectacle was that the public intervened there. As in the bull-fights of Spain, the audience commanded, ruled the incidents, ordered the blows, judged the incidents of death or life. The exasperation against the Christians was such that they called aloud against them for more terrible punishments.

The red-hot iron chair was the most infernal thing that the art of the executioner had invented. Maturus and Sanctus were seated there; a repulsive odour of roasted flesh filled the amphitheatre, and only further intoxicated these furious savages. The firmness of the two martyrs was admirable. They could draw from Sanctus only one word, ever the same, "I am a Christian." It appeared as if the two martyrs could not die. The beasts on the other hand appeared to shun them. They were obliged to finish them, to put them out of their misery, as in the case of the beasts and gladiators.

Blandina during all this time was fixed to a stake and exposed to the beasts whom they urged on to devour her; she did not cease to pray, her eyes raised to heaven. No beast that day would touch her. That poor naked body exposed to those thousands of spectators, whose curiosity was restrained only by the close band which the law ordered to be worn by actresses and condemned women, did not excite any pity from the audience; but it presented to the other martyrs a mystic signification. Blandina's stake appeared to them as the cross of Jesus. The body of their friend shining by its whiteness to the other extremity of the amphitheatre recalled to their minds that of Christ crucified. The joy of thus seeing this image of the sweet Lamb of God rendered them insensible. Blandina from that moment was Jesus to them. From that moment, in their cruellest sufferings, a look cast upon their sister on the cross filled them with joy and ardour.

Attalus was known throughout the whole town, thus the crowd called eagerly for him. They compelled him to make the tour of the amphitheatre, having borne before him a tablet inscribed HIC EST ATTALIS CHRISTIANUS. He walked with firm step, with the peace of a sound conscience. The people called for the most cruel punishments for him. But the imperial legate, having learned that he was a Roman citizen, made them cease, and ordered him back to prison. Thus ended the day.

Blandina, attached to a stake, waited in vain for the teeth of some beast. They unloosed her hands, and led her back to the depot, that she might serve again for the amusement of the people.

The case of Attalus was not isolated; the number of accused increased daily. The legate felt himself compelled to write to the emperor, who about the middle of the year 177 A.D. was, it appears, at Rome. Some weeks had to pass before a reply. During this interval the prisoners abounded in mystic joys. The example of the martyrs was contagious, all those who had denied returned to repentance, and demanded to be interrogated anew. Many Christians doubted the validity of such conversions, but the martyrs settled the question by stretching out their hands to the renegades, and communicating to them some of the grace that was in them. They declared that the living in such a case could revivify the dead; that in the great community of the Church those who had too much could give to those who had not enough; that he who had been rejected from the bosom of the Church, like an abortion, could in some manner re-enter it; to be connected a second time with the virginal bosom, to be placed in communication with the sources of life. The true martyr was thus looked upon as having the power of forcing the devil to vomit from his maw those whom he had already devoured. His privilege became a privilege of indulgence, grace and charity.

That which was admirable among the Lyonese confessors is that glory did not fascinate them, their humility equalled their courage and their holy liberty. Those heroes who had proclaimed their faith in Christ two or three times, who had faced the beasts, whose bodies were covered with scars, with stripes, dared not claim the title of martyr, nor were they allowed to attribute such a name to themselves. If any one of the faithful, by letter or the living voice, called them so, they quickly rejected the title; they reserved the title of martyr first for Christ, "the faithful and true witness, the first begotten again from the dead," the imitator of the life of God, then to those who had already obtained by dying, while confessing their faith, and whose title was in a manner sealed and ratified; as to themselves they were only modest and humble confessors, and they asked only from their brethren to pray for them without ceasing that they might make a good end. Far from showing themselves proud, haughty, or hard upon the poor apostates as pure Montanists did, and as certain martyrs of the third century did, they had for them the bowels of a mother, and poured out for their establishment continual tears; they did not accuse anyone; they prayed for their executioners, and found extenuating circumstances for all their faults; they absolved, and did not condemn them. Some rigorist found them too indulgent to the renegades; they quoted for example St. Stephen, saying, "If he prayed for those who stoned him, would he not have been permitted to pray for his brethren?" Good minds on the contrary said with justice that it was the love of the accused that made their strength and secured their triumph. Their perpetual desire was peace and concord; thus there were left after them, not like certain confessors, courageous besides, some discords and disputes among their brethren, but an exquisite souvenir of joy and perfect love.

The good sense of the confessors was not less remarkable than their courage and love. Montanism, by its enthusiasm and ardour for martyrdom which it inspired, could not all at once displease them, but they saw excess in it. This Alcibiades, who lived on nothing but bread and water, was among the confessors; he wished to carry out this régime in the prison. The confessors looked with an evil eye upon these peculiarities. Attalus, after the first combat which he had in the amphitheatre, had a vision on this matter; it was revealed to him that the way of Alcibiades was not good; that he had the fault of avoiding systematically the use of things created by God, and caused thus a scandal to his brethren.

Alcibiades allowed himself to be persuaded, and ate henceforth all foods without distinction, giving thanks to God for them.

The accused, thus believed also that they possessed in their bosom a permanent fire of inspiration, and received direct counsels from the Holy Spirit. But that which in Phrygia raised nothing but abuse was here a principle of heroism. Montanists, by the ardour of martyrdom, the Lyonese, by the absence of all pride, were profoundly Catholic.

The imperial reply arrived at last; it was hard and cruel. All those who persevered in their confession were to be put to death, all the renegades were to be released. The great annual festival which was celebrated at the altar of Augustus, and when all the peoples of Gaul were represented, was commencing. The affair of the Christians occurred to increase the interest in it.

So as to strike the people, a sort of theatrical audience was organised, where all the accused were pompously paraded. They were asked simply if they were Christians. Upon an affirmative reply, they beheaded those who appeared to have the right of Roman citizenship, and reserved the others for the beasts. Pardon was also extended to several. Not a single confessor was weak, as might have been expected. The Pagans hoped that those who had formerly apostatised would renew their anti-Christian declaration. They questioned them separately, in order to exclude them from the influence of the others. They showed them that immediate liberty would be given as the result of their denial. There was here, in some sense, the decisive moment, the crisis of the struggle. The hearts of the faithful who remained free, and who witnessed this scene, beat with anguish. Alexander the Phrygian, who knew them all as a physician, and whose zeal knew no bounds, kept himself as near the tribunals as possible, and made the most energetic signs with the head to those who were interrogated to make them confess. The Pagans took him for one that was "possessed." The Christians saw in his contortions something which recalled to them the convulsions of child-birth. The act by which the apostate re-entered the Church seemed to them a second birth. Alexander and grace fascinated them.

Apart from a little number of unfortunates whom punishments had frightened, the apostates retracted and avowed themselves Christians. The anger of the Pagans was extreme. They accused Alexander of being the cause of these culpable retractations. They stopped him and presented him to the legate. "Who art thou?" asked he. "A Christian," replied Alexander. The enraged legate condemned him to the beasts. The execution was fixed for the next day.

Such was the enthusiasm of the faithful band that they cared much less for the frightful death which they had before their eyes than for the torture of the apostates. The horror which the martyrs conceived against those who relapsed was extreme. They treated them as sons of perdition, wretches who covered their Church with shame; people in whom remained no longer a trace of faith, nor of respect for their nuptial robe, nor fear of God. On the contrary, those who had repaired their first fault were reunited to the Church, and fully reconciled.

On the first of August, in the morning, in the presence of all Gaul assembled in the amphitheatre, the horrible spectacle began. The people thought much of the punishment of Attalus, after Pothin the true head of Lyonese Christianity. We cannot see how the legate, who once had snatched him from the beasts because he was a Roman citizen, could give him up this time; but the fact is certain; it is probable that the title of Attalus to Roman citizenship was not found sufficient. Attalus and Alexander entered first into the sandy and carefully raked arena. They passed like heroes all the instruments of punishment with which the arrangements were made. Alexander did not pronounce one word, did not utter a cry; collecting himself he communed with God. When they seated Attalus in the red-hot iron chair, and his body, burned on all sides, exhaled an abominable odour and smoke, he said to the people in Latin, "It is you who are eaters of men. As to us, we do nothing evil." They asked him, "What is God's name?" "God," said he, "has not a name like a man." The two martyrs received the coup de grâce, after having exhausted with full knowledge all that was most atrocious that Roman cruelty could invent.

The fêtes lasted several days; every day the combats of the gladiators were relieved by the punishment of the Christians. It is probable that they introduced the victims two and two, and that every day saw one or other pair of martyrs perish. They put in the arena those who were young and those thought feeble, that the sight of their friends' suffering might frighten them. Blandina and a young man of fifteen years of age, named Ponticus, were kept to the last day. They were thus witnesses of all the trials of the others, but nothing shook them. Each day there was a strong attempt made on them; it was sought to make them swear by the gods; they refused with disdain. The people, much irritated, would listen to no sentiment of shame or pity. They made the poor girl and her young friend exhaust all the hideous series of the punishments of the arena; after each trial they proposed that they should swear. Blandina was sublime. She had never been a mother; this boy by her side became her son, born in the tortures. Attentive only to him, she followed him in each of his halting-places of pain, to encourage him, and to exhort him to persevere to the end. The spectators saw this and were struck by it. Ponticus expired after having submitted to the complete series of torments.

Of all the holy band there remained only Blandina. She triumphed and shone with joy. She looked like a mother who has seen all her sons proclaimed conquerors, and presents them to the great King to be crowned. That humble slave was shown to be the inspirer of heroism in her companions; her ardent voice had been the stimulant which had upheld the weak nerves and failing hearts. Thus she was thrust into the bitter career of tortures which her brothers had passed through, as if it had been a nuptial festival. The glorious and near issue of all these trials made her leap with pleasure. She placed herself at the end of the arena, not to lose any of the ornaments which each punishment engraved upon her flesh. There was first a cruel scourging which tore her shoulders, then they exposed her to the beasts, who contented themselves with biting her and drawing her about. The odious burning chair was not spared her. At last they enclosed her in a net and exposed her to a furious bull; this animal, seizing her with its horns, threw her many times into the air and let her fall heavily. But the blessed one felt nothing any longer; she rejoiced already with supreme felicity, lost as she was in internal communion with Christ. It was necessary to finish her like the others. The crowd ended by being struck with admiration, they spoke of nothing but the poor slave. "Truly," said the Gauls, "never have we seen a woman in our country suffer so much."

CHAPTER XX

RECONSTITUTION OF THE CHURCH OF LYONS--IRENÆUS

The rage of the fanatics was not satisfied, it gratified itself upon the corpses of the martyrs. The bodies of the confessors who had died stifled in prison were thrown to the dogs, and a guard was set night and day lest any of the faithful might give them burial. As to the others, each day there were taken from the arena broiled bones, scraps torn by the teeth of the beasts, limbs roasted or blackened in the fire, heads which had been cut off, mutilated trunks; and these were left likewise without burial, and in the sewers, exposed to the air, with a guard of soldiers watching over them for six days. This hideous spectacle excited varied reflections among the Pagans. Some thought that they had sinned by excess of humanity, and that the martyrs ought to have been subjected to still more cruel punishments. Others mingled irony with a shade of pity. "Where is their God?" they said. "Of what use was this worship to them who preferred it to life?" The Christians felt a deep grief at not being able to conceal in their graves the remains of the holy bodies. The excess of cruelty on the part of the Pagans appeared to them the proof of a malice which had reached its height, and the sign of an approaching judgment from God. "Come," said they, "this is not enough," and they added, as they remembered their Apocalypse, "Ah, let the sinner triumph more that the good may more improve." They sought to take away the bodies during the night, trying the effect of money and entreaties upon the soldiers. All was useless; the authorities guarded those wretched remains with tenacity. The seventh day having come, the order was given to burn the infected mass, and to throw the ashes into the Rhone, which flowed hard by, so that there might remain no trace of them upon the earth. There had been in this way of acting more than a mental reservation. They imagined by the complete disappearance of the corpses to take away from the Christians the hope of resurrection. This hope appeared to the Pagans the origin of all the evil. "It is by the trust they have in the resurrection," they said, "that they introduce among us this new strange worship, that they contemn the most terrible punishments, that they walk to death with eagerness and even with joy. Let us see then if they will rise again, and if their God is able to take them out of our hands." The Christians were reassured by the thought that they could not conquer God, and that he knew well how to recover the remains of his servants. They believed indeed in a later age that miraculous apparitions had revealed the ashes of the martyrs, and all the middle ages believed that they possessed them, as if the Roman authorities had not destroyed them. The people used to call these innocent victims by the name of Macchabees.

The number of the victims had been forty-eight. The survivors of the churches so cruelly tried rallied very quickly. Vettius Epagathus was found what he really was, the good genius, the guardian of the Church of Lyons. He was not yet bishop. Already the distinction of the ecclesiastic by profession and of the layman who shall be always a layman is felt. Ireæeus, the disciple of Pothin, and who had, if one may express it so, an education in clerical habits, took his place in the direction of the Church. It was perhaps he who indited, in the name of the communities of Lyons and Vienna, that admirable letter to the churches of Asia and Phrygia, of which the larger portion has been preserved, and which includes all the account of the combats of the martyrs. It is one of the most extraordinary pieces which any literature possesses. Never has a more striking picture been traced of the degree of enthusiasm and devotion to which human nature can reach. It is the ideal of martyrdom, with as little pride as possible on the part of the martyr. The Lyonese narrator and his heroes were certainly credulous men; they believed that the Antichrist would come to ravage the world; they saw in everything the action of the Beast, the wicked demon to whom the good God grants (one cannot tell why) that he should triumph momentarily. Nothing more strange that God, who makes a garland of flowers from the sufferings of his servants, and pleases himself to arrange his designs, expressly devoting some to the beasts, others to decapitation, the others to suffocation in prison. But the enthusiasm, the mystical tone of the style, the spirit of sweetness and good sense which mark the whole recital, inaugurate a new rhetoric, and make this piece the pearl of the Christian literature of the second century.

To the circular epistle, the brethren of Gaul added the letters relative to Montanism written by the confessors in the prison. This question of Montanist prophecies assumed such an importance that they believed they were obliged to give their own opinion on this point. Irenæus was probably again their spokesman. The extreme reserve with which he expresses himself in his writings on Montanism, the love of peace which he imported into all controversies, and which caused it to be said so often that no one had been better named than he--Irenæus (peaceful)--leads us to believe that his opinion was impressed with a lively desire of reconciliation. With their ordinary judgment, the Lyonese pronounced without doubt against the excesses, but recommended a tolerance which, unfortunately, was not always sufficiently observed in these burning debates.

Irenæus, settled henceforth at Lyons, but in constant correspondence with Rome, presented there the model of the accomplished ecclesiastic. His antipathy for the sects (the gross millenarianism which he professed, and which he held from the Presbyteri of Asia, did not appear to him a sectarian doctrine), the clear view he had of the dangers of Gnosticism, made him write those vast books of controversy, the work of a mind limited no doubt, but with a most healthy moral conscience. Lyons, thanks to him, was for a moment the centre of the emission of the most important Christian writings. Like all the great doctors of the Church, Irenæus found means to associate with his supernatural beliefs, which appear to us at this day irreconcilable with a right mind, the rarest practical sense. Very inferior to Justin in philosophic spirit, he is much more orthodox than he was, and has left a strong trace in Christian theology. To an enthusiastic time he united a moderation which is astonishing, to a rare simplicity he joined profound science, with ecclesiastical administration the government of souls; finally, he possessed the clearest conception which had yet been formulated in the universal Church. He has less talent than Tertullian; but how superior is he in heart and life! Alone, among the Christian polemics who combated heresies, he shows some charity for the heretic, and puts himself on guard against the calumnious inductions of orthodoxy.

The relations between the churches of the Upper Rhone and Asia becoming more and more rare, the surrounding Latin influence became greater little by little. Irenæus and the Asians who surrounded him followed already the Western custom for Easter. The Greek custom was lost; Latin was soon the language of these churches, which, in the fourth century, were not essentially distinguished from that of the rest of Gaul. Yet the traces of Greek origin effaced themselves very slowly; several Greek customs were preserved in the liturgy at Lyons, Vienne, Autun, until the middle ages. An ineffaceable souvenir was inscribed in the annals of the universal Church; this little Asiatic and Phrygian island, hidden in the midst of the darkness of the West, had thrown forth an unequalled brilliancy. The solid goodness of our races, joined to the brilliant heroism and the love of Orientals for glory, produced sublime episodes. Blandina, on the cross at the extremity of the amphitheatre, was like a new Christ. The sweet, pale slave, attached to her stake on this new Calvary, showed that the servant, when a holy cause is concerned, is equal to the free man and sometimes excels him. We say nothing of the rights of man. The ancestors of these are very old. After having been the town of Gnosticism and Montanism, Lyons shall be the town of the Vaudois, of the Pauperes of Lugduno, and shall become the grand battlefield where the opposing principles of modern conscience shall engage in the most impassioned struggle. Honour to those who suffer for such a cause! Progress shall bring in, I trust, the day when these grand constructions, which modern Catholicism raises imprudently upon the heights of Montmartre and Fourvières, shall become temples of the supreme Forgiveness, and shall include a chapel for all causes, for all victims, for all martyrs.

CHAPTER XXI

CELSUS AND LUCIAN

The determined conservative who, in passing near some mutilated corpses of the martyrs of Lyons, said to himself, "They have been too gentle; some more severe punishments must be invented!" was not more narrow than those politicians who, in all ages, have believed they could arrest religious or social movements by punishments. Religious and social movements are fought with by time and the progress of reason. The sectarian socialism of 1848 has disappeared in twenty years without special laws of repression. If Marcus-Aurelius, instead of employing the lions and the red-hot chair, had used the primary school and the teaching of a rationalist State, it would have better prevented the seduction of the world by Christian supernaturalism. Unfortunately, they were not placed upon the true ground. To combat religions by maintaining, by exaggerating even the religious principle, is the worst calculation. To show the emptiness of everything supernatural, this is the radical cure for fanaticism. Now scarcely any one was at that point of view. The Roman philosopher Celsus, an educated man, of great good sense, who had anticipated on several points the results of modern criticism, wrote a book against Christianity, not to prove to Christians that their style of conceiving of the intervention of God in the affairs of the world was contrary to what we know of the reality, but to show that they were wrong in not practising the religion which they found established.

This Celsus was the friend of Lucian, and appears at bottom to have shared the scepticism of the great laugher of Samosate. It was at his request that Lucian composed the intellectual essay upon Alexander of Abonoticus, where the foolishness of believing in the supernatural is so well exposed. Lucian, with him heart to heart, represents him as an unreserved admirer of that grand liberating philosophy which has saved man from the phantoms of superstition, and which preserves him from all vain beliefs and errors. The two friends, exactly like Lucretius, look upon Epicurus as a saint, a hero, a benefactor of the human race, a divine genius, the only one who had seen the truth and has dared to speak it. Lucian, on the other hand, speaks of his friend as an accomplished man; he boasts of his wisdom, his justice, his love of the truth, the sweetness of his manners, and the charm of his conversation. His writings appear to him the most useful and beautiful of the age, capable of opening the eyes of all those who have any reason. Celsus in fact has taken as his speciality to discover the snares to which poor humanity is subject. He had a strong antipathy to the Goetes and the introducers of false gods after the manner of Alexander of Abonoticus. As to general principles, he appears to have been less firm than Lucian. He wrote against magic, rather to unveil the charlatanism of the magicians than to show the absolute emptiness of their art. His criticism in what concerns the supernatural is identical with that of the Epicureans; but he does not stop there. He puts upon the same footing astrology, music, natural history, magic, and divination. He repels most spells as impostures, but he admits some. He does not believe in the legends of Paganism, but he considers them great, marvellous, and useful to men. Prophets in general appear to him charlatans, and yet he does not treat as a simple dream the art of foretelling the future. He is eclectic, deistical, or, if it is preferred, a Platonist. His religion resembles much that of Marcus-Aurelius, Maximus of Tyre, and that which later shall be the religion of the Emperor Julian.

God, universal order, delegates his power to some special gods, a sort of demons or ministers, to whom is presented the worship of polytheism. This cult is lawful, or at least very acceptable, when it is not carried to excess. It becomes a strict duty when it is the national religion, each one having as his duty the adoration of the divine according to the form which has been transmitted to him by his ancestors. True worship is to hold always one's thoughts raised towards God, the common father of all men. Internal piety is essential, the sacrifices are nothing but the sign. As to the adorations which people make to the demons, those obligations are of little consequence and may be satisfied by a movement of the hand, although it is good to treat them seriously. The demons do not need anything, and it is necessary not to delight too much in magic or magical operations; but one must not be too ungrateful, and, besides, all piety is salutary. To serve the inferior gods is to please the great God whom they extol. Christians may well yield some extraordinary honours to a son of God appearing recently in the world! Like Maximus of Tyre, Celsus has a philosophy of religion which allows him to admit all cults. He would admit Christianity on the same footing as the other beliefs if Christianity had only a pretension limited to the truth.

Providence, divination, the prodigies of the temples, the oracles, the immortality of the soul, future rewards and punishments appeared to Celsus as integral parts of a State doctrine. It must be recollected that the possibility of magic was at that time almost a dogma. They were Epicureans, atheists, impious, and ran the risk of their lives who dared to deny it. All sects, the Epicureans excepted, taught its reality. Celsus seriously believed in it. His reason shows him the falsity of generally admitted supernatural beliefs; but the insufficiency of his scientific education and his political prejudices prevented him from being consequent; he maintains, at least in principle, certain beliefs quite as little rational as those he combats. The feeble knowledge which people had then of the laws of nature made all such credulousness possible. Tacitus has certainly an enlightened mind, and yet he does not dare to repel completely the most puerile prodigies. The apparitions of the temples and divine dreams were considered to be facts. Elien was soon to write his books to demonstrate, by pretended facts, that those who deny the miraculous manifestations of the gods are "more unreasonable than children," that those who believe in the gods are blessed, while the most fearful adventures happen to the incredulous and blasphemers.

What Celsus was eminently is, a subject devoted to the emperor--a patriot. We suppose him to have been a Roman or Italian; it is certain that Lucian, loyal as he is, has not such a pronounced sympathy for the empire. The fundamental reasoning of Celsus is this: the Roman religion has been a phenomenon concomitant with the Roman grandeur; therefore, it is true. Like the Gnostics, Celsus believes that every nation has its gods, who protect it in proportion as it adores them as they wish to be adored. To abandon its gods is, for a nation, the equivalent of suicide. Celsus is thus the reverse of a Tatian, the bitter enemy of Hellenism and Roman society. Tatian sacrifices the Hellenic civilisation entirely to Judaism and Christianity. Celsus attributes all that is good among the Jews or Christians to the borrowings made from the Greeks. Plato and Epictetes are for him the two poles of wisdom. If he had not known Marcus-Aurelius he would have certainly loved and admired him. From such a point of view, he could not look on Christianity but as an evil; but he does not indulge in calumnies, he acknowledges that the manners of the sectaries are gentle and well regulated; it is the grounds of credibility in the sect which he would discuss. Celsus made a thorough investigation on the subject, read the Christian and Jewish books, and conversed with both classes. The result of his researches was a work entitled A True Discourse, which naturally enough has not come down to us, but which it is possible to reconstruct from the quotations and the analyses which Origen has given of it.

It is beyond doubt that Celsus knew better than any other Pagan writer Christianity, and the books which served as its basis. Origen, in spite of his remarkable Christian instruction, is astonished to have so many things to learn from him. As to erudition Celsus is a Christian doctor. His journeys in Palestine, Phoenicia, and Egypt have opened his mind on the matters of religious history. He has read attentively the Greek translations of the Bible, Genesis, Exodus, the Prophets, including Jonah, Daniel, Enoch, and the Psalms. He knew the Sibylline writings, and he saw their fraud; the emptiness of the tentatives of allegorical exegesis did not escape him. Among the writings of the New Testament he knew the four Canonical Gospels and many others, perhaps the Acts of Pilate. While decidedly preferring Matthew, he takes good account of the different retouchings to which the Gospel texts have been subjected, especially in view of the Apology. It is doubtful if he had in his hands St. Paul's writings; like St. Justin he never names him; yet he recalls some of his maxims and is not ignorant of his doctrines. As to ecclesiastical history he has read the dialogue of Jason and Papiscus, numerous Gnostic and Marcionite writings, especially the Heavenly Dialogue, a writing of which there is no mention elsewhere. He does not appear to have had the writings of St. Justin, although the way in which he thinks of Christian theology, Christology, and the Canon are exactly agreeable to the theology, Christology, and Canon of St. Justin. The Jewish legend of Jesus was familiar to him. The mother of Jesus had committed adultery with the soldier, Pantherus; she had been rejected by her husband, the carpenter. Jesus wrought his miracles by means of the secret sciences which he had learned in Egypt.

It was especially in exegesis that Celsus astonishes us by his penetration. Voltaire has not triumphed better over Biblical history, the impossibilities of Genesis taken in its natural sense, that which is artlessly childish in the stories of the creation, of the deluge and the ark. The bloody, hard egotistical character of Jewish history; the bizarrerie of the divine choice in fixing on such a race to make of them the people of God, are well brought to light. The bitterness of the Jewish scoffs against the other sects is set forth in a lively manner as acts of injustice and pride. All the Messianic plan of the Judeo-Christian history, having as its base the exaggerated importance which men, and in particular the Jews, claim in the universe, is refuted by the hand of a master. Why should God come down to earth? Could it be to know what was passing among men? But does he not know all things? Is his power so limited that he cannot correct anything without coming into the world or sending some one here? Could this be known? It is to impute to him an emptiness entirely human. And then why so late? Why rather at one moment than another? Why rather in one country than another? The Apocalyptic theories of the final conflagration and of the Resurrection are in the same way victoriously refuted. Bizarre pretension, to render immortal dust, putrefaction! Celsus triumphs by opposing to this religious materialism his pure idealism, his absolute God who does not manifest himself in the progress of finished things.

"Jews and Christians present to me the effect of a lot of field mice or pismires leaving their hole, or frogs settled in a marsh, or worms in the corner of a ditch . . . . . and saying among themselves: It is to us that God reveals and announces everything; he has no concern for the rest of the world; he leaves the heavens and the earth to roll on at their own fancy, to occupy himself with us alone. We are the only beings with whom he communicates by his messengers, the only ones with whom he desires to have society, for he has made us like himself. Everything is subordinated to us, the earth, the water, the air, and the stars, all has been done for us and destined for our service, and it is because it has so happened that certain among us have sinned that God himself will come or will send his own Son to burn up the wicked, but to make us enjoy eternal life with him.'"

The discussion on the life of Jesus is conducted exactly according to the method of Reimarus and Strauss. The impossibilities of the Gospel history, if one may take it as history, have never been better shown. The appearance of God in Jesus appears to our philosophy unseemly and useless, the evangelical miracles are paltry, the walking magicians have done quite as much without being regarded as the Son of God. The life of Jesus is that of a miserable Goëte hatred of God. His character is provoking, his manner of speaking decidedly indicates a man who is powerless to persuade; it is unseemly for a God or even a man of sense. Jesus ought to have been beautiful, strong, majestic, eloquent. Now his disciples confess that he was little, uncomely, and without nobleness. Why, if God wished to save the human race, did he send his Son only to a corner of the world? He should rather have sent his Spirit into many bodies, and commanded his celestial envoys in different directions, since he knew that the messenger destined to the Jews should be put to death. Why also two opposing revelations, that of Moses and that of Jesus? Jesus has risen, do they say? That is reported of a crowd of others, Zamolxis, Pythagoras, Rhampsinit.

Perhaps it first ought to be made a subject of examination whether any man really dead has risen with the same body. Why treat the adventures of others as fables without verisimilitude, as if the issue of your tragedy had a better appearance and was credible, with the cry that your Jesus threw on high from the cross while expiring amid the shaking of the earth and the darkness? Living he has been able to do nothing for himself; dead do you say he rose, and showed the marks of his suffering, the holes in his hands? But who has seen all that? A woman with an evil spirit, as you yourselves confess, or otherwise possessed in the same way, whether the pretended witness had dreamed that which his troubled spirit suggested to him, or that his abused imagination had given a substance to its desires (which happens so open), or rather that he had wished to strike the minds of men by a marvellous story, and by the help of this imposture to furnish material for charlatans.. . . . At his tomb there were present, some say, one angel, others say two, to announce to the women that he had risen; for the Son of God, as he appeared to be, had not the power alone to open his tomb; he needed some one to come and displace the stone. . . . If Jesus wished really to make his divine power to shine he must have shown it to his enemies, to the judge who had condemned him, to the whole world, for since he was dead, and God besides, as you pretend, he had nothing more to fear from anyone and that was not apparently that he should remain concealed that he had been sent. By the some necessity, to place his divinity in the full light, he ought to have disappeared all at once from the cross. . . Dead he only causes himself to he seen in secret by a woman and her companions. His suffering had had innumerable witnesses; his resurrection has only one. It is the reverse of what should have taken place.

"If you had such a strong desire to do something new, how much better would it have been to choose to deify some one of those who died manfully, and who are worthy of a divine fable. If you object to take Hercules or Æsculapius, or any one of the ancient heroes, who already are honoured with worship, you have Orpheus, an inspired man, as no one disputes, and who perished by a violent death. Perhaps you will say that there were no more to take. Be it so; but then you have an Anaxarcus, who, cast one day into a mortar that they might pound hint, cruelly made game of his executioner. Pound pound, the case of Anaxarcus, for as for himself you cannot touch him'--a word full of a divine spirit. Here again will it be said you have been prevented. . . . Ah, well, then will you not take Epictetes? As his master twisted his leg, he, calm and smiling, said, You are breaking it,' and the leg was indeed broken. I told you that you were going to break it.' What has your God said like that in his agonies? And the sibyl, whose authority many of you quote from, why do you not take her? You would have had the best grounds for calling her the daughter of God. You are content to introduce wrongly, and across each other fraudulently, a number of blasphemies into his books, and you give us for a God a personage who has finished by a wretched death an infamous life. Come, you would have been better to choose Jonas, who escaped safe and sound from a great fish; or Daniel, who escaped from the lions; or some other one, concerning whom you have told us things more ridiculous still."

In his judgments upon the Church, such as it was at his time, Celsus shows himself singularly malevolent. Apart from some honest and gentle men the Church appears to him to be a mass of sectaries hurting one another. It is a new race of men, born yesterday, without country, without ancient traditions, leagued against civil and religious institutions, pursued by justice, marked with infamy, and glorying in public execration. Their assemblies are clandestine and unlawful; they bind themselves there by an oath to break the laws and to suffer everything for a barbarous doctrine, which would in any case need to be perfected and purified by Greek reason. A secret and dangerous doctrine! The courage which they put forth to sustain it is praiseworthy; it is good to die rather than abjure or feign to abjure the faith which one has embraced. But yet it is necessary that faith should be founded on reason, and should not have for its only foundation a part taken upon no examination. The Christians besides have not invented martyrdom; every creed has given examples of ardent conviction. They mock at powerless gods who do not know how to revenge their injuries. But has the supreme God of the Christians revenged his crucified Son? Their presumption in deciding questions over which the wisest hesitate is the act of people who only know how to seduce the simple. All that they have of good, Plato and the philosophers have said better before them. The Scriptures are nothing but a translation in a gross style of what the philosophers, and especially Plato, have said in an elegant style.

Celsus is struck by the divisions of Christianity, and by the anathemas which the different churches pronounce upon each other. At Rome, where, according to the most likely opinion, the book was written, all sects flourished. Celsus knew the Marcionites and the Gnostics. He saw, nevertheless, that in the midst of this labyrinth of sects there was the orthodox Church, "the Great Church which had no other name than that of Christian." The Montanist extravagances, the sibylline impostures inspire him naturally only with contempt. Certainly, if he had known better the learned Episcopate of Asia, such men as Melito for example, who dreamed of concordats between Christianity and the empire, his judgment would have been less severe. What hurt him was the extreme social meanness of the Christians, and the small intelligence of the means by which they exercised their propaganda; those whom they wished to gain were base people--slaves, women, and children. Like charlatans, they avoided as much as they could honest people who would not allow themselves to be deceived, taking into their nets the ignorant and the foolish, the ordinary provender of knaves.

"What harm is it then to be well educated, to love fine learning, to be wise, and to pass for such? Is that an obstacle to the knowledge of God? Are they not rather helps to attain to the truth? What are these fair-runners, these jugglers doing? Do they address themselves to men of sense, to tell them their good news? No, but if they see somewhere a group of children, of street porters, or low people, it is there they ply their industry and cause themselves to be admired. It is the same way inside families; here are some wool-carders, some shoemakers, some fullers, some people of the lowest ignorance, and quite destitute of education. Before masters, men of experience and judgment, they dare not open their mouths; but if they surprise the children of the house, or women who have no more reason than themselves, they set themselves to work wonders. Only such can believe; the father and the preceptors are fools who do not know the true good and are incapable of understanding it. Those preachers alone know how they ought to live; the children are found following them, and through them good fortune will come to all the family. If while they are speaking some serious person, one of the preceptors, or the father himself, come in unexpectedly, the more timid keep silence; the bolder are not allowed to excite the children to shake off the yoke, insinuating in a low voice what they would not say before their father or preceptor, so as not to expose themselves to the brutality of those corrupted people who would chastise them. Those who want to know the truth have only to brave the father and preceptors, and go with the women and brats to their part of the house, or to the bootmakers' stall, or the fullers' shop, to understand the absolute! See how they act to gain converts. . . . Whoever is a sinner, whoever is without understanding, whoever is weak in mind, in a word whoever is miserable, let him draw near; the kingdom of God is for him."

One may imagine how such an overturning of the authority of the family in education would he hateful to a man who perhaps exercised the functions of a tutor. The whole Christian idea that God had been sent to save sinners revolts Celsus. He only wants justice. The privilege of the prodigal son is to him incomprehensible.

"What harm is there in being free from sin? Let the unjust, they say, humble himself by the feeling of his misery, and God will receive him. But if the righteous, trusting in his virtue, raises his eyes towards God, what! will he be rejected? Conscientious magistrates do not suffer the accused to melt into lamentations, lest they should be seduced into sacrificing justice to pity. God, in his judgments, is then accessible to flattery? Why has he such a preference for sinners? . . . Did these theories come from the desire of drawing around him a more numerous clientèle? Will it be said that it is proposed by this indulgence to improve the sinners? What an illusion! The nature of people does not change; the bad are not improved either by force or gentleness. Would God not be unjust it he showed himself complaisant to sinners, who know the art of affecting him, and if he abandon the good, who have not the talent for that?"

Celsus would have no bounty extended to false humility, to importunity, to humble prayers. His God is the God of noble and right minds, not the God of pardon, the consoler of the afflicted, the patron of the wretched. He evidently sees a great danger, from the point of view of politics and also from the point of view of his profession as a man of public instruction, that it should be permissible to say that, to be dear to God, it is good to have been guilty, and that the humble, the poor, and the minds without culture have because of this special advantages.

"Listen to their professors. The sages,' they say, repel our teaching, led away and prevented as they are by their wisdom.' What man of judgment, in fact, could allow himself to accept a doctrine so ridiculous? It is sufficient to look at the crowd who embrace it to despise it. Their masters seem like quacks who offer to give healing to a sick person, on condition that the learned doctor shall not be called in, lest they should discover their ignorance. They are obliged to show suspicious knowledge. Leave me to do it,' they say; I will save you, I only; the ordinary doctors kill those whom they boast that they will cure.' They speak like drunken men, who among themselves accuse men of being overcome by wine, or the short-sighted who would persuade those like themselves that those who have good eyes do not see at all."

It is especially as a patriot and friend of the State that Celsus shows himself the enemy of Christianity. The idea of an absolute religion, without distinction of nations, appears to him a chimera. All religion is, in his eyes, national; religion has no raison d'être but as national. He certainly does not love Judaism; he thinks it full of pride and badly-founded pretensions, inferior in everything to Hellenism; but inasmuch as the religion of the Jews is national, Judaism has its rights. The Jews ought to conserve the customs and beliefs of their fathers as other peoples do, although the powers to whom Judea has been entrusted may be inferior to the gods of the Romans who conquered them. One is a Jew by birth; one is a Christian by choice. That is why Rome never seriously thought of abolishing Judaism, even after the fearful wars of Titus and Hadrian. As to Christianity, it is the national religion of no one; it is the religion which men adopt as a protest against the national religion by a collective and corporate spirit.

"They refuse to observe the public ceremonies and to render homage to those who preside; then they renounce also the wearing of the manly robe, marriage, becoming fathers, or filling the functions of life; let them go forth altogether far from here, without leaving the least seed of themselves, and that the earth may be disembarrassed of their breed! But if they would marry, if they would have children, if they would share in the things of life, good as well as evil, it is proper that they should render to those who are charged with administering everything the proper honours. . . . We ought continually, both in word and action, and even when we do not speak or act, to have our souls raised towards God. This being granted, what harm is there in seeking the good of those who have received this power from God, and specially that of the kings r.nd the powerful of the earth? It is, indeed, not without the intervention of a divine energy that they have been raised to the rank they occupy."

In good logic Celsus was wrong. He does not limit himself to demand political confraternity; he would have also religious confraternity. He is not limited to say to them, "Keep your beliefs; serve the same country with us, and we demand nothing contrary to your principles." No, he would have Christians taking part in ceremonies opposed to their ideas. He makes some bad reasonings, to show them that the Polytheistic cult should not horrify them.

"Doubtless," he says, "if a pious man were compelled to commit impious action, or to pronounce some shameful word, it would be right for him to endure all punishments rather than act thus; but it is not the same when we command you to honour the sun or to chant a beautiful hymn in honour of Athene. There are there certain forms of piety, and we cannot have too much piety. You believe in angels: why don't you admit the existence of demons or secondary gods? If the idols are nothing, what harm is there in taking part in the public festivals? If there are demons, servants of the all-powerful God, should not pious men render them homage? You would appear, indeed, so much the more to honour the great God as you would glorify these secondary divinities. By applying itself thus to everything, piety becomes more complete."

To which the Christians had the right to reply: "That concerns our conscience; the State is not to reason with us on that point. Speak to us of civil and military duties, which have no religious character, and we shall fulfil them." In other words, nothing which connects us with the State should be of a religious character. This solution appears very simple to us; but how are we to reproach politicians of the second century with not having put it into practice when in our days we find so many difficulties surrounding it?

More admirable, certainly, is the reasoning of our author as regards the oath in the name of the emperor.

There was there a simple adhesion to the established order, an order which was in itself only the defence of civilisation against barbarism, and without which Christianity would have been swept away like all the rest. But Celsus appears to us to be wanting in generosity, when he mixes up threatening with reasoning. "You do not pretend, doubtless," said he, "that the Romans should abandon, to embrace your beliefs, their religious and civil traditions, that they should leave their gods, and put themselves under the protection of your Most High, who has not known how to defend his own people? The Jews no longer possess a rood of earth, and you, drawn from all parts, vagabonds, reduced to a small number, we should seek to end it with you?"

What is singular in fact is that, after having fought Christianity to the death, Celsus sometimes seems to come near it himself. We can see that at bottom Polytheism is only an embarrassment, and he envies it its one God. The idea that one day Christianity shall be the religion of the empire shone before his eyes, as before those of Melito. But he turns with horror from such a prospect. That would be the worst manner of dying. "A power more enlightened and far-seeing," he said to them, "will destroy you root and branch, rather than perish itself through you." Then his patriotism and his good sense show him the impossibility of such a religious policy. The book, which had commenced by the most bitter refutations, closes with proposals of conciliation. The State runs the greatest risks; it is concerned in saving civilisation; the barbarians are coming over on every side; gladiators and slaves are enrolled. Christianity shall lose as much as established society in the triumph of the barbarians. Concord is therefore easy. "Help the emperor with all your force; share with him in the defence of right; fight for him if circumstances demand it; aid him in the management of his provinces. For that purpose cease to decline the duties of civil life and military service; take your part in the public functions, if it be necessary for the safety of the laws and the cause of piety."

That was easy to say. Celsus forgot that those whom he wished to rally thus were continually menaced with the cruellest torments. He especially forgot that, in maintaining the established cult, he asked the Christians to admit greater absurdities than those he combated among themselves. This appeal to patriotism could not be listened to. Tertullian said, proudly, "To destroy your empire we have only to withdraw; without us there would be nothing but inertia and death." Abstention has always been the revenge of defeated conservatives. They know that they are the salt of the earth; that without them society is impossible. It is then natural that in their moments of annoyance they should simply say, "Pass us by!" To tell the truth, no one in the Roman world, at the time of which we speak, was prepared for liberty. The principle of the State religion was that of nearly all. The plan of the Christians is already to become the religion of the empire. Melito shows Marcus-Aurelius the establishment of the revealed religion to be the best use of his authority.

The book of Celsus was very little read at the time of its appearance. It was only seventy years after that Christianity knew of its existence. It was Ambrose, that Alexandrinian bibliophile and scholar, the teacher of Origen, who discovered the impious book, read it, sent it to his friend, and begged him to reply to it. The effect of the book was then very little felt. In the fourth century, Hierocles and Julian used it, and almost copied it; but it was too late. Celsus had not probably taken away a single disciple of Jesus. He was right from the point of view of good natural sense, but simple good sense, when it finds itself opposed to the wants of mysticism, is very little listened to.

The soil had not been prepared by a good ministry of public instruction. It must be remembered that the emperor was not himself free from all belief in the supernatural; the best minds in the century admitted the medical dreams and the miraculous cures in the temples of the gods. The number of pure rationalists, if considerable in the first century, is very much limited now. Those spirits who, like Cæcilius and Minucius Felix, professed a sort of atheism, held only more forcibly to the established religion. In the second half of the second century, we really only see a single man who, being above all superstition, had a good right to smile at all human follies, and to pity them likewise. That man, that mind, at once the most solid and the most charming of his age, was Lucian.

Here there is more ambiguity. Lucian absolutely rejected the supernatural. Celsus admits all religions; Lucian denies them all. Celsus thinks he is conscientiously bound to study Christianity up to its sources; Lucian, who anticipates what it will lead to, takes up a very superficial notion of it. His ideal is Demonax, who, quite unlike Celsus, made no sacrifices, nor initiated himself into any mystery, had no other religion than gaiety and universal benevolence.

This entire difference in the point of departure made Lucian to be less at a distance from the Christians than Celsus. He who had the best right of any one to be severe as to the supernatural shows himself, on the contrary, at times indulgent enough to them. Like the Christians, Lucian is a demolisher of Paganism, a subject resigned, but not loving, to Rome. Never was there any disquieted patriotism with him, or a single one of those anxieties for the State which devoured his friend Celsus. his laugh is like that of Peres, his diasyrnios made a chorus to that of Hermias. lie spoke of the immorality of the gods, of the contradiction of the philosophers, almost like Tatian. His ideal city singularly resembled a church. The Christians and he were allied in the same war, war against local superstitions, goëtes, oracles, and thaumaturges.

The chimerical and Utopian side of the Christians could not but displease him. It seemed, indeed, that he had thought often of them in tracing, in the Fugitives, that picture of a society of Bohemianism, impudent, ignorant, and insolent, raising a real tribute under the name of alms, austere in words, in reality debauchés, seducers of women, enemies of the Muses, people of pale face and shaven heads, parties in shameful orgies. The picture is less gloomy, but the allusion is perhaps more contemptuous, in Peregrinus. Certainly Lucian did not see, like Celsus, a danger for the State in those base sectaries, whom he shows us living as brethren and animated by the most ardent charity for each other. It is not he who shall ask who persecutes them. There are enough of fools in the world! Those are not by any means the most wicked.

Lucian certainly formed a strange idea of "the crucified sophist who introduced those new mysteries and succeeded in persuading his disciples not to adore him." He pities such credulity. How should those unfortunates, who have taken it into their heads that they are immortal, be exposed to all aberrations? The cynic who vaporises himself at Olympia, the Christian martyr who seeks for death to be with Christ, appear to him fools of the same order. In view of these pompous deaths sought for willingly, his reflection is that of Arrius Antoninus: "If you so much desire to be roasted, do it among yourselves at your ease and without this theatrical ostentation." This care to gather together the remains of the martyr, to raise them to the altars, this claim to obtain from them miracles of healing, to erect its pyre in a sanctuary of prophecy--common enough follies these to all sectaries. Lucian is of opinion that one might laugh at this if knavery were not mixed up with it. He did not regard the victims with favour, because they provoked the executioners.

It was the first appearance of this form of human genius, of which Voltaire has been the perfect incarnation, and which, in many points of view, is the truth. Man being incapable of resolving seriously any metaphysical problems which he had imprudently raised, what would the sage do in the middle of the war of religions and systems? To abstain, to smile, to preach tolerance, humanity, benevolence without pretension, that is to render a simple service to poor humanity. The radical remedy is that of Epicurus, who destroyed at a blow religion, and its object and the evil it brings with it. Lucian appears to us like a wise man wandered in a world of fools. He hates nothing, he laughs at everything, serious virtue excepted.

But at the time when we stop this history men of this kind become rare; they may be counted. The very intellectual Apulerius of Madaurus is, or at least affects to be, very much opposed to these strong minds. He had been invested with the priesthood. He detested the Christians as impious. He repelled the accusation of magic, not as chimerical, but as a fact not proved; all is complete for him, the gods and the demons. The true thinker was in some sort an isolated being, badly seen, and obliged to dissimulate. We produce with horror the history of a certain Euphronius, an obdurate Epicurean, who fell sick, and whose parents brought him into a temple of Æsculapius. There a divine oracle signified to him this recipe: "Burn the books of Epicurus, knead the ashes of them with soft wax, rub the belly with this liniment, and wrap the whole round with bandages." We read also of the history of a cock of Tanagre which, wounded on the leg, was sent among them who sung a hymn to Æsculapius, and accompanied them with its song, while showing to the god its wounded leg. A revelation being made to bring about its cure, "they saw the cock beating its wings, lengthening its stride, raising its neck and shaking its comb, to proclaim that Providence which considers creatures wanting in reason."

The overthrow of good sense was accomplished. The delicate railleries of Lucian, the just criticisms of Celsus, fell only as powerless protests. In one generation man in entering life shall have no other choice than that of superstition, and soon even that choice he shall have no longer.

CHAPTER XXII

NEW APOLOGIES--ATHENAGORAS, THEOPHILUS OF ANTIOCH, MINUCIUS FELIX

Never was the struggle more ardent than in those last years of Marcus-Aurelius. Persecution was at its highest period. The attacks and replies crossed each other. The parties borrowed one after the other the weapons of dialectic and irony. Christianity had its Lucian in a certain Hermias, who calls himself "philosopher," and who seems to set himself to the task of adding to all the exaggerations of Tatian on the mistakes of philosophy. His writing, probably composed in Syria, is not only an apology: it is a sermon addressed to the assembled believers. The author has published it under the title of Diasyrmos, or "Tales of the Philosophers outside." The pleasantry was heavy and weak enough. It recalls the attempts which have been produced in our age, in the bosom of Catholicism, to employing the irony of Voltaire to the profit of the good cause, and to make the apology for religion in the style of a Tertullian in good humour. The sarcasms of Hermias do not only strike at the exaggerated claims of philosophy; they reach to the most legitimate attempts of science, the desire to know the things which are now perfectly discovered and known. According to the author, science has for its origin the apostasy of the angels. These are the unhappy perverse beings who have taught men philosophy, with all its contradictions. The knowledge of the old schools which the author possesses is wide, but not very profound; as to the philosophical spirit, never was a man so completely without it.

The clemency of the emperor, his known love of truth, called forth, year after year, new petitions, where the generous advocates of the persecuted religion tried to show what was monstrous in those persecutions. Commodus, associated with the empire from the end of the year 176, had his part in these entreaties, to which--strange thing!--he later on gave better heed than his father. "To the emperors, Marcus-Aurelius Antoninus and Marcus?Aurelius Commodus of Armenia, Sarmatia (and whatever was their greatest title) philosophers." . . . Thus began an apology, written in a very good antique style by Athenagoras, an Athenian philosopher, who appears to have been converted to Christianity by his own efforts. The exceptional position allowed to Christians, under a reign full of mildness and happiness, and which had given peace and liberty to the whole world, was scandalous. All the cities enjoyed a perfect self-government. All people were permitted to live according to their laws and their religion. The Christians, although very loyal towards the empire, were the only men who were persecuted for their creed. And even if the authorities had contented themselves by taking away their property and life! But what was still more insupportable was the official calumnies with which they were loaded--atheism, the eating of human flesh, and incest.

If the Christians were guilty of atheism, philosophers were guilty of the same crime. The Christians admitted that supreme intelligence, invisible, impassable, incomprehensible, which is the "last word" of philosophy. Why make that a reproach to them which was praised in others? What the Christians said of the Son and the Spirit complements philosophy--does not contradict it. The Son of God is the Word of God, the eternal reason of the Eternal Spirit. The Christians rejected the sacrifices, the idols and the fables of Paganism. Who can blame them? The gods were often only men deified. The miracles of healing in the temples are the work of demons.

Athenagoras has no difficulty in demonstrating that the crimes with which Christians are reproached have no verisimilitude about them. He affirms the perfect purity of their morals, notwithstanding the objections directed against the kiss of peace.

"According to the difference in age, we treat some as sons and daughters, others as brothers and sisters, others again as fathers and mothers; but these titles of relationship bring with them no stain. The Word tells as in fact: If anyone shall repeat the kiss to procure the enjoyment of pleasure . . .' and it adds, There must be great scrupulousness concerning the kiss, and with stronger reason in that which concerns the proscyneme, since, if it were obtained by the slightest impure thought, it would deprive us of eternal life.' The hope of eternal life makes us contemn the present life, even as far as the pleasures of the mind. Each of us uses his own spouse according to certain rules we have laid down, and in the manner necessary for the procreation of children; even as the workman, after he had entrusted his grain to the soil, waits for the harvest without sowing above it. You will find among us many persons of both sexes who have grown old in celibacy, hoping thus to live nearer God. . . . Our doctrine is that each one ought to remain as he is born or be content with a single marriage. Second marriages are only adultery decorously disguised. . . .

"If we were to ask our accusers if they have seen what they say, there would be none impudent enough to assert it. We have slaves, some of us more, some less; we do not think of concealing them, and nevertheless not one among them has made any of these lying statements against us. We cannot endure the sight of a man who has been put to death, even justly. Who can look with cheerfulness upon the spectacles of the gladiators and the beasts, especially when it is you who give them? Ah well, we have renounced these spectacles, believing that there is hardly any difference between looking on at a murder and committing it. We hold as a murderess the woman who procures abortion, and we believe that is to kill a child only to expose it. . . .

"What we ask is the common justice, it is not to be punished for the name we bear. When a philosopher commits a crime they judge him for that crime, and they do not make his philosophy responsible. If we are guilty of the crimes of which they accuse us, spare neither age or sex, exterminate along with us our wives and children. If these are inventions without any other foundation than the natural enmity of vice to virtue, it is for you to examine our life, our doctrine, our devoted submission to you, to your house, to the empire, and to do us the same justice that you do to our adversaries."

Extreme deference, almost obsequiousness, towards the empire is the character of Athenagoras as of all the apologists. He flatters in particular the ideas of heredity, and assures Marcus-Aurelius that the prayers of the Christians will have the effect of assuring the succession of his son.

"Now that I have replied to all these accusations, and that I have shown our piety towards God as well as the purity of our minds, I ask nothing more from you than a sign from your royal head. Oh! Princes whom nature and education have made so excellent, so moderate, so humane. Who is more worthy of being favourably listened to by the sovereign whose government we pray for, that the succession may be established between you and your son according to what is most just, and that your empire, receiving without ceasing new accretions, should reach over the whole earth? And in praying thus we pray for ourselves, since the tranquillity of the empire is the condition through which we may in the bosom of a gentle and tranquil life apply ourselves entirely to the observance of those precepts which have been imposed upon us.

The dogma of the resurrection of the dead was that which caused the greatest difficulty to minds which had received a Greek education. Athenagoras devoted to this a special conference, seeking to reply to the objections drawn from the case where the body loses its identity. The immortality of the soul is not sufficient. Some commandments, such as those which concern adultery and fornication, do not regard the soul, since the soul is not capable of such misdeeds. The body has its part in virtue, it ought to have its part in the recompense. Man is not complete without being made up of body and soul, and all that is said of the end of man is applied to the complete man. Notwithstanding all these reasonings the Pagans obstinately said, "Show us one who has risen from the dead, and when we have seen him we will believe," and they were not wrong.

Theophilus, Bishop of Antioch, about the year 170, was, like Athenagoras, a convert from Hellenism, who, when he was converted, did not believe that he did anything but change one philosophy for another which was better. He was a very fertile teacher, a catechist endowed with a great talent for exposition, a clever polemic according to the ideas of the age. He wrote against the dualism of Marcion and against Hermogenes, who denied creation and asserted the eternity of matter. He commented upon the Gospels, and he wrote, they say, a concord or harmony. His principal work which has been preserved to us was a treatise in three books, addressed to a certain Autolycus, probably a fictitious personage under whose name Theophilus represents the instructed Pagan held in error by the prejudices spread against Christianity. According to Theophilus, one is a Christian by the heart, it is the passions and the vices which keep one from seeing God. God is immaterial and without form, but his works reveal him. The gods of the Pagans are men whom they cause to be adored, and the worst of men.

Theophilus speaks already of the Trinity, but his trinity had not the appearance of that of Nice, it is composed of three persons, God, the Word, and Wisdom. His trust in the reading of the prophets, as a means for the conversion of the heathen, may appear exaggerated. His scholarship is abundant, but his criticism is totally defective, and the exegesis which he gives of the first chapters of Genesis is very weak. What shall we say of the assurance with which he quotes to Pagans as a decisive authority the Judæo-Christian Sibyl whose authenticity he fully admits?

To sum up, Theophilus approaches much nearer the narrow and malignant spirit of Tatian than the liberal spirit of Justin and Athenagoras. Sometimes he admits that the philosophers and the Greek poets have anticipated revelation, notably in what concerns the final conflagration of the world, but most frequently he finds them stained by enormous errors. The Greeks have plundered Genesis by altering it. The Greek wisdom is but a pale, modern, and very feeble plagiarism from Moses. Even as the sea would dry up if it were not ceaselessly fed by the rivers, so would the world perish by the wickedness of man if the law and the prophets had not established truth and justice. The Catholic Church is like an island prepared by God in the midst of a sea of errors. But let them not be deceived; there are heresies, islands of reefs without water, without fruit, full of fierce beasts. Beware of the pirates who would attack and destroy you there. Theophilus is never so triumphant as when he reduces to nothing the absurd calumnies with which they pursued his co-religionists. Otherwise he is feeble, and Autolycus is not wrong after such arguments to persist in his incredulity. The pearl of this apologetic literature of Marcus Aurelius is the dialogue composed by the African, Minucius Felix. It is the first Christian work written in Latin, and one feels already that the Christian Latin literature, theologically inferior, will become greater than the Greek Christian literature, because of the shades and manliness of its style. The author, originally from Cirta, remained at Rome, and exercised there the profession of an advocate. Born a Pagan, he had received a most liberal education, and had embraced Christianity upon reflection. He knew his classics perfectly, imitated them, and occasionally copied them. Cicero, Seneca, and Sallust were his favourite authors. Among his contemporaries no one wrote in Latin better than he. The book of his compatriot Fronton struck him: he wished to reply to the attack. He did so, taking, it would seem, his style from the illustrious rhetorician, and making more than one borrowing. Perhaps he had also read Celsus' work, and refers to it more than once without naming it.

A learned Pagan, belonging to the leading family of Cirta, Cæcilius Natalis, and two Christians, Octavius and Minucius, went down to the seashore, near Ostium, during the autumn recess. Cæcilius, perceiving a statue of Serapis, put his hand to his mouth, according to custom. A discussion ensued. Cæcilius commences by a long discourse, which one may consider as a nearly textual reproduction of Fronton's argument. It is a perfect representation of the objections a Roman such as he would have to Christianity. The tone is that of a conservative, who does not much disguise his haughty incredulity, and defends his religion without believing in it. Sceptical on the foundation of things, disdainful of all speculation, Cæcilius holds to the established religion only through decency and habit, and because the dogmatism of Christians displeased him. The schools of philosophy have only produced disputes; the human mind knows not how to bridge the space which separates it from God. The wiser give it up. What shall we say of the presumption of certain people, drawn from the basest classes, without education or science, strangers to all literature, pretending to decide questions as to which, for centuries back, philosophy has deliberated? Is it not much wiser, leaving these, the higher questions, in our humility, to follow the worship established by our ancestors? The old ages, thanks to their ignorance and simplicity, had certain privileges, particularly that of seeing the gods near them and having them for kings. In such a matter antiquity is everything; the truth--that is what has been believed for a long time past. Rome has deserved to reign over the world by accepting the rites of the entire globe. How can one think of changing a religion so useful? This old cult has seen the beginnings of Rome, has defended it against the barbarians, has braved at the Capitol the assault of the Gauls. Would you have it that Rome should renounce this to please some factious people who abuse the credulity of women and children?

Thanks to rare skilfulness in language, Cæcilius shows that all is fabulous and yet true in what concerns divination, the cults, the miraculous cures, and the dreams. His position is that of Celsus. At bottom he is an Epicurean; he believes little in Providence or supernatural interventions; but his attachment to the religion of the State renders him crafty.

"Man and the animals are born, live and grow by a sort of spontaneous concretion of elements which divide, dissolve, dissipate. Everything comes back on itself, returns to its source, without any being playing in that the position of fabricator, judge or creator. Thus the reunion of the fiery elements makes suns shine unceasingly, and then other suns still. Thus the vapours which are extracted from the earth are gathered together in masses, rise to the clouds and fall in rains. The winds whistle, the hail rattles, the thunder rolls in the breaking of the clouds, the lightnings shine, the thunderbolts gleam; all this athwart and across; the lightning smites the mountains, strikes the trees, touches without distinction sacred and profane spots, slays guilty men, and often religious men. What shall we say of those blind and capricious forces, which hurry away everything without order and without trial; in shipwrecks, the fate of good and evil confounded, merits made ex æquo; in fires, the innocent surprised by death as well as the guilty; when the sky is infected with pestilential virus, death without distinction to all; in the midst of the fury of battle, the bravest falling; in time of peace, wickedness not only equal to virtue, but privileged so much so that many ask whether it is better to detest their wickedness or to ask the good fortune of these for themselves? If the world were governed by a higher Providence, and by the authority of some divinity, would Phalaris and Dionysius have deserved the crown, Rutilius and Carmilla exile, or Socrates poison? Look at the trees covered with fruits, a harvest, and an exuberant vintage; the rain spoils everything, the hail breaks everything; so true is it the truth is concealed and forbidden to us, or rather that chance without law reigns alone across the infinite unreachable variety of cases."

The picture which Cæcilius, interpreter of the prejudices of high Roman society, made of the Christian morals was most gloomy. They had reason for hiding themselves--these sectaries; it is that they dare not show themselves. Their secret and nocturnal assemblies are only conventicles for infamous pleasures. Disdaining all that is honourable, the priesthood, the purple, public honours, incapable of saying a word in honourable assemblies, they take refuge in corners to dogmatise. These people in rags, and half naked! O height of audacity! despising present torments through belief in torments future and uncertain. Through fear of dying after their death, they do not fear to die now.

"They know each other by marks or secret signs; they almost love each other before being known. Then debauch becomes their religion, the bond which binds them together. They are called without distinction brothers and sisters, so that by the use of this sacred name that which would only be adultery or fornication becomes incest. It is so that this vain and foolish superstition boasts of its crimes. If there had not been in these stories a foundation of truth, it is impossible that public report, always wise, should have spread so many monstrous tales about them. I have heard it said that they worship the head of the most ignoble beast, rendered sacred in their eyes by the most baseless arguments; a worthy religion in truth, and made expressly for such morals! Others tell. . . . If there are falsehoods there I don't know; there are at least the suspicions which secret and nocturnal rites naturally provoke. And after all, when we attribute to them the worship of a man punished by the last penalty for his misdeeds, as well as the presence in their ceremonies of the inauspicious wood of the cross, they only put upon their altars what befits them: they worship what they deserve.

"The picture of the initiation of the neophytes is also known to be abominable. A child, covered with paste and flour to deceive those who are not in the secret, is placed before him who is about to be initiated. He is invited to strike him; the floury crust makes him believe in everything most innocently; the child dies under his secret blind blows; and then--oh, horror!--they greedily lick his blood, they tear in pieces his limbs; henceforth their federation is sealed by a victim--the mutual knowledge they have of their crime is the pledge of their silence. No one knows anything of their feast; they speak of it on all sides, and the discourse of our compatriot of Cirta has made it believed. On solemn days some people of every age, men and women, meet together at a banquet with the children, sisters, and mothers. After a plentiful repast, when the guests are heated, and drunkenness has excited in them the fire of incest, there passes what follows:--A dog is attached to the candelabra; they draw it; they make it leap from the place where it is attached by throwing to it a little cake. The candelabra is overturned; then, disembarrassed of all disagreeable light, in the bosom of the darkness, complaisant to all immodesties, they are confused by the chance or lot in copulation, with an infamous lubricity, all incestuous, if not in actual fact, at least by complicity, since the vow of all pursues that which may result from the act of each.

"I pass on; for already these are enough of allegations, all or nearly all proved by the sole fact of the darkness of that perverse religion. Why, indeed, should they be obliged to conceal the object of their religion, such as it is, when it is proved that good loves publicity, and that crime alone seeks secrecy? Why have they not altars, temples, and known images? Why should they never speak in public? Why this horror for free assemblies, if what they adore with so much mystery was not either punishable or shameful? Who is this unique God, solitary in sorrow, who does not know a free nation or a kingdom, nor even the lowest degree of Roman superstition? Alone, the miserable Jewish nationality honours this one God, but at least it honours him openly with its temples, altars, victims, ceremonies: a poor effete God, dethroned, since he is now captive with his nation to the Roman gods. . . . The larger part of you suffer, you confess, from misery, cold, fatigue, hunger, and your God permits it--takes no notice of it! Either he does not wish to, or he cannot, succour his own; he is either powerless or unjust.

"Threatenings, punishments, torments, that is your lot; the cross--it is not a question of adoring it but of mounting it; the fire which you predict and which you fear you actually submit to. Where is, then, this God who can save his servants when they live again, and can do nothing for them when they are living now? Is it by the grace of your God that the Romans rule, command, and are your masters?--and you during this time always in suspicion and disquieted. You abstain from all honest pleasures, you desert the fêtes, public banquets, sacred festivals. As if you dreaded the gods whom you deny, you hold in horror the meats from which a part has been cut for sacrifice, the drinks part of which have been poured out. You do not surround your heads with flowers, you refuse perfume for your bodies, reserving them for funerals. Yell deny even crowns to the tombs; pale, trembling, worthy of pity. . . . Thus unhappy you shall not rise again, and meanwhile you do not live. If, then, you have any wisdom, any feeling of ridicule, cease to lose yourselves in those heavenly spaces, and to seek anxiously the destinies and the secrets of the earth. It is enough to look at one's feet, especially for ignorant and unpolished people, without education and without culture, to whom it is not given to comprehend human things, and who with greater reason cannot have the right to speak upon divine things."

The merit of the author of this curious dialogue lies in having diminished in no way the forces of the reasons of his adversaries. Celsus and Fronton have not expressed with more energy what was contrary to the simplest ideas of natural science in those perpetual announcements of the conflagration of the world by which the simple are frightened. The Christian ideas on the doctrine of the Resurrection are not criticised with less vigour. Whence comes that horror of the pyre and the cremation of corpses, as if the earth would not do in a few years what the pyre does in some hours? What does it matter if the corpse is broken by the beasts, or buried in the sea, or covered by the soil, or absorbed by the flame?

Octavius replies weakly to these objections, inherent in some sort to his dogma, and which Christianity shall carry with it during the whole course of its existence. God, said the advocate of Christianity, has created the world; he can destroy it. If he has made man out of nothing, he can surely raise him from the dead. The doctrine of the conflagration is taught in the philosophical systems. If the Jews have been conquered it is their own fault. God has not abandoned them; it is they who have abandoned God.

Octavius shows himself more subtle still when he pretends that the sign of the cross is the basis of all religion, and especially of the Roman religion; that the Roman standard is a gilded cross; that the trophy represents a man on a cross; that the vessel with its yards, the yoke of a chariot, the attitude of a man in prayer, are figures of the cross. His explanation of auguries and oracles by the action of perverse spirits is also a little childish. But he eloquently refutes the aristocratic prejudices of Cæcilius. The truth is the same for all; all can find it and ought to seek it. God is manifest in the mind; Providence follows with a glance of the eye cast upon the order of the world and man's conscience. This truth is even revealed, although obliterated in the Pagan traditions. At the foundation of all religions and all poetry is found the idea of an all-powerful Being, father of the gods and of men, who sees all, and is the universal cause. Octavius proves his thesis by some passages borrowed from Cicero. Monotheism is the natural religion of man, since he, in his erudition, says simply: "O God!" The providence of God is the "last word" of Greek philosophy, and especially of Plato, whose doctrine would be divine if it were not injured by too much complaisance for the principle of State religion. This principle Octavius attacks with extreme vivacity. The reasons drawn from the grandeur of Rome affect him little; this grandeur is nothing in his eyes but a tissue of violence, perfidies, and cruelties.

Octavius excels in showing that the Christians are innocent of the crimes of which they are accused. They have put them to the torture; not one has confessed, and yet the confession would have saved them. The Christians are neither statues, nor temples, nor altars. They are right. The true temple of the Divinity is the heart of man. What sufferings are equivalent to a good conscience, an innocent heart? To practise righteousness is to pray; to cultivate virtue is to sacrifice; to save one's brother is the best of offerings. Among Christians, the most pious is the most righteous. Octavius triumphs especially in the courage of the martyrs.

"What a fine spectacle for God, when the Christian fights with sorrow; when he gathers himself up against all menaces, punishments and torments; when he laughs at the horrible noise of death and the terror of the executioner; when he maintains his liberty before kings and princes; bends only before God, to whom he belongs; when, as triumphant and conquering, he braves him who pronounces on him his sentence of death! To conquer, in fact, is to know how to attain one's end! . . . The Christian may, therefore, appear unhappy; he never is so. You raise to heaven such men as Mucius Scævola, whose death was certain if he had not sacrificed his right hand. And how many of us have suffered without a complaint not only that their right hand, but that their whole body should be burned, when it was in their power to have saved them! . . . Our children, our wives play themselves with the crosses, the torments, the beasts, all the utensils of punishment--thanks to a patience which is inspired in them from on high."

How the magistrates who preside at these horrors tremble. God does not allow honours and riches but to cause them to be lost; raised the higher, their fall shall be the heavier. There are some victims fattened and already crowned for death. Escorts, fasces, purple, nobility of blood, what vanities! All men are equal, virtue alone makes the difference between them.

Conquered by these arguments, Cæcilius, without allowing Minucius time to conclude, declares that he believes in Providence and the religion of the Christians. Octavius, in his explanation, scarcely leaves pure Deism. He mentions neither Jesus, nor the Apostles, nor the Scriptures. His Christianity is not that of which the Shepherd dreams; it is a Christianity of men of the world who do not shun gaiety, or talent, or an amiable taste for life, nor a search for elegance in style. How far are we from the Ebionite or even the Jew of Galilee! Octavius is Cicero, or better, Fronton become Christian. It is really by intellectual culture that he arrives at Deism. He loves nature, he is pleased by the conversation of well-educated people. Men made upon this model would not have created either the Gospel or the Apocalypse, but, on the other hand, without such adherents, the Gospel, the Apocalypse, the Epistles of Paul, would have remained the secret writings of a narrow sect which, like the Essenes or the Therapeutics, would have finally disappeared.

Minucius Felix gives even more than the Greek Apologists the tone which prevails among the defenders of Christianity in all ages. He is a skilful advocate addressing himself to people less versed in dialectics than the Greeks of Egypt or Asia, concealing three-fourths of his dogma to secure the adhesion to the whole without discussion of detail, using the appearances of the lettered to convert the lettered, and to persuade them that Christianity does not compel them to renounce the philosophies and the writers whom they admire. "Philosophers, Christians . . . . but what? it is only one and the same thing. Dogmas repugnant to reason! . . . . come, then! but the Christian dogma is in its own terms what Zeno, Aristotle, Plato said, and nothing more. You treat us as barbarians; but we cultivate the good authors as well as you do." Of special beliefs in religion as it is preached, not a word; to inculcate Christianity they avoid pronouncing the name of Christ. Minucius Felix is the preacher of Notre Dame, speaking to people of the world easy to please, making himself all things to all men, studying the weaknesses and the fancies of the people he wishes to conquer, affecting under his cope of lead the behaviour of the easy man, straining his symbol to render it acceptable. Make a Christian upon the faith of this pious sophist, nothing could be better, but remember that all this was a bait. The next day he who was represented as accessory shall become the principal; the bitter bark which they have wished to make you swallow in small compass and reduced to its simplest expression shall recover all its bitterness. They had told you that the gallant man, to be a Christian, has scarcely any need to change his maxims; now that the trick is played, they tell you to pay as superaddition an enormous sum. This religion, which was, they say, only natural morals, implies over the market price an impossible physique, a bizarre metaphysic, a chimerical history, a theory of divine and human things which is in everything contrary to reason.

CHAPTER XXIII

PROGRESS OF ORGANISATION

In the midst of circumstances so difficult in appearance, the organisation of the Church was completed with a surprising rapidity. At the point at which we have arrived, the Church of Jesus is something solid and substantial. The great danger of Gnosticism, which was to divide Christianity into sects without number, is exorcised. The word Catholic Church flashes from all quarters like the name of that great body, which will henceforth pass through the ages without breaking to pieces. And we can see well already what is the character of this Catholicity. The Montanists are looked upon as sectaries, the Marcionists are conquered by straining the Apostolic teaching, the different Gnostic schools are being more and more repelled from the bosom of the general Church. There is then something which is neither Montanism nor Marcionism, nor Gnosticism, which is unsectarian Christianity; the Christianity of the majority of the bishops resisting heresies and using them all, not having, if it be desired, anything except negative characters, but preserved by those negative characters from pietistic aberrations and from the rationalistic solvent. Christianity, like all who wished to live, puts itself under discipline and retrenches its own excess. It joins to mystic enthusiasm a fund of good sense and moderation which shall kill Millenarianism, the charismas, the speaking with tongues and all spiritual primitive phenomena. A handful of enthusiasts, like the Montanists, rushing to martyrdom, discouraging penitence, condemning marriage, is not the Church. The just mean triumphs; it shall not be given to radicals of any sort to destroy the work of Jesus. The Church is always of average opinion, she is the affair of all the world, not the privilege of an aristocracy. The pietistic aristocracy of the Phrygian sects and the speculative aristocracy of the Gnostics are equally dismissed with their claims. There are in the Church the perfect and the imperfect, all can have part in it. Martyrdom, fasting, and celibacy are excellent things, but one can without heroism be a Christian and a good Christian.

It was the Episcopate without any intervention of the civil power, without any support from police or tribunals, which established order above liberty in a society founded at first upon individual inspiration. That is why the Ebonites of Syria, who had no Episcopacy, had not the idea of Catholicity either. At the first glance the work of Jesus was not born viable; it was a chaos. Founded upon a belief in the end of the world, which the years rolling by ought to convince of error, the Galilean assembly appeared only to be capable of breaking up into anarchy. Free prophecy, the charismas, the speaking with tongues and individual inspiration; this was more than was necessary for all to be confined within the proportions of an ephemeral chapel, as one sees so much of in America and England. Individual inspiration created, but destroyed at once what it had created. After liberty, rule was necessary. The work of Jesus might be considered saved on the day in which it was admitted that the Church had a direct power--a power of presenting that of Jesus. The Church from that moment dominated the individual, and chased him if need were from his own. Soon the Church, a body unstable and changing, was personified in the Elders; the powers of the Church became the powers of a clergy, the dispensatory of all the graces, the intermediary between God and the believer. Inspiration passes from the individual to the community. The Church has become everything in Christianity; one step more and the bishop becomes everything in the Church. Obedience to the Church, then to the bishop, is set forth as the first of duties, innovation is the mask of the false, schism shall henceforth be for the Christian the worst of crimes.

Thus the Primitive Church had at the same time order and excessive liberty. The pedantry of scholasticism was as yet unknown. The Catholic Church quickly accepted the fertile ideas which took birth among the heretics, keeping back what they contain of sectarianism. The spontaneity of theology surpassed everything which has been seen later. Without speaking of the Gnostics who pushed fancy to the utmost limits, St. Justin, the author of the Confessions, Pseudo-Hermas, Marcion, and those innumerable masters appeared from all parts, cutting out the full dress, if one may express it so; each one made a Christology according to his own fancy. But in the midst of the enormous variety of opinions which filled the first Christian age, there was constituted a fixed point, the opinion of Catholicism. To convince the heretic it is not necessary to reason with him. It is sufficient to show him that he is not in communion with the Catholic Church, with the great churches which can reckon the succession of their bishops up to the apostles. Quod semper, quod ubique became the absolute rule of truth. The argument of prescription, to which Tertullian shall give such an eloquent form, sums up all the Catholic controversy. To prove to any one that he is an innovator, one lately come into theology, is to prove that he is in the wrong. An insufficient rule, since by a singular irony of fate the very doctor who developed this method of refutation in a style so imperious died a heretic!

The correspondence between the churches became soon a habit. The circular letters from the chiefs of the great churches, read on Sunday to the assembly of the faithful, were a continuation of the apostolic literature. The Church, like the synagogue and the mosque, is a thing essentially city-like. Christianity (we might almost say as much of Judaism and Islamism) shall be a religion of towns, not a religion of rustics. The countryman, the paganus, shall be the last resistance which Christianity shall encounter. The Christian rustics, not very numerous, went to church at the nearest town.

The Roman town thus became the cradle of the Church, as the country districts and the little towns received the Gospel from the great towns. They received also their clergy from them, always subject to the bishop of th e large town. Among the towns the civitas alone had a real church, with an Episcopos; the little town was in ecclesiastical dependence upon the large town. This primacy of the great towns was a principal fact. The great town once converted, the little town and the country followed the movement. The diocese was thus the original unity of the Christian conglomerate.

As to the ecclesiastical province, implying the precedence of the great churches over the small, it corresponds in general to the Roman province. The founder of the limits of Christianity was Augustus, the divisions of the worship of Rome and of Augustus were the secret law which ruled everything. The towns, which had a flamen or archiereus, were those which later on were an arch-bishopric; the flamen civitatis became the bishopric. At the beginning of the third century the flamen duumvir occupies in the city the rank which a hundred or a hundred and fifty years after was that of the bishop in the diocese. Julian tried later on to oppose these flamens to the Christian bishops and the curés to the augustates.

It is thus that the ecclesiastical geography of a country is very nearly the same in almost everything as the geography of the same country at the Roman epoch. The picture of the bishoprics and archbishoprics is that of the ancient civitates according to their bonds of subordination. The empire was like the mould where the new religion coagulated. The interior framework, the hierarchical divisions, were those of the empire. The ancient positions in the Roman administration, and the registers of the Church in the middle ages and even in our days, scarcely differ.

Rome was the point where this great idea of Catholicism elaborated itself. Its Church had an undisputed primacy. It owed that partly to its holiness and its excellent reputation. Everybody recognised now that this Church had been founded by the apostles Peter and Paul; that these two apostles had suffered martyrdom at Rome, that John even had there been plunged into boiling oil. They showed the places sanctified by these apostolic acts, partly true and partly false. All this surrounded the Church of Rome with an unequalled halo. Doubtful questions were brought to Rome to receive arbitration, if not solution. They led this argument, that, since Christ had made of Cephas the corner-stone of his Church, this privilege should be extended to his successors. The bishop of Rome became the bishop of bishops, he who admonished the others. Pope Victor (189-199) pushed this claim to an excess which the wise Irenaeus restrained. But the blow was struck, Rome had proclaimed her right (dangerous right!) to excommunicate those who did not move in everything with her. The poor Artemonites (a sort of anticipative Arians) had complained much of the injustice of the lot which made heretics of them, while up to Victor's time all the Church of Rome thought with him. The Church of Rome put itself from that time above history. The spirit which, in 1870, shall proclaim the infallibility of the Pope may be recognised already from the end of the second century by certain signs. The work, of which the fragment known under the name of Canon de Muratori, written at Rome about 180, shows us already Rome ruling the Canon of the churches, giving for a basis to Catholicism the Passion of Peter, repelling alike Montanism and Gnosticism. The attempts at symbols of the faith also commenced, in the Roman Church, about this time. Irenæus refuted all the heresies by the faith of this Church, "the greatest, the most ancient, the most illustrious; which possesses, by a continued succession, the true tradition of the apostles Peter and Paul; to which, by reason of its primacy, the rest of the Church should defer." Every Church reputed to have been founded by an apostle had a privilege; what should be said of the Church which was believed to have been founded by the two greatest apostles at once?

This precedence of the Church of Rome did nothing but increase to the third century. The bishops of Rome showed a rare ability, avoiding theological questions, but always in the first rank in the questions of organisation and administration. Pope Cornelius conducted everything in the matter of Novatianism: we can see this especially in removing the bishops of Italy and giving them successors. Rome was thus the central authority of the churches of Africa. Aurelian, in 272, judges that the real bishop of Antioch is he who is in correspondence with the bishop of Rome. When is this superiority of the Church of Rome to suffer an eclipse? When Rome ceases to be really the unique capital of the empire, at the end of the third century: when the centre of great affairs is transported to Nicæa, to Nicomedia, and especially when the Emperor Constantine creates a new Rome on the Bosphorus. The Church of Rome, from Constantine to Charlemagne, had really fallen from what it was in the second and third century. It rose more powerful than ever when, by its alliance with the Carlovingian house, it became for eight centuries the centre of all the great affairs of the West.

We may say that the organisation of the churches has known five degrees of advancement, of which four have been traversed in the period embraced by this work. First, the primitive ecclesia, where all the members are equally inspired by the Spirit. Then the elders presbyteri taking in the ecclesia a right of considerable power and absorbing the ecclesia. Then the president of the elders, the episcopos, absorbs in a little nearly all the powers of the elders, and consequently those of the ecclesia. Then the episcopi of the different churches, corresponding to them, form the Catholic Church. Between the episcopi there was one, that of Rome, which was evidently destined to a great future. The Pope, the Church of Jesus transformed in monarchy with Rome for its capital, may be perceived in a distant obscurity; but the principle of this last transformation is still weak to the end of the second century. Let us add that this transformation has not had, like others, the universal character. The Latin Church alone is favoured by it, and even, in the bosom of this Church, the tentative of the papacy ended by bringing in revolt and protestation.

Thus the grand organisms which still form such an essential part of the moral and political life of the European peoples have all been created by these artless and sincere men, whose faith has become inseparable from the moral culture of humanity.

At the end of the second century the episcopate is thoroughly ripe, the papacy exists in germ. The oecumenical councils were impossible; the Christian could alone permit of those great assemblies: but the provincial synod was used in the Montanist and Easter affairs: the presidence of the bishop of the provincial capital was admitted without contest. An active epistolary correspondence was, in the apostolic age, the soul and condition of the whole movement. In the case of Novatianism, about 252, the different provincial assemblies, communicating with each other, constitute a true council by correspondence, having the Pope Cornelius as president. In the process against Privatus, bishop of Lambesa, and in the question of the baptism of heretics, things passed in the same way.

A writing which shows well the rapid progress of this internal movement of the churches towards the constitution, let us rather say towards the exaggeration of the hierarchical authority, is the supposed correspondence of Ignatius, of which the reasonable letter of Polycarp is perhaps an appendix. One can suppose that these writings appear about the time at which we have arrived. Who better than these two great bishop martyrs, whose memory was everywhere revered, could counsel the faithful to submit to order?

"Obey the bishop as Jesus Christ obeys the Father, and the presbyterial body like the apostles; revere the deacons like the very commandment of God. Let nothing which concerns the Church be done without the bishop. As to the act of the Eucharist, that ought to be held as good which is administered by the bishop or by him to whom he has entrusted the duty.

"Then where the bishop is visible, let the people be; even as where Christ Jesus is, there is the Catholic Church. It is not permitted to baptize nor to make the agape without the bishop; the episcopal approbation is the mark of what pleases God, the firm and sure rule to follow in practice.

"It is seemly therefore that you should support the bishop, as also you do. For your venerable presbyterial body, worthy of God, is with the bishop in the same harmonious sympathy as the chords to the harp. It is by the effect of your union and your affectionate concord that Jesus Christ is praised. Let each one of you be then as in a chorus, so that, in full accord and unanimous, receiving the chromatique from God in perfect unity, you sing with one voice through Jesus Christ to the Father, so that he hears you and recognises you, by your good actions, as members of his Son."

Already the name of Paul and his relations with Titus and Timothy had been used to give to the Church a kind of little canonical code upon the duties of the faithful and the clergy. They did the same under the name of Ignatius. A piety quite ecclesiastical took the place of the ardour which, during more than a hundred years, kept up the memory of Jesus. Orthodoxy is now the sovereign good; docility is what saves; the old man must bow before the bishop as well as the young. The bishop ought to occupy himself with everything, and know the names of all his subordinates. Thus, by force of pushing to their extreme the principles of Paul, they arrived at some ideas which would have revolted Paul. He who would not that he should be saved by his works, would he have admitted that he could be saved by simple submission to his superiors On other points, pseudo-Ignatius is a very genuine disciple of the great apostle. At an equal distance from Judaism and Gnosticism, he is one of those who speaks in the most exalted manner of the divinity of Jesus Christ. Christianism is for him, as for the author of the Epistle Diognetes, a religion entirely separate from Mosaism. All the primitive distinctions have, besides, disappeared before the dominant tendency which drew the most opposed parties towards unity. Pseudo-Ignatius gives the hand to the Judeo-Christian pseudo-Clement, to preach obedience and respect for authority.

A very striking example of this abdication of differences which had filled the Church of Christ for more than a hundred years was that given by Hegesippus. Having left Ebionism, but fully received by the orthodox Church, this respectable old man completed at Rome his five books of "Memoirs," the first basis of ecclesiastical history. The work commenced with the death of Jesus Christ. It is doubtful, however, whether it is written in chronological order. In many points of view, it was a polemical book against heresies, and the apocryphal revelations written by the Gnostics and Marcionites. Hegesippus showed that many of these apocryphas were composed quite recently.

The memoirs of Hegesippus would have been priceless to us, and their loss is not less regrettable than those of the writings of Papias. It was the whole treasury of the Ebionite traditions, rendered acceptable to the Catholics, and presented in a spirit of lively opposition to the Gnosis. What concerns the Jewish sects and the family of Jesus was much developed, evidently according to some special information. Hegesippus, whose mother-tongue was Hebrew, and who did not receive a Hellenic education, had the credulity of a Talmudist. He is repelled by no bizarrerie. His style appeared to the Greeks simple and dull, doubtless because he had borrowed from the Hebrew, like him of the Acts of the Apostles. We have had a curious specimen of it in this story of the death of James, a piece of such a singular tone that one is tempted to believe that it has been borrowed from an Ebionite work written in rhymed Hebrew.

No one was less like a sectary than the pious Hegesippus. The idea of Catholicism held a place in his mind such as with the author of the pseudo-Ignatian epistles. His object is to prove to the heretics the truth of the Christian doctrine, by showing them that it has been taught uniformly in all the churches, and that it had always been taught in the same manner since the apostles. Heresy, starting from that of Thebuthis (?), arises from pride or ambition. The Roman Church, in particular, has replaced for authority the old Jewish discipline, and created in the West a centre of unity like that which constituted at the very first in the East the episcopate of the parents of Jesus, issued like him from the race of David.

We see that the old Ebion was much sweetened. After Hegesippus we do not see this variety of Christianity, unless it be in the heart of Syria. There Julius Africanus, about 215, found still some primitive Nazarenes, and received from them traditions very analogous to those among which Hegesippus lived. The latter underwent some progress, or rather some narrowing of orthodoxy. They read him little and they copied him less. Origen and St. Hippolytus did not know of his existence. Only the curious in history, like Eusebius, would know him, and from these precious pages those have been saved which the more modern chonographers have inserted in their pages.

Another sign of maturity is the epistle addressed to a certain Diognetus, a fictitious personage, no doubt, by an eloquent and fairly good anonymous writer, who recalls sometimes Celsus and Lucian. The author supposes his Diognetus to be animated by a desire to know "the new religion." The Christians, replied the apologists, are at an equal distance both from Greek idolatry and from superstition, a disquieted spirit, and from the vanity of the Jews. All the work of the Greek philosophy is but a mass of absurdities and charlatan tricks. The Jews, on the other side, had the habit of honouring the one God in the same manner as the polytheists adored their gods; that is to say, by sacrifices, as if that could be agreeable to him. Their over-scrupulous precautions as to food, their superstition as to the Sabbath, their boasting in regard to circumcision, their paltry preoccupation as to fasts and new moons, were ridiculous. It is not permitted that one should distinguish between the things which God has created, to consider the one pure, and to reject the others as useless and superfluous. To pretend that God forbids to do on the Sabbath day an action which has nothing dishonourable, what could be more impious? To present the mutilation of the flesh as a sign of election, and to imagine that, for that, God would love him, what could be more grotesque?

"As to the mystery of the Christian religion, no one may hope to understand it. The Christians indeed are not distinguished from other men either by country, by tongue, or by manners; they do not dwell in towns of their own, nor do they use a separate dialect; their life is not marked by any particular asceticism; they do not lightly adopt the fancies and dreams of disturbed minds; they do not attach themselves, as so many others, to sects bearing this or that name; but dwelling in the Greek and barbarian towns, just as fortune places them, conform themselves to the local customs in the habits, government, and other things of life, astonishing everybody by the truly admirable organisation of their republic. They dwell in some special countries, but in the manner of people who are only on a visit; they share in the duties of the citizens, and they support the charges of strangers. Every foreign land is to them a native country, and every country is to them a foreign land. They marry, as all others do, and have children; but they never abandon their new-born babes. They eat in common, but their table is not common for all that. They are in the flesh, yet do not live according to the flesh. They remain on the earth, but are citizens of heaven. They obey the established laws, and by their principles of life they are raised above the laws. They love everybody, and they are persecuted by everybody, misunderstood, and condemned. They meet death, and through that are assured of life. They are poor and they enrich others; they want everything and yet abound. They are crushed down with insults, and by the insults they arrive at glory. They are calumniated and the moment after they proclaim their justice; injured, they bless; they reply to insult by respect; doing nothing but good, they are punished as malefactors; punished, they rejoice as if they had been gratified with life. The Jews make war on them as on the Gentiles; they are persecuted by the Greeks, and those who hate them cannot say why.

"In short, that which the soul is in the body the Christians are in the world. The soul is diffused among all the members of the body, and the Christians are diffused among all the towns in the world. The soul lives in the body, and yet it is not of the body; in the same way the Christians dwell in the world without being of the world. The invisible soul is held prisoner in the visible body; besides, the presence of the Christians in the world is of public notoriety: but their worship is invisible. The flesh hates the soul and fights with it, without doing it any other harm than to keep it from enjoyment. The world also hates the Christians, although the Christians do no harm except make opposition to pleasure. The soul loves the flesh which hates it; in the same way the Christians love those who detest them. The soul is imprisoned in the body, and yet it is the bond which preserves the body. In like manner the Christians are held in the prison of the world, and yet they are those who maintain the world. The immortal soul dwells in a mortal body; thus the Christians are provisionally domiciled in corruptible habitations, waiting for the incorruptibility of heaven. The soul is softened by the sufferings of hunger and thirst; the Christians, punished every day, multiply more and more. God has assigned to them a post which he will not permit them to desert."

The spiritual apologist puts his own finger on the explanation of the phenomenon which he would represent as supernatural. Christianity and the empire are looked on as two animals which would devour each other without giving an account of the causes of their hostility. When a society of men takes up such an attitude in the bosom of a great society, when it becomes in the State a separate republic, supposing it were composed of angels, it is a pest. It is not without reason that they were detested, these men in appearance so gentle and well-doing. They really demolished the Roman empire; they absorbed its energy; they laid hold of its functions, in the army especially, as its choicest subjects. It does not serve to say that the Christian was a good citizen because he paid his contributions, and that he was generous in alms, and steady, when he is really a citizen of heaven, and when he considers the terrestrial fatherland only as a prison in which he is chained side by side with wretches. The fatherland is an earthly thing; he who would become an angel is always a poor patriot. Religious enthusiasm is bad for the State. The martyr may maintain that he does not rebel, that he is the most submissive of subjects; the fact of anticipating penalties, of putting the State to the alternative of persecuting him or subjecting the law to the theocracy, is more prejudicial to the State than the worst of revolts. It is never without reason that he is the object of every one's hatred; nations have, in that matter, an instinct which never deceives. The Roman empire felt, at bottom, that this secret republic was killing it. Let us hasten to add that, by persecuting it violently, it permitted itself to act on the worst policy, and that it accelerated the result while wishing to prevent it.

CHAPTER XXIV

SCHOOLS OF ALEXANDRIA AND EDESSA

Many things were ended; others had begun; the school and books replaced tradition. No one had any longer a claim to have seen either the apostles or their immediate disciples. Reasonings such as that set forth by Papias forty years back, that disdain for books, and that avowed preference for the people who had known the original, would pass no longer. Hegesippus shall be the last who shall make journeys to study on the spot the doctrine of the churches. Irenæus found these researches useless. The Church is a vast depot of truth from which one has but to draw. If we except the barbarians who did not know how to write, no one had any more need to consult oral tradition.

They set themselves therefore resolutely to write; the doctor, the ecclesiastical scribe, replaced the traditionist; the time for the creation of beginnings has gone by; ecclesiastical history commences; we say ecclesiastical, and not clerical. The doctor, in fact, at the time at which we have arrived, is very often a layman. Justin, Tatian, Athenagoras, and the majority of the apologists are neither bishops nor deacons. The doctors of the school of Alexandria have a distinct place outside of the clerical hierarchy; the institution of the catechumenate served to the development of that institution. Some postulants, often educated people, prepared outside of the Church for acceptance by baptism, demanded a separate instruction more accurate than that of the faithful. Origen is the catechist and preacher, with the permission of the bishop of Cæsarea, without having any defined rank among the clergy. St. Jerome shall hold a situation analogous to this, which, even in his time, is full of difficulties. It was natural indeed that, little by little, the Church should absorb the ecclesiastical teaching, and that the doctor should become a member of the clergy subordinated to the bishop.

We have seen that Alexandria, through the disputes on Gnosticism, and perhaps in imitation of the Muséon, had a catechetical school of sacred letters, distinct from the Church, and some doctors to comment upon the scriptures sensibly. This school, a species of Christian university, was prepared to become the centre of the movement of all theology. A young Cecilian convert named Pantænus was the chief of it, and carried into the sacred instruction a breadth of ideas which no Christian chair had as yet known. Everything pleased him--philosophers, heresies, and the strangest religions. Out of them all he made his honey, Gnostic in the best sense, but removed from the chimeras which Gnosticism nearly always implied. From this moment there were grouped around him some youths at once lettered and Christian, especially the young convert Clement, about twenty years of age, and Alexander, the future bishop of Jerusalem, who played, in the first half of the third century, a rôle so considerable. The vocation of Pantænus was especially oral teaching; his voice had a peculiar charm; he left among his disciples more celebrated than himself a profound feeling. Not less favourable than Justin to philosophy, he conceived of Christianity as the worship of all that is beautiful. Of happy genius, brilliant, luminous, kindly to all, he was in his age the most liberal and open spirit the Church had possessed till then; and he marked the dawn of an extraordinary intellectual movement, perhaps superior to all the attempts of rationalism which have ever been produced in the heart of Christianity. Origen, at the date at which we stand, is not born yet, but his father, Leonidas, nourished in his heart that ardent idealism which made a martyr of him and the first master of that son whose bosom he shall kiss during his sleep as the temple of the Holy Spirit.

The Pagan East did not always inspire in Christians the same antipathy as Greece. The Egyptian Polytheism, for example, was treated by them with less severity than the Hellenic Polytheism. The Sibylline poet of the second century announces at Isis and Serapis the end of their reign with more sadness than insult. His imagination is struck by the conversion of an Egyptian priest who in his turn shall convert his compatriots. He speaks in enigmatical terms of a great temple raised to the true God, who shall make out of Egypt a sort of holy land which shall not be destroyed till the end of time.

The East, on its side, always given to syncretism, and by advance in sympathy with all that which bears the character of disinterested speculation, rendered to Christianity this large tolerance. If we should compare to the strict patriotism of a Celsus, a Fronton, the open mind of a thinker such as Numenius of Apamea, what a difference! Without being exactly Christian or Jew, Numenius admires Moses and Philo. He equalled Philo to Plato; he called the latter an ancient Moses; he knew even the apocryphal compositions on Jamnes and Mambre. To the study of Plato and Pythagoras, philosophy ought, according to him, to unite the knowledge of Brahman, Jewish, magical, and Egyptian institutions. The result of the inquiry, we may say in advance, will be that all these people are in accord with Plato. As Philo allegorises the Old Testament, Numenius explains symbolically certain facts in the life of Jesus Christ. He admits that the Greek philosophy is originally from the East, and owes the true notion of God to the Egyptians and the Hebrews; he proclaims this philosophy insufficient, even in its most venerated masters. Justin and the author of the Epistle to Diognetes said scarcely anything more. Numenius, however, does not belong to the Church; the sympathy and admiration for a doctrine did not in an eclectic carry him to a formal adhesion to this doctrine. Numenius is one of the precursors of Neo-platonism; it is by him that the influence of Philo and a certain knowledge of Christianity penetrated into the school of Alexandria. Ammonius Saccas, at the time when we finish this history, perhaps frequents the Church from which philosophy shall not delay to make him depart. Clement, Ammonius, Origen, Plotin! What a century is to open for the city which nourishes all these great men, and becomes more and more the intellectual capital of the East!

Syria numbered many of these independent spirits who showed themselves favourable to Christianity, without on that account embracing it. Such was that Mara, son of Serapion, who looked on Jesus as an excellent legislator, and admitted that the destruction of the nationality of the Jews had arisen from their having put to death "their wise king." Such was also Longinus, or the author, whoever he may be, of the treatise, On the Sublime, who read with admiration the first pages of Genesis, and places the expression, "Let light be and light was" among the most beautiful words he knows.

The most original among the mobile and sincere minds which the Christian law charmed, but not in a style exclusive enough to make them detach themselves from everything else and make of them simple members of the Church, was Bardesanes of Edessa. He was, if one may so express it, a man of the world, rich, amiable, liberal, educated, well placed at court, versed at once in Chaldean science and Hellenic culture, a sort of Numenius, acquainted with all the philosophies, all religions, and all the sects. He was sincerely Christian; he was even an ardent preacher of Christianity, almost a missionary; but all the Christian schools he went through lacked something to his mind; no one took possession of him. Marcion alone, with his austere asceticism, displeased him thoroughly. Valentinianism, on the contrary, in its Oriental form, was the teaching to which he always returned. He delighted in the syzgies of æons and denied the resurrection of the body. He preferred to this material conception the views of Greek spiritualism on pre-existence and the survival of the soul. The soul, according to him, is neither born nor dies; the body is only a passing instrument. Jesus had not a true body; he was united to a phantom. It seems that towards the end of his life Bardesanes came nearer the Catholics; but, definitively, orthodoxy repelled him. After having fascinated his own generation by his brilliant preaching, by his ardent idealism, and by his personal charm, he was covered with anathemas; they classed him among the Gnostics, he who never wished to be classed at all.

One only of Bardesanes' treatises found favour among orthodox readers; it was a dialogue in which he combated the worst errors of the East, the Chaldean error, astrological fatalism. The form of the Socratic conversations pleased Bardesanes. He liked to pose before the public surrounded by his friends, and discussing with them the highest problems of philosophy. One of his disciples named Philip drew out or was thought to have drawn out the conservation. In the dialogue on fatality, the principal interlocutor of Bardesanes is a certain Aoueid tainted by the errors of astrology. The author opposes to these a truly scientific reasoning: "If man is dominated by means and circumstances, how is it that the same should produce human developments quite different from each other? If man is dominated by race, how can a nation changing its religion, for example, making itself Christian, become quite different from what it was?" The interesting details which the author gives on the manners of unknown countries piqued curiosity. The last editor of the romance of the Confessions, then Eusebius, then St. Cesaire, made capital out of it. It is singular that, being in possession of such a writing, we should still ask what Bardesanes thought upon the question of the influence of the stars on the acts of men, and in the events of history. The dialogue expresses itself on this point with all the clearness which one could desire. Yet St. Ephrem, Diodorus and Antiochus combat Bardesanes as if he had accepted the errors of his masters of Chaldea. Sometimes his school would appear as a profane school of astronomy as much as of theology. It pretended to fix by certain calculations the duration of the world at six thousand years. It admitted the existence of sidereal spirits residing in the seven planets, especially in the sun and moon, whose monthly union preserves the world by giving it new forces.

What Bardesanes was without contradiction was the creator of Christian Syriac literature. Syriac was his tongue; although he knew Greek he did not write in that idiom. The work necessary to render the Aramean idiom flexible for the expression of philosophical ideas belongs entirely to him. His works, moreover, were translated into Greek by his pupils under his own eyes. Allied to the royal family of Edessa, having been, as it appears, educated as the companion of Abgar VIII. bar Manou, who was a fervent Christian, he contributed powerfully to the extirpation of Pagan customs, and had a most important social and literary position. Poetry had always been awanting in Syria; the old Aramean idioms had only known the old Semitic parallelism. Bardesanes composed, in imitation of Valentin, a hundred and fifty hymns, of which the cadenced rhythm, partly imitated from Greek, fascinated everybody, especially young people. It was at once philosophical, poetical, Christian. The strophe was composed of eleven or twelve verses of five syllables, scanned according to the accent. They sang the hymns in chorus, to the accompaniment of the cithara, to Greek airs. The civilising influence of this beautiful music was considerable. Nearly all Osrhoene became Christian. Unfortunately Abgar IX., son of Abgar VIII., was dethroned in 216 by Caracalla; this phenomenon of a little principality founded on the principles of a liberal Christianity, disappeared; Christianity continued to make some progress in Syria, but in the orthodox direction, and by giving up every day more of the speculative liberties which were at first allowed it.

The connections of Bardesanes with the Roman empire are obscure. According to certain appearances the persecutions of the last years of Marcus-Aurelius gave him the idea of presenting an apology to that emperor. Perhaps it was in connection with Caracalla or Heliogabalus, whom it is very easy to confound in the texts with Marcus-Aurelius. It seems that he composed a dialogue between himself and a certain Apollonius, a special friend of the emperor, in which this latter asks that he should deny the Christian name. Bardesanes replied courageously like Demetrius the Cynic: "Obedience to the orders of the emperor does not relieve me from the necessity of dying."

Bardesanes left a son, named Harmonius, whom he had sent to study at Athens, and who continued the school, making it lean still more to the side of Hellenism. In imitation of his father he expressed the most elevated ideas of Greek philosophy in Syriac hymns. There resulted from all this a discipline too marked in respect to the medium which Christianity allowed. It was necessary to be a member of such a Church, to have intellect and instruction. The worthy Syrians were frightened. The fate of Bardesanes much resembled that of Paul of Samosata. They treated him as a dangerous charmer, a woman seducer, irresistible in private. His hymns, like the Thalia of Arius, were treated as a magical work. Later, St. Ephrem found no other means to dethrone these hymns, and to keep children from their charm, than to compose orthodox hymns to the same airs. From that time, whenever there was produced in the Church of Syria any remarkable person having independence of mind and a great knowledge of the Scriptures, they said with terror, "This will be a Bardesanes."

His talent and the services he rendered were, however, not forgotten. His birthday was marked in the Chronicle of Edessa among the great anniversaries of the city. His school lasted during all the third century, but produced no very celebrated man. Later on, the germ of dualism which was in the teaching of the master approached the Manichæan school. The Byzantine chroniclers and their disciples the Arabic polygraphists constituted a sort of trinity of evil, composed of Marcion, Ibn-Daïsan and Manes. The name "Daïsanites" became synonymous with atheist, zendik; those Daïsanites were reckoned as Mussulmans among the secret sects affiliated to Parseeism, the cursed trunk of all heresies.

CHAPTER XXV

STATISTICS AND GEOGRAPHICAL EXTENSION OF CHRISTIANITY

In a hundred and fifty years the prophecy of Jesus was accomplished. The grain of mustard seed had become a tree which began to cover the world. In the hyperbolic language which is customary in such a matter, Christianity had spread "everywhere." St. Justin had affirmed already, about 150, that there was not a corner of the earth, even among the most barbarous peoples, where people did not pray in the name of the crucified Jesus. St. Irenæus expresses himself in the same manner: "They push and spread like the evil herd; their places of meeting multiply on all sides," say the ill-disposed. Tertullian, on the other hand, writes twenty years after: "We are of yesterday, and already we fill your whole framework, your cities, your strong places, your councils, your camps, your tribes, your decuries, the palace, the senate, the forum; we have only left out your temples. Without betaking ourselves to arms, in which we have little experience, we could combat you by separating from you; you would be afraid of your solitude, of a silence which would appear like the stupor of a dead world."

Up to the time of Hadrian the knowledge of Christianity is the act of those who are in the secrets of the police, and a small number of the curious. Now a new religion rejoices in the greatest publicity. In the Oriental part of the empire no one was ignorant of its existence; the lettered class spoke about it, discussed it, borrowed from it. Far from being enclosed in the Jewish circle, the new religion gathers from the Pagan world the greatest number of her converts, and, at least at Rome, surpasses in number the Jewish Church, from which it has come. It is neither Judaism nor Paganism; it is a third definitive religion, destined to replace all that precedes it.

The figures are in such a matter impossible to fix, and certainly they differ much according to the provinces. Asia Minor continued to be the province where the Christian population was more dense. It was also the hearth of piety. Montanism appeared in the leaven of the universal ardour which burns in the spiritual body of the Church. Indeed, while they fought they were animated by what appeared to them a sacred flame. In Hierapolis and in many towns of Phrygia the Christians must have formed the majority of the population. Since the reign of Septimus Severus, Apamea of Phrygia put upon its coins a Biblical emblem, Noah's Ark, with an allusion to his name of Kibotos. In the West, we have seen, in the midst of the third century, some towns destroying their ancient temples, converted en masse. All the neighbouring region of the Propontides shared in the movement. Greece, properly speaking, on the contrary, was slow to leave the old religion, which she did not abandon till the middle ages, and then almost with her heart against the change.

In Syria, about 240, Origen found that, in connection with the assemblage of the people, the Christians are "not very numerous;" what they say of Protestants and Israelites in Paris. When Tertullian says to us, "Fiunt non nascuntur, Christiani," he indicates to us that the earlier Christian generation had counted few souls. The Church of Rome, in 251, possessed forty-six priests, seven deacons, seven sub-deacons, forty-two acolytes, fifty-two exorcists, readers, and porters; it had more than fifteen hundred widows or poor, and, it was supposed, about thirty or forty thousand believers. At Carthage, about the year 212, the Christians formed the bulk of the population. All the Greek portion of the empire possessed flourishing Christian bodies; there was not a town of any importance which had not its church and its bishop. In Italy, there were sixty bishops; even little towns almost unknown had them. Dalmatia was evangelised. Lyons and Vienne had Christian colonies composed of Asians and Syrians, using Greek, but exercising their apostleship among the neighbouring peoples who spoke Latin or Gallic. The Gallo-Roman and Hispano-Roman world, nevertheless, was really scarcely broached. A very superstitious local Polytheism presented in these vast continents a mass most difficult to pierce.

Britain had no doubt already seen the missionaries of Jesus. Her claims on that point are founded much less upon fables, of which the Isle of Saints, like all the great Christian communities, surrounded the cradle of its faith, than upon a leading fact, viz.: the observance of Easter according to the quarto-deciman rite, that is to say, the old style of Asia Minor. It is possible that the first churches of Britain owed their origin to some Phrygians, some Asians, like those who founded the churches of Lyons and Vienne. Origen says that the virtue of the name of Jesus Christ had passed the seas to seek the Britons in another world.

The condition of the believers was in general very humble. With some exceptions, all open to doubt, we do not see any great Roman family passing over to Christianity with its slaves and clients, before Commodus. A man of the world, a knight, or functionary, ran against impossibilities in the Church. The rich were out of their element there. Life in common with people who had neither their fortune nor social rank was full of difficulties, and the relations of society were found almost forbidden to them. Marriage above all presented enormous difficulties; because many Christians espoused Pagans rather than give themselves to a poor husband. Thus when we find in the Christian cemeteries, from the time of Marcus-Aurelius and the Severuses, the names of the Cornelii, Pompeii; Cæcilii, it is hazardous to conclude that there had been believers among these great names by right of blood. The clients and the slaves were the origin of these ambitious agnomina. The intellectual standard was likewise very low at first. That high culture of reason which Greece had inaugurated was generally wanting in the first two generations. With Justin, Minucius Felix, the author of the epistle to Diognetes, the average was raised; soon, with Clement of Alexandria and Origen, it rose still higher; at the beginning of the third century, Christendom shall possess men on a level with the enlightened of the century.

Greek was still essentially the Christian tongue. The most ancient catacombs are all Greek. In the middle of the third century, the sepulchres of the popes have Greek epitaphs. Pope Cornelius wrote to the churches in Greek. The Roman liturgy was in the Hellenic tongue; even when Latin had prevailed, it was often written in Greek characters; some Greek words, pronounced in the fashion of the iota, frequently occurring, which was that the Eastern people, remained as marks of its origin. One country alone had a Church speaking Latin, that was Africa. We have seen Minucius Felix open the Latin Christian literature by a chef d'oeuvre. Tertullian, twenty years later, after having hesitated between the Greek and Latin tongues for the composition of his writings, shall fortunately prefer the second and present the strangest literary phenomenon; an unheard of mixture of talent, flexibility of mind, eloquence and bad taste; a great writer, if we admit that to sacrifice all grammar and correctness to effect is to write well. At last Africa shall give to the world a fundamental book--the Latin Bible. One at least of the first Latin translations of the Old and New Testaments was made in Africa; the Latin text of the mass, some leading portions of the Liturgy, appear also to be of African origin. The lingua vulgata of Africa contributed thus to the formation of the ecclesiastical language of the West, and thus exercised a decided influence over our modern tongues. But there resulted from that another consequence; it was that the fundamental texts of the Latin Christian literature were written in a language which the lettered of Italy found barbaric and corrupt, which later on gave occasion on the part of the rhetoricians for endless objections and epigrams.

From Carthage, Christianity shone powerfully into Numidia and Mauritania. Cirta produced both adversaries and defenders of the most ardent kind for the faith of Jesus. A town concealed in the depths of the province of Africa, Scillium, fifty leagues from Carthage, furnished some months after the death of Marcus-Aurelius a group of twelve martyrs, led by a certain Speratus, who showed an unbreakable firmness, struggled with the pro-consul, and gloriously opened the series of African martyrs.

Edessa became day by day a Christian centre of high importance. Placed in the vassalage of the Parthians, Osrhoene had submitted to the Romans since the campaign of Lucius Verus (165); but it kept its dynasty of Abgars and Manous till about the middle of the third century. This dynasty, which was related to the Jewish Izates of Adiabene, showed itself extremely favourable to Christianity. In 202, at Edessa, a church was destroyed by an inundation. Osrhoene possessed numerous Christian communities at the end of the second century. A certain Palut, bishop of Edessa, ordained by Serapion of Antioch (190-210), remains celebrated by his contests with the heretics. At last Abgar VIII. bar Manou (176-213) definitely embraced Christianity in the time of Bardesanes, and, in sympathy with that great man, made rude war upon the Pagan customs, especially the practice of emasculation, a vice deeply rooted in the usages of the Syrian cults. Those who continued to honour Targatha in that strange manner had their hand cut off. Bardesanes, against the theory of climates, remarks that the Christians spread in Parthia, Media, Hatra, and into the most remote countries, not conforming themselves in any way to the laws of these countries. The first example of a Christian kingdom, with a Christian dynasty, was given at Edessa. This state of things, which caused much displeasure, especially among the great, was overturned in 216 by Caracalla; but the Christian faith scarcely suffered. From that time were probably composed those apocryphal works intended to prove the holiness of the town of Edessa, and especially that pretended letter from Jesus Christ to Abgar, of which Edessa later on grew so proud.

Thus was founded, alongside the Latin literature of the churches of Africa, a new branch of Christian literature --the Syriac literature. Two causes created it, the genius of Bardesanes and the need of possessing an Aramean version of the sacred books. The Aramean writing had been for a long time used in these countries, but had not yet been used to establish a true literary work. Some Judeo-Christians laid the foundation of an Aramean literature by translating the Old Testament into Syriac. Then came the translation of the writings of the New; then were composed apocryphal stories. This Syrian Church, destined later on to a vast development, appeared to have included at that time the greatest varieties, from the Judeo-Christian up to the philosophy such as Bardesanes and Harmonius.

The progress of the Church outside of the Roman empire was much less rapid. The important

Church of Bosra had probably some suffragan churches among the independent Arabs. Palmyra no doubt already reckoned some Christians. The numerous Aramean populations subject to the Parthians embraced Christianity with the earnestness which the Syrian race showed always for the worship of Jesus. Armenia received, about the same time, the first germs of Christianity, to which it is possible that Bardesanes was not a stranger. Martyrs in Persian Armenia are spoken of from the third century.

Some fabulous traditions, greedily received at the beginning of the fourth century, attributed to Christianity certain very remote conquests. Each apostle was reputed to have chosen his part of the world to convert. India especially, by the geographical indecision of the name it bears and the analogy of Buddhism with Christianity, made some singular illusions. It was claimed that St. Bartholomew had brought Christianity there, and had left a copy of the Gospel of St. Matthew in Hebrew. The celebrated Alexandrian doctor Pantænas had returned there upon the steps of the apostle, and found this Gospel. All this is doubtful. The use of the word India was extremely vague; whoever had embarked at Clysina and made the voyage of the Red Sea was reported to have been in India. Yemen was often described by that name. In any case there certainly resulted from these travels of Pantæas no durable church. All that the Manicheans have written concerning the missions of St. Thomas in India is fabulous, and it is artificially that they have connected later on with this legend the Syrian Christian communities which were established in the Middle Ages on the coast of Malabar. Probably there was mixed up with this tissue of fables some confusion between Thomas and Gotama. The question of the influence which Christianity could exercise upon Brahmanic India, and specially upon the cult of Krichna, is beyond the limits at which we should stop.

CHAPTER XXVI

THE INTERIOR MARTYRDOM OF MARCUS-AURELIUS --HIS PREPARATION FOR DEATH

While all these strange moral revolutions were being accomplished the excellent Marcus-Aurelius, casting upon everything a loving and calm regard, bore always his pale visage, his gentle resigned face, and his sickness of heart. He spoke no longer, except in a low voice, and he walked with short steps. His strength sensibly diminished; his sight failed. One day he was obliged to lay down the book he held in his hand. "I am not allowed to read thee any more," he wrote, "but it is always permitted thee to repulse violence from thy heart, it is always permitted thee to scorn pleasure and pain, it is always permitted thee to be superior to vainglory, it is always permitted thee to declaim against fools and ingrates; better still it is permitted thee to do them good." Enduring life without pleasure, as without revulsion, resigned to the lot which nature had reserved for him, he did his duty every day, having without ceasing in his mind the thought of death. His wisdom was complete, that is to say, that his weariness was boundless. War, court, the theatre, all alike exhausted him, and yet he did all the good he could, for he did it as his duty. At the point at which he had arrived the love and the hatred of men are one and the same thing. Glory is the last of illusions; yet how vain is it! The memory of the greatest man disappears so quickly! The most brilliant courts are those of Hadrian, those great parades in the style of Alexander; what are they if this is not a decoration which passes away, and which is thrown aside as refuse? The actors change, the emptiness of the play is the same.

When some enthusiastic Christians came to realise that they could not any longer hope to see the kingdom of God realising itself, except by fleeing to the desert, the Ammoniouts, the Nils, and the Pacômes shall proclaim the renunciation and disgust of things as the supreme law of life. These masters of the Thebaïde shall not equal in complete separation their crowned brother. He has made some ascetic operations, some receipts like those of the fathers for spiritual life, so as to convince himself by irresistible deductions of universal vanity.

"To scorn the song, the dance, the pancratium, it is sufficient to separate them into their elements. As to music, for example, if you divide any one of the harmonies into sounds, and you ask, concerning each sound, is it there that the charm lies, there would be no longer a charm. In the same way as to dancing; divide the movement into attitudes. In the same way look at the pancratium; in a word, in regard to everything that is not virtue, reduce the object to what composes it by a complete analysis, and by this division you will come to despise it. Apply this process to the whole of life."

His prayers had a humility and resignation quite Christian.

"Wilt thou, therefore, be one day, my soul, good, simple, perfectly one, naked, more transparent than the material body which enwraps? When wilt thou stay the joy fully of loving all things, when wilt thou be satisfied, independent, without any longing, without the least necessity for a living or inanimate being for thy joys? When wilt thou have no longer need nor time to prolong thy pleasures, nor of space or place, or serenity of gentle climates, or even of the society of men? When wilt thou be happy with thy actual condition, content with the present good, persuaded that thou hast all which thou oughtest to have, that everything is good which concerns thee, that everything comes from the gods, that in the future everything shall be equally good--I mean all that they will decide for the preservation of the living being, perfect, good, just, beautiful, who has produced everything, includes everything, contains and comprehends all individual things, which only dissolve themselves to form new like the first? When shalt thou be such, O my soul, that thou shalt be able to live in the city of gods and men in such a way as never to address a complaint to them and never again to need their pardon?"

This resignation became day by day more necessary. For the will which had been thought for a moment to be mastered by the government of the philosophers raised its head in all directions. At bottom the progress wrought by the reigns of Antonine and Marcus-Aurelius had only been superficial. Everything was bordered by a varnish of hypocrisy, by exterior appearances which were taken as caused by the unison of the two wise emperors. The mass of the people was gross, the army had grown weak, the laws only had been improved. What reigned throughout all was a deep gloom. Marcus-Aurelius had in one sense succeeded too well. The ancient world had taken the monk's cowl like those descendants of the noblesse of Versailles who become to-day Trappists or Carthusians. Unhappy end of those old aristocracies which after the excesses of a youthful folly become all at once virtuous, humane, and steady! There is here a symptom that they are about to die. The saintliness of the emperor had obtained in what concerned public opinion a result greater than what could have been looked for, it had made him in some sort sacred in the eyes of the people. There is here a fact honourable to human nature, and which history should no longer omit like so many other melancholy facts. Marcus-Aurelius was exceedingly beloved; popularity, so subject to misunderstand the deserts of men, for once at least has been just. The best of sovereigns has been the best appreciated. But the wickedness of the age took its revenge in other directions. Three or four times the goodness of Marcus-Aurelius injured him.

The great inconvenience of real life, and what renders it unbearable to the higher man, is that, if we bring into it ideal principles, qualities become defects, so much so that very often the accomplished man succeeds less in it than he who has. motives of egotism or vulgar routine. The conscious honesty of the emperor made him commit a prime fault in being persuaded to associate in the government Lucius Verus, towards whom he was under no obligation. Verus was a frivolous and worthless man. It needed miracles of goodness, and delicacy would have been required, to prevent him from making disastrous blunders. The wise emperor, serious and earnest, took about with him in his litter the foolish colleague he had given himself. He always determinedly took him to be serious, he did not once rebel against this tiresome companionship. Like people who have been well brought up, Marcus-Aurelius was annoyed continually; his own manners had always dignity and grace. Minds of this kind, whether it be not to give pain to others, or out of respect to human nature, are resigned not to confess that they observe evil. Their life is a perpetual dissimulation. Faustina was in the life of the pious emperor another source of sadness; providence, which guards the education of great minds and works without ceasing to perfect them, prepared in her for him the most painful trials, a woman who did not understand. She began, it would seem, by loving him; probably she even found at first some happiness in that villa at Lorium, when in that beautiful retreat of Lanuvium, under the highest slopes of the Albanian mountains, which Marcus-Aurelius described to Fronton as a residence full of the purest joys. Then she grew weary of too much wisdom. Let us tell all; the fine sentences of Marcus-Aurelius, his austere virtue, his perpetual melancholy, his aversion to everything which resembled a court, must have appeared wearisome to a young woman, capricious, with an ardent temperament, and of marvellous beauty. Some careful researches have reduced to a small matter the deeds which calumny has been pleased to ascribe to the spouse of Marcus-Aurelius. That which remains to her charge is nevertheless grave: she did not love her husband's friends; she did not enter into his life; she had tastes quite apart from him. The good emperor perceived this, suffered, and was silent. His determined principle to see things as they ought to be, and not as they are, did not give way. In vain did they dare to show him on the stage as a deceived husband. The comedians even went so far as to name Faustina's lovers in public. He would consent to hear nothing. He would not depart from his constant gentleness. Faustina always remained "his very good and very faithful spouse." They never succeeded even after she was dead in making him abandon this monstrous falsehood. In a bas-relief, which may be seen to this day in Rome, in the museum of the Capitol, while Faustina is raised to heaven by Fame, the excellent emperor follows her from the earth with a look full of love. What is most extraordinary is, that in his beautiful private prayer to the gods, which he wrote upon the banks of the Gran, he thanks them for having given him "a wife so kind, so affectionate, and so simple." He had come in those last days to create an illusion for himself and to forget everything. But what a struggle he must have gone through to arrive at that! During long years an internal complaint slowly consumed him. The despairing effort which made up the essence of his philosophy, pushed sometimes even to sophism, concealed at bottom a terrible wound. How he must have said adieu to happiness to arrive at such extremes! We can never comprehend all this poor blighted heart suffered, how much bitterness was concealed by that pale face, always calm and half smiling. It is true that the adieu to happiness is the beginning of wisdom, and the most certain means of finding happiness. There is nothing so sweet as the return of joy which follows the renunciation of joy, nothing so lively, so profound, so charming as the enchantment of being disenchanted.

A martyrdom much harder was inflicted upon Marcus-Aurelius in the person of his son Commodus. Nature, by a cruel sport, had given as a son to the best of men a sort of stupid athlete, only skilful at exercises of the body, a superb boy-butcher, ferocious, liking nothing except to kill. His little mind inspired him with a hatred of the intellectual society which surrounded his father. He fell into the hands of blackguards of the lowest kinds, who made of him one of the most odious monsters that have ever been seen. Marcus-Aurelius saw better than any one the impossibility of drawing anything out of this mean being, and nevertheless he neglected nothing to educate him well. The best philosophers lectured before the youth. He listened, something in the way in which a young lion would have done, while they taught, and allowed them to say on, yawning and showing long teeth to his masters. Marcus-Aurelius was misled in this matter by his want of practical finesse. He did not bring out his habitual sentiments on the benevolence which should be brought into the opinions and the consideration we owe to those who are not so good as we. The new motives for indulgence which he can give show us his charming good nature. "What evil can the most wicked of men do if thou remainest determinedly gentle to him, if on occasion thou dost exhort him quietly, and givest him, when he would injure thee, some lessons like this: No, no, my child, we are born for other things. It is not I who will bear the harm, but thou thyself, my son.' Show him dexterously by a general consideration that such is the rule, that neither the bees nor any other animals who live naturally in bands act as he does. No, give him not mockery or insult: let everything be said with a tone of true affection, as coming from a heart which anger has not embittered; do not speak to him as they do at school, nor with a view of obtaining the admiration of the audience, but speak to him with the same ease as if you were alone together." Commodus (if it is of him he is speaking) was no doubt little sensitive to this paternal rhetoric. There was evidently but one means of preventing the fearful evils that threatened the world; it was, by virtue of the right of adoption, to substitute a person more worthy of that which the chance of birth had designated. Julian particularises even more, and believes that Marcus-Aurelius should have associated in the government his son-in-law Pompeius, who would have continued to rule on the same principles as himself.

There are here some things which it is easy to say when the obstacles are no longer there, and when one can reason far from the facts. It is forgotten, first, that the emperors since Nerva who made the adoption system so fruitful had no sons. Adoption, including the disinheriting of son or grandson, we see in the first century of the empire, but not with good results. Marcus-Aurelius, by principle, approved of direct heredity, in which he sees the advantage of preventing competition. Since Commodus was born in 161, he presented him alone to the legions, although he was a twin; often he took him when quite little into his arms and renewed this act, which was a sort of proclamation. Marcus was an excellent father: "I have seen thy little brood," Fronton writes to him, "and nothing has given me so much pleasure; they resemble thee to such a degree that there has never been in the world such a resemblance. I see thee doubled, so to speak; on the right, on the left, it is thee whom I believe I see. They have, thanks to the gods, the appearance of health, and a good style of crying. One of them holds a morsel of very white bread, like a royal infant; the other, a morsel of house bread, like a true son of a philosopher. Their little voices appear to me so sweet and so gentle that I believe I recognise in their babble the clear and charming sound of thy voice." These sentiments were those of the whole world; in 166 it is Lucius Verus who asks that the two sons of Marcus, Commodus and Annius Verus, should be made Cæsars. In 172, Commodus shares with his father the title of Germanicus. After the repression of the revolt of Avidius, the senate, to recognise in some way the disinterestedness in family matters which Marcus-Aurelius had shown, demanded by acclamation the empire and the tribunal power for Commodus. Already the natural badness of the latter was betrayed by more than one sign known to his pedagogues, but how can one pre-judge by such evil marks the future of a child of twelve years? From 176-177 his father made him imperator, consul, august. It was surely an imprudence, but they were bound by former acts; Commodus, besides, kept himself yet within bounds towards the end of the life of Marcus-Aurelius. The evil revealed itself all at once; at each page of the last books of the Thoughts we see the trace of internal sufferings in the excellent father, the accomplished emperor, who saw a monster growing up beside him, ready to succeed him, and ready to take in everything by antipathy the reverse of what he had seen done among good people.

The thought of disinheriting Commodus must then without doubt have come to Marcus-Aurelius for the first time. But it was too late. After having associated him in the empire, after having proclaimed him so many times as perfect and accomplished before the legions, to go in face of the world, declaring him unworthy, would be a scandal. Marcus-Aurelius was taken by his phrases, by that style of an acknowledged benevolence which was too habitual to him; and after all Commodus was seventeen years of age, and who could be sure he wouldn't improve? Even after the death of Marcus-Aurelius they could hope. Commodus showed at first an intention to follow the counsels of deserving persons by whom his father had surrounded him. Is it not evident besides that if Pompeius or Pertinax succeeded Marcus-Aurelius, Commodus would become at once the chief of the military party, a continuation of that of Avidius, who held philosophy and the friends of the wise emperor in honour?

We believe, then, that we must judge leniently the conduct of Marcus-Aurelius in these circumstances. He was morally right; but the facts made him wrong. At sight of this wretch, losing the empire by his disgusting life, dragging shamefully among the valets of the circus and the amphitheatre a name consecrated by virtue, one curses the goodness of Marcus; one regrets that the exaggerated optimism which had made him take Verus as his colleague, and which perhaps would never allow him to see all the faults of Faustina, should have made him commit a fault much more grave. According to the public voice, he could so much the better have disinherited Commodus that a story was told, according to which Marcus would have been freed as to this paternal duty. By a sentiment of pious indignation, it was declared that Commodus was not the son of Marcus-Aurelius. To absolve Providence from such an absurdity, they calumniated the mother. When they saw the unworthy son of the best of men fighting in the amphitheatre and comporting himself like an actor of the lowest kind: "He is not a prince," they said, "he is a gladiator. No, there is no son of Marcus-Aurelius there." They soon discovered in the band of gladiators some individual in whom they found a resemblance to him, and they affirmed that he was the true father of Commodus. The fact is that all the monuments show the resemblance of Commodus to Marcus, and confirm fully the evidence of Fronton.

Without reproaching Marcus-Aurelius with not having disinherited Commodus, we can only regret that he could not do it. The perfection of the man injured the inflexibility of the sovereign. Capable of endurance, he would perhaps have saved the world, and he would not in anywise have borne the responsibility of the frightful decadence which followed. His misfortune was to have had a son. He forgot that the Cæsar is not a man like another, that his first duty is to enter into an arrangement with fate; that is, to divine what the time has marked as a sign. The heredity of dynasties is feudal, in unapplied Cæsarism. This régime is that which of all others produces the best or the worst fruits. When it is not excellent, it is execrable. Atrocious in the first century of our era, while a law of demi-heredity was followed, Cæsarism became splendid in the second, when the principle of adoption had definitely been brought in. The decadence commenced on the day when, by a weakness pardonable since it was inevitable, the best of princes whom adoption had brought to the empire did not follow a custom which had given for leaders to humanity the finest series of good and great princes the world has ever had. To crown the evil, he did not succeed in founding heredity. During the whole of the third century the empire was in the throes of intrigue and violence. The ancient world succumbed then.

For some years Marcus-Aurelius endured this punishment, the most cruel that could be inflicted on a man of heart. His friends of infancy and youth were no more. All this excellent world formed by Antoninus, this solid and distinguished society which believed so profoundly in virtue, had gone down to the grave. Remaining alone in the midst of a generation which knew him no longer, and even desired to be rid of him, with a son at his side making him drink deep of grief, he had before him only the horrible prospect of being the father of a Nero, a Caligula or a Domitian.

"Do not curse death, but make it welcome, since it is of the number of those phenomena which nature wills. The dissolution of our being is a fact as natural as youth, old age, growth, or full maturity. But if thou hast need of a very special reflection which should make thee kindly towards death, thou hast only to consider that from which it separates thee, and the moral world with which thy mind shall no longer be mixed. It is not that it is necessary to confound yourself with them; far from that; thou oughtest to love them, to endure them with gentleness. Only it is very necessary to tell thee that there are no people who share the sentiments that thou art leaving; the only motive which could attach us to life and retain us there would be to have the good fortune of finding ourselves with some men who hold the same opinions as we. But, at this hour, thou seest what lacerations are in thy bosom, so that thou criest, O death, do not delay thy coming, lest I should not come, I also, to forget myself!'

"He was an honest man; he was a wise man!' some will say; what shall keep another from saying, See us delivered from this pedagogue; let us breathe! Certainly he was not bad to any of us, but I felt that in his heart he disapproved of us!' As to the bed of death, this reflection will make thee quit life very readily: I leave this life whence my travelling companions (for whom I have struggled so much, made so many vows, and taken such trouble) desire that I should go, hoping that my death will put them more at their ease.' What motive could make us, therefore, desire to remain longer here?

"Do not, although in parting, show less benevolence to them; preserve in their view thy habitual character; remain affectionate, indulgent, gentle, and do not assume the appearance of a man who is leaving. It is nature which has formed thy connection with them. See how it breaks it. Ah, well, adieu, friends; I go without force being required to draw me from your midst; for this very separation is only conformable to nature."

The last books of the Thoughts are connected with this period, in which Marcus-Aurelius, remaining alone with his philosophy which no one shares now, has only one thought--that of leaving the world quite gently. It is the same melancholy as in the philosophy of Carnoute; but the hour in the life of the thinker is quite another. At Carnoute, and on the banks of the Gran, Marcus-Aurelius meditates that he may be rendered brave in life. Now, all his thought is only a preparation for death, a spiritual exercise, to arrive adorned as for the altar. All the motives by which we can seek to persuade ourselves that death is not a sovereign injustice for virtuous man he presents to himself; he goes even to sophism, that he may absolve Providence, and prove that man in dying ought to be satisfied.

"The time which the life of man lasts is only a point; his being is a perpetual flux; his sensations are obscure; his body, composed of different elements, tends with himself to corruption; his soul is a whirlwind; his destiny is an insoluble enigma; glory is an undetermined thing. In a word, all that concerns the body is a flowing river; all that concerns the soul is but a dream and smoke; life is a battle, a sojourn in a strange country; posthumous fame is forgotten. What, then, can serve as a guide? One thing, one only--that is philosophy; and philosophy it is to act on the genius who keeps us pure from all stain, stronger than pleasures or sufferings; accepting events and fate as emanations from the source from which it comes itself, at last waiting with a serene frame for death, which it takes to be the simple dissolution of the elements of which every living being is composed. If for the elements themselves, this is not an evil like submitting to perpetual metamorphoses, why look with sadness on the change and the dissolution of all things? This change is agreeable to the laws of nature, and nothing is evil that is so."

Thus, by analysing life, he dissolves it, and renders it little different from death. He arrives at perfect goodness, absolute indulgence, and comparative indifference through pity and disdain. "To pass his life resigned amidst lying and unjust men" --that is the sage's programme. And he was right. The most solid goodness is that which is founded on perfect weariness, on the clear view of this fact, that everything in this world is frivolous and without any real foundation. In that absolute ruin of everything what remains? Wickedness? Oh! that ought not to be any trouble. Wickedness supposes a certain serious faith in life, faith at least in pleasure, faith in revenge and ambition. Nero believed in art; Commodus believed in the circus; and that made them cruel. But the disabused man who knows that every object of desire is frivolous, why should he give himself the pain of a disagreeable feeling? The goodness of the sceptic is the most secure, and the pious emperor was more than a sceptic; the movement of life in this soul was almost as gentle as the little sounds of the inmost atmosphere of a grave. He had attained the Buddhist nirvana--the peace of Christ. Like Jesus, Çakya-Mouni, Socrates, Francis d'Assisi, and three or four other sages, he had totally conquered death. He could smile at it, for it had really no more meaning for him.

CHAPTER XXVII

DEATH OF MARCUS-AURELIUS—THE END OF THE OLD WORLD

On the 5th August, 178, the holy emperor quitted Rome to return, with Commodus, to those interminable wars of the Danube, which he wished to crown by the formation of solidly-constituted frontier provinces. The success was brilliant. They seemed to touch the limit so much longed for, and which had only been retarded by the revolt of Avidius. Some months afterwards the most important military enterprise of the second century is being terminated. Unfortunately the emperor was very weak. His stomach was so ruined that he often lived a whole day on some grains of theriac. He ate nothing except when he had to address the soldiers. Vienna on the Danube was, it would appear, the headquarters of the army. A contagious malady reigned in the country, for some years back, and it decimated the legions.

On the l0th March, 180, the emperor fell sick. He at once hailed death as welcome, abstained from all nourishment and all drink, and he spoke and acted henceforth only as from the brink of the grave. Having made Commodus come to him, he begged him to complete the war so as not to appear to betray the State by a precipitate departure. On the sixth day of his sickness he called his friends together, and spoke to them in his customary tone, that is to say, with a slight irony, as to the absolute vanity of things and the small importance he attached to death. They shed abundant tears. "Why weep for me?" he said to them. "Think of saving the army. I do nothing but precede you. Adieu!" They wished to know to whose care he recommended his son. "To you," said he, "if he is worthy, and to the immortal gods." The army was inconsolable; for they adored Marcus-Aurelius, and they saw too well into what an abyss of evils they were about to fall after his death. The emperor had still energy enough to present Commodus to the soldiers. His art of preserving peace in the midst of the greatest griefs made him keep, in this cruel moment, a calm countenance.

On the seventh day he felt his end approaching. He only received his son now, and he sent him away after a few moments, lest he might contract the malady from which he was suffering: probably this was only an excuse to free himself from his odious presence. Then he covered his head as if to sleep. The following night he yielded up his soul.

They brought his body to Rome and interred it in Hadrian's mausoleum. The effusion of the popular piety was touching. Such was the affection they had for him that they never called him by his name or titles. Each one, according to his age, called him "Marcus, my father, brother, son." On the day of his obsequies scarcely any tears were shed, all being certain that he had only returned to the gods who had lent him for a moment to the world. During the very funeral ceremony they proclaimed him "Propitious God," with an unexampled spontaneity. They declared it sacrilege for any one, if his means permitted it, not to have his portrait in their houses. And this cult was not like so many ephemeral apotheoses. A hundred years after the statue of Marcus-Aurelius was seen in a great number of collections of lares among the penates. The emperor Diocletian had a separate worship for him. The name of Antoninus was henceforth sacred. It became, like that of Cæsar and Augustus, a sort of attribute of the empire, a sign of human and civil sovereignty. The numen Antoninum was like the beneficent star of that government whose admirable programme remained for the century which followed it, a reproach, a hope, a regret. We see some minds as little poetical as that of Septimus Severus, dreaming of it as of a lost heaven. Even Constantine bowed before that clement divinity, and wished that the golden statue of the Antonines might be reckoned among those of the ancestors and guardians of his power, founded nevertheless under quite different auspices.

Never was cult more legitimate, and it is ours still to-day. Yes, such as we are, we carry in heart a mourning for Marcus-Aurelius, as if he had died yesterday. With him philosophy has reigned. For a moment, thanks to him, the world has been governed by the best and greatest man of his century. It is of importance that this experience should have been made. Will it ever occur a second time? Shall modern philosophy, like the ancient, ever reign in its turn? Shall it have its Marcus-Aurelius, supported by his Fronton and Junius Rusticus? Will the government of human things belong once more to the wisest? What does it matter, since that reign would be for only a day, and since the reign of fools would succeed it once more? Accustomed to contemplate with a calm and smiling eye the everlasting mirage of human illusions, modern philosophy knows the law of the passing creators of opinion. But it would be curious to seek for what should come forth from such principles, if they ever should arrive at power. It would be a pleasure to construct, à priori; the Marcus-Aurelius of modern times, to see what a mixture of force and feebleness could create, in a chosen soul called to the largest action, the kind of reflection particular to our age. One would like to see how criticism would ally itself to the highest virtue and to the most lively ardour for the good, what attitude a thinker of that school would observe before the social problems of the nineteenth century, by what art he would seek to turn them, lull them to sleep, elude them or solve them. What is certain is that the man called to govern his fellow-men ought always to contemplate the exquisite model of the sovereign which Rome in her best days presents. If it is true that it might be possible to surpass him in certain parts of the science of government, who does not know that in modern times the son of Annius Verus will always remain inimitable by his force of soul, his resignation, his accomplished nobility, and the perfection of his goodness?

The day of Marcus-Aurelius' death may probably be taken as the decisive moment when the ruin of the old civilisation was decided. In philosophy, the great emperor had raised such a high ideal of virtue that no one cared to follow him; in politics, the fault of having so profoundly separated the duties of the father from those of the Cæsar, he reopened without desiring it the era of tyrants and anarchy. In religion, through being too much attached to a State religion, whose weakness he saw thoroughly, he prepared the violent triumph of the non-official worship, and he left to be laid to his memory a reproach unjust, it is true, but whose shadow ought not to have met us in a life so pure. In everything, except the laws, feebleness could be felt. Twenty years of kindness had relaxed the administration and favoured abuses. A certain reaction in the sense of the ideas of Avidius Cassius was necessary; in place of that, there had been a thorough uprooting. Horrible deception for good people! So much virtue, so much love, only ending in placing the world in the hands of a knacker of beasts--a gladiator. After this beautiful apparition of an Elysian world on earth, to fall into the hell of the Cæsars' which was believed to be closed for ever! Faith in good was then lost. After Caligula, Nero, and Domitian one was able to hope. Experiences had not been decisive. Now, it is after the greatest effort of governmental rationalism, after eighty-four years of an excellent régime, after Nerva, Trajan, Hadrian, Antoninus, Marcus-Aurelius, that the reign of evil recommences, worse than ever. Adieu, virtue! adieu, reason! Since Marcus-Aurelius could not save the world, who shall save it? Now, long live the fools, the absurd, the Syrian and his ambiguous gods! The grave physicians can do nothing. The invalid is worse than ever. Let the quacks come in, they often know better than honourable practitioners what the people need.

What is sad in this is really that the day of Marcus-Aurelius' death, so evil for philosophy and civilisation, was a splendid day for Christianity. Commodus, having taken up the task of doing everything contrary to what he had seen, showed himself much less unfavourable to Christianity than his illustrious father. Marcus-Aurelius is the accomplished Roman with his traditions and prejudices. Commodus is of no race. He liked the Egyptian cults; he personally, with his head shaved, presided at the processions, carried the Anubis, and went through all the ceremonies with which the women were so pleased. He had himself represented in that attitude in the mosaics of the circular porticos of his gardens. He had Christians in his household. His mistress Marcia was almost a Christian, and used the love he gave her with credit, so as to alleviate the lot of the confessors condemned to the mines of Sardinia. The martyrdom of the Sicilians which took place on 17th July, 180, four months therefore after the ascension of Commodus, was no doubt the result of orders given before the death of Marcus, which the new government had not had time to withdraw. The number of victims under Commodus appears to have been less considerable than under Antoninus and Marcus-Aurelius. So true is it that between the Roman maxims and Christianity the war was to the death. Decius, Valerian, Aurelian, Diocletian, who sought to elevate the maxims of the empire, shall turn out to be ardent persecutors, while the emperors foreign to Roman patriotism, such as Alexander Severus, Philip the Arabian, and the Cæsars of Palmyra, will show themselves tolerant.

With a principle less disastrous than that of an unbridled military despotism, the empire, even after the ruin of the Roman principle by the death of Marcus-Aurelius, would have been able to live still, and to give place to Christianity a century sooner than it did, and to avoid the rivers of blood that Decius and Diocletian made to flow from pure wastefulness. The rôle of the Roman aristocracy was ended; after having used folly in the first century, it used virtue in the second. But the hidden forces of the great Mediterranean Confederation were not exhausted. Just as, after the falling down of the political edifice built under the title of the family of Augustus, there was formed a provincial dynasty, the Flavii, to restore the empire; just as, after the falling to pieces of the edifice built by the adoption of the high Roman nobility, there were found some among Provincials, Orientals, and Syrians, for the restoration of the grand association where all would find peace and profit, Septimius Severus did again without moral elevation, but not without glory, what Vespasian had done before.

Certainly the men of that new dynasty are not comparable to the great emperors of the second century. Even Alexander Severus, who equals Antoninus and Marcus-Aurelius in goodness, is far inferior to them in intelligence and nobility. The principle of the government is detestable. It is the outbidding of complaisance among the legions, revolt placed at a price; one does not address soldiers except with the purse in the hand. Military despotism never clothed itself in a more shameless form, but military despotism can have a long life. By the side of hideous spectacles, under those Syrian emperors whom they despise, what reforms are there? What a progress in legislation! What a day was that (under Caracalla) when every free man dwelling in the empire obtained equality of the laws! The advantages which this equality offered at that time must not be exaggerated; words, moreover, are never always empty in politics. Some excellent things were inherited. Philosophers of the school of Marcus-Aurelius had disappeared; but the juris-consulti replaced them. Papinian, Ulpian, Paul, Gaius, Modestinus, Florentinus, Marcian, during these execrable years, produced the chef-d'oeuvres, and really created the law of the future. Very inferior to Trajan and to the Antonines in political traditions, the Syrian emperors, inasmuch as they were not Romans, and had no Roman prejudices, often gave evidence of an openness of mind which the great emperors of the second century could not have, all so deeply conservative. They permitted, encouraged even, colleges or syndicates. Allowing themselves to go in that matter even to excess, they desired to have bodies of tradesmen organised in castes with special dresses. They opened the two leaves of the doors of the empire. One of them, the son of Mammæa, that good and affecting Alexander Severus, equals nearly, by his plebeian goodness, the patrician virtues of the great centuries; the highest thoughts pale before some righteous effusions of his heart.

It is especially in religion that the emperors called Syrian inaugurated a breadth of ideas and a tolerance alike unknown till then. These Syrian ladies of Emesa, handsome, intelligent, rash even to Utopianism, Julia Domna, Julia Mæsa, Julia Mammæa, Julia Sæmia, were not restrained by any tradition or social rule. They dared what no Roman lady had dared to do; they entered the Senate, deliberated there, effectively governed the empire, repeated Semiramis and Nitocris over again. Faustina never could have done this, in spite of her lightness; she would have been stopped by tact, by the feeling of ridicule, by the rules of good Roman society. The Syrian ladies drew back before nothing. They had a senate of women, who decreed every extravagance. The Roman cult appeared cold and insignificant to them. Not being restrained by any family reasons, and their imagination finding itself more in harmony with Christianity than with Italian Paganism, these women amused themselves with accounts of the travels of the gods on the earth; Philostratus enchanted them with his Apollonius; probably they had a secret affiliation with Christianity. During this time the last respectable ladies of ancient society, like that aged daughter of Marcus-Aurelius, honoured by all, whom Caracalla caused to be killed, assisted in darkness at an orgie which formed a strange contrast to their recollections of youth.

The provinces, and especially the provinces of the East, much more active and awake than those of the West, went definitely forward. Certainly Heliogabalus was a madman; and while his chimera of a central monotheistic cult, established at Rome, and absorbing all the other cults, showed that the strict circle of the Antonine idea was quite broken, Mamma and Alexander Severus went farther; while the juris-consulti continued to transcribe with the quietness of routine their old cruel maxims against liberty of conscience, the Syrian emperor and his mother were instructed in Christianity, testifying their sympathy with it. Not content to give security to the Christians, Alexander introduced Jesus among his lares, by a touching eclecticism. Peace seemed made, not as under Constantine, by the humbling of one of the parties, but by a large reconciliation. There was certainly in all this an audacious attempt at reform, inferior in its rational aspect to that of the Antonines, but more capable of succeeding, for it was much more popular; it heldin more esteem the province and the East. In such a democratic work people without ancestors, like those Africans and Syrians, had more chances of success than people with an irreproachable style like the aristocratic emperors. But the profound vice of the imperial system revealed itself for the tenth time. Alexander Severus was assassinated by the soldiers on the 19th March, 235 A.D. It was clear that the army could no longer tolerate tyrants. The empire had gradually fallen from the high Roman nobility to the officers of the province, now it passed to sub-officials and military assassins. While up to Commodus the assassinated emperors were intolerable monsters, at present it is the good emperor who creates some new discipline, he who represses the crimes of the army, who is surely marked out for death.

Then opens that hell of a half-century (235-284 A.D.) when all philosophy, all civility, all delicacy foundered. The bidding, as at auction, the soldiery masters of everything, sometimes ten tyrants at once, the barbarian penetrating through all the fissures of the cracked world; Athens demolishing her ancient monuments to surround herself with evil walls against the terror of the Goths. If anything proves to what a degree the Roman empire was necessary, by intrinsic reason, it is that it was not totally dislocated in this anarchy. It is that it kept breath enough to revive under the powerful action of Diocletian, and to complete a course of two centuries yet. Among all orders the decadence was frightful. In fifty years they had forgotten the art of sculpture. Latin literature ceased completely. It seemed as if a bad genius brooded over this society, drinking its blood and its life. Christianity took to itself what was good in it, and impoverished to that extent civil order. The army was dying for want of a good recruitment of officers; the Church drew everything to itself. The religious and moral elements of the State have a very simple manner of punishing the State which does not give them the position to which they think they have a right; it is to retire to their tents. For a State cannot go away from them. Civil society has nothing thenceforth but the refuse intellects. Religion absorbs everything in it that is good. People leave a country which does not represent anything but a principle of material force. People chose their country in the ideal or rather in the institution which takes the place of the overthrown city and country. The Church became exclusively the bond of souls, and as it increased by the very misfortunes of civil society they comforted themselves easily for these misfortunes, in which it was easy to show a revenge of Christ and his saints.

"If we were permitted to render evil for evil," said Tertullian, "one night and some torches would be enough for our revenge." They were patient, for they were sure of the future. Now, the world slew the saints; but to-morrow the saints shall judge the world. "Look at our faces well, for you will recognise us at the last judgment," said one of the martyrs of Carthage to the Pagans. "Our patience," said the most moderate, "comes to us from the certainty of being revenged; it heaps coals of fire on the heads of our enemies. What a day will that be when the Most High shall reckon up his faithful, shall send away the guilty to Gehenna and make our persecutors burn in the furnace of eternal fires! What a tremendous spectacle; what shall be my transports, my admiration, and my laughter! flow shall I applaud as I see in the depths of darkness, with Jupiter and their own worshippers, so many princes who have been declared received into heaven after their death! What joy to see the persecuting magistrates of the Lord's name consumed by flames more devouring than those the executioners lit up for the Christians!"

CHAPTER XXVIII

CHRISTIANITY AT THE END OF THE SECOND CENTURY--DOGMA

In the space of time which passed from the death of Augustus to the death of Marcus-Aurelius a new religion was produced in the world; it called itself Christianity. The essence of that religion consisted in believing that a grand celestial manifestation was made in the person of Jesus of Nazareth, a divine being, who, after a quite supernatural life, was put to death by the Jews, his compatriots, and rose again on the third day. Thus, the conqueror of death, he waits, at the right hand of God, his Father, the propitious hour to reappear in' the clouds to preside at the general resurrection, of which his own has been but the prelude, and to inaugurate, upon a purified earth, the kingdom of God; that is to say, the reign of the risen saints. While waiting thus, the assembly of the faithful, the Church, represents a kind of city of the saints presently living, always governed by Jesus. It was believed, in fact, that Jesus had delegated his powers to apostles, who established bishops and all the ecclesiastical hierarchy. The Church renews its communion with Jesus by means of the breaking of bread and the mystery of the cup, a rite established by Jesus himself, and by virtue of which Jesus becomes for the moment but really present in the midst of his own people. As consolation in their waiting, in the midst of the persecutions of a perverse world, the faithful have the supernatural gifts of the Spirit of God, that Spirit which formerly animated the prophets and which is not extinguished. They have especially the reading of the books revealed by the Spirit; that is to say, the Bible, the Gospels, the letters of the apostles, and those of the writings of the new prophets which the Church has adopted for reading in the public assemblies. The life of the believers ought to be a life of prayer, asceticism, renunciation, and separation from the world, since the present world is governed by the prince of evil, Satan, and since idolatry is nothing else than the worship of devils.

Such a religion would appear at first as if it had come from Judaism. The Jewish Messianism is its cradle. The first title of Jesus, a title become inseparable from his name, is Christos, the Greek translation of the Hebrew word Mesih. The grand sacred book of the new worship is the Jewish Bible; its festivals, at least as to names, are the Jewish festivals; its prophecy is the continuation of the Jewish prophecy. But the separation between the mother and the child is made thoroughly. The Jews and the Christians, in general, detest each other; the new religion tends more and more to forget its origin and what it owes to the Hebrew people. Christianity is looked upon by most of its adherents as an entirely new religion, without any tie to that which precedes it.

If we now compare Christianity, such as it existed about the year 180, with the Christianity of the Middle Ages, with the Christianity of our day, we find that it really has been augmented in a very small degree in the centuries which have passed away. In 180 the New Testament was closed; no other new book shall be added. Slowly the epistles of Paul have conquered their place after the gospels in the sacred code and in the liturgy. As to dogmas, nothing was fixed; but the germ of everything existed; scarcely any idea can appear which could not find authorities in the first and second centuries. There has been too much, there have been contradictions; the theological work shall rather consist in pruning, cutting away superfluities, than in inventing anything new. The Church shall allow to fall to the ground a crowd of matters badly begun; it will come away from these difficulties. It has still two hearts, so to speak; it has many heads; these anomalies shall pass away; but no dogma truly original shall form itself henceforth.

The Trinity of the doctors of the year 180, for example, is undecided. Logos, Paraclete, Holy Spirit, Christ, and Son are words employed confusedly to designate the divine entity incarnate in Jesus. The three persons are not counted, numbered, if one may express it in that way; but the Father, the Son, and the Spirit are well enough designated by the three terms which shall be maintained as distinct, without, nevertheless, dividing the indivisible Jehovah. The Son shall increase exceedingly. That species of vicarship which Monotheism, from a certain time, is pleased to give to the Supreme Being shall in a singular manner obscure the Father. The bizarre formulas of Nicea shall establish some equalities contrary to nature; the Christ, the sole active person of the Trinity, shall be changed with the whole work of creation, and providence shall become God himself. But the epistle to the Colossians is only one step in such a doctrine; to arrive at these exaggerations only a little logic is needed. Mary, the mother of Jesus, is herself destined to increase to colossal proportions; she shall become indeed a person of the Trinity. Already the Gnostics have divined this future, and inaugurated a worship called by an immoderate importance.

The dogma of the divinity of Jesus Christ exists complete; only, there is not agreement as to the formulas which serve to express it; the Christology of the Judeo-Christian of Syria and that of the author of the Hermas or the Confessions differ considerably; the work of theology shall be to choose, not to create. The millenarianism of the first Christians became more and more distasteful to the Greeks who embraced Christianity. Greek philosophy exercised a kind of violent thrust in order to substitute its dogma of the immortality of the soul for the old Jewish ideas (or Persian ideas if you will) of the resurrection and a Paradise on earth. The two formulas yet coexist. Irenæus surpassed all the millenarians in gross materialism, since already, fifty years back, the fourth gospel, so purely spiritualistic, proclaimed that the kingdom of God commences here below, that one carries it in himself. Caius, Clement of Alexandria, Origen, and Dionysius of Alexandria sought soon to condemn the dream of the first Christians, and to envelop the Apocalypse in their antipathy. But it is too late to suppress anything so important. Christianity will subordinate the appearance of Christ in the clouds and the resurrection of the body to the immortality of the soul; so that the old primitive dogma of Christianity shall be almost forgotten and relegated, like a theatrical piece out of vogue, to the background of a last judgment, which has as little meaning since the fate of each one is fixed at death. Many declare that the torments of the damned will never end, and that these pains shall be a condiment to the joy of the righteous; others believe that they will finish or be mitigated.

In the theory of the constitution of the Church, the idea that the apostolic succession is the foundation of the bishop's power, who is thus looked on not only as a delegate of the community, but as continuing the apostles' office, and being the depository of their authority, came more and more uppermost. Yet many Christians hold still to the much more simple conception of the Ecclesia in Matthew, where all the members are equal. In the fixing of the canonical books, agreement reigns as to the grand fundamental texts; but an exact list of the writings of the new Bible does not exist, and the limits, if we may so express it, of this new sacred literature are entirely undecided.

The Christian doctrine is thus already one so compact that nothing essential shall be joined to it, and that any considerable retrenchment shall not be possible. Up to Mahomet, and even after him, there were in Syria some Judeo-Christians, Elkasaïtes, and Ebionites. In addition to these minim or Nazarenes of Syria, whom the erudite among the Fathers alone knew, and who did not cease even in the fourth century to inveigh against St. Paul in their synagogues, and to treat the ordinary Christians as false Jews, the East has never ceased to reckon some Christian families observing the Sabbath and practising circumcision. The Christians of Salt and Kerak appear to be, in our day, a kind of Ebionites. The Abyssinians are real Judeo-Christians, practising all the Jewish precepts, often with more rigour than the Jews themselves. The Koran and Islamism are only a prolongation of that old form of Christianity, Docetism, the suppression of the cross. On the other hand, in the full nineteenth century, the communist and apocalyptic sects of America make of millenarianism and an approaching last judgment the foundation of their belief, as in the first days of the first Christian generations.

Thus, in that Christian Church of the end of the second century, everything was already said. There is not an opinion, not a course of ideas, not a fable which has not had her defender. Arianism was in germ in the opinions of the monarchists, Artemonites, Praxeas, Theodotus of Byzantium, and those made the remark with reason that their belief had been that of the majority of the Church of Rome up to the time of Pope Zephyrin (about the year 200). That which is wanting in this age of unbridled liberty is what shall later on bring about councils and doctors--namely, discipline, rule, and the elimination of contradictions. Jesus is already God, and yet many people have a repugnance to call him by this name. The separation from Judaism is accomplished, and yet many Christians practise still all Judaism. Sunday replaces Saturday, which does not prevent certain of the faithful observing the Sabbath. The Christian passover is distinguished from the Jewish passover; and yet some entire churches always follow the ancient usage. In the supper, most churches use ordinary bread; many, nevertheless, especially in Asia Minor, use only unleavened bread. The Bible and the writings of the New Testament are the base of the ecclesiastical teaching, and at the same time a crowd of other books are adopted by some and rejected by others. The four Gospels are fixed, and yet many other evangelical texts circulate and obtain favour. The majority of the faithful, far from being enemies of the Roman empire, only waited the day of reconciliation, admitting already the thought of a Christian empire; others continue to vomit against the capital of the Pagan world the most sombre apocalyptic predictions. An orthodoxy is formed and already used as a touchstone to set aside heresy; but, lest this reason of authority should be abused; the most Christian doctors rail hotly against what they call the "plurality of error." The primacy of the Church of Rome commenced to be marked out; but those even who submitted to this primacy would have protested if it had been said that the bishop of Rome would one day aspire to the title of sovereign of the universal Church. To resume, the differences which separate in our days the most orthodox Catholic and the most liberal Protestant there is very little difference, except such disagreements as existed then between two Christians who have not remained less in perfect communion with each other.

What makes the unequalled interest of this creating period? Accustomed to study only the reflected periods of history, nearly all those who in France have given forth views upon the origins of Christianity have considered only the third and fourth centuries. The centuries of celebrated men and oecumenical councils, symbols and rules of faith, Clement of Alexandria, and Origen, the Council of Nicea and St. Athanasius, are for them the summits and the highest figures. We do not deny the importance of any epoch in history, but there are not beginnings there. Christianity was entirely made before Origen and the Council of Nicea, and who made it? A multitude of great anonymous persons, unconscious groups, writers without name or pseudonyms, the unknown author of the Epistles to Titus and Timothy, attributed to Paul, have contributed more than any Council to the constitution of ecclesiastical discipline. The obscure authors of the Gospels have apparently more real importance than their most celebrated commentators. And Jesus? It will be confessed, I hope, that there had been some reason for which his disciples loved him to the point of believing that he had risen from the dead, and to see in him the accomplishment of the Messianic ideal, the superhuman being destined to preside at the complete renovation of heaven and earth.

Fact in such a matter is the mark of right, success is the grand criterion. In religion and morals, invention is nothing. The maxims of the Sermon on the Mount are as old as the world; no one has the literary property of them. The essential thing is to realise these maxims and to give them as a basis to a society. That is why, in the case of the religious founder, the personal charm is the leading thing. The grand work of Jesus has been to make himself loved by a score of people, or rather to have made them love the idea in him up to a point which triumphs over death. It was the same with the apostles and with the second and third generations. Founders are always obscure; but in the eyes of the philosopher the glory of these unnamed ones is the true glory. They were not great men, those humble contemporaries of Trajan and Antoninus, who have decided the faith for the world. Compared with them the celebrated personages of the Church of the third and fourth centuries make a much better figure. And yet these last have built upon the foundation which the first have laid. Clement of Alexandria and Origen were only half Christians. These are Gnostics, Hellenists, and Spiritualists, placing the essence of Christianity in metaphysical speculation, not in the application of the merits of Jesus or the Biblical Revelation. Origen confesses that if the Law of Moses be understood in its proper sense it would be inferior to the laws of the Romans, the Athenians, and the Spartans. St. Paul had already denied the title of Christian to a Clement of Alexandria, saving the world by a gnosis where the blood of Jesus Christ plays scarcely any part.

The same reflection may be applied to the writings which these ancient ages have left us. They are flat, simple, gross, artless, analogous to letters without orthography, which in our days the most despised communist sectaries would write. James, Jude recall Cabet or Babick, the fanatic of 1848 or the fanatic of 1871, convinced, but not knowing his language, expressing by fits and starts, in a touching manner, his artless aspiration of conscience. And yet these are the stammerings of a kind of people who have become the second Bible of the human race. The upholsterer Paul wrote Greek as badly as Babick did French. The rhetorician governed by literary consideration, for whom French literature commences at Villau; the doctrinaire historian who thinks only of reflected developments, and for whom the French constitution commences with the pretended Constitutions of St. Louis, cannot understand these apparent bizarreries.

The age of beginnings is chaos, but a chaos rich in life; it is the fertile plain where a being is prepared to exist, a monster still, but endowed with a principle of unity, of a type strong enough to remove impossibilities and to give himself essential organs. What are all the efforts of the conscious centuries if we compare them with the spontaneous tendencies of the embryo age--a mysterious age where the being, in process of making himself, cuts away a useless appendage, creates for himself a nervous system, and stretches out a limb? It is in these moments that the Spirit of God broods over his work, and that the group which works for humanity can truly say:--

"Est Deus in nobis, agitante calescimus illo."

CHAPTER XXIX

WORSHIP AND DISCIPLINE

The history of a religion is not the history of a theology. The subtleties without value with which they have ornamented this name are the parasite which devours the religions.

Jesus had no theology, he had the most lively feeling that could be of Divine things, and of the filial communion of man with God. Thus he did not institute a worship, properly speaking, outside of what he already found established by Judaism. The "breaking of bread," accompanied by the action of grace or the eucharist, was the only rite a little symbolic which he adopted; and yet Jesus does nothing but give it importance and appropriate it, for the beraka (benediction) before breaking the bread had always been a Jewish usage. However this may be, this mystery of bread and wine is considered as being the body and blood of Jesus, so much so, that those who eat and drink of them partake of Jesus, become the generating element of a whole religion. The ecclesia or assembly was the foundation. Christianity has never gone from that. The ecclesia, having for central object the communion or eucharist, became the mass: now the mass has always reduced the remainder of the Christian cult to the rank of accessory and secondary practice.

They were far, about the time of Marcus-Aurelius, from the primitive Christian assembly, during which two or three prophets, often women, fell into ecstasy, speaking at the same time, and demanding from each other after the attack what wonderful things they had said. That was no longer seen among the Montanists. In the immense majority of the churches the elders and the bishops presided over the assembly, ruling the readings, they only speaking. Women are seated apart silent and veiled. Order reigns throughout, thanks to a considerable number of secondary employés having distinct functions. Little by little the seat of the episcopos and the seats of the presbyteri constitute a central half circle choir. The eucharist demands a table before which the celebrant pronounces the prayers and the mysterious words. Soon they established a rood-loft for the readings and the sermons, then a chancel of separation between the presbyterium and the remainder of the hall. Two reminiscences ruled all this infancy of Christian architecture; first a vague remembrance of the Temple at Jerusalem, of which a part was accessible to the priests alone in a preoccupation of the grand heavenly liturgy found in the Apocalypse. The influence of this book upon the liturgy was of the first order. The desire was to do on earth what the twenty-four old men and the beast-shaped singers did before the throne of God. The service of the Church was thus modelled upon that of heaven. The use of incense doubtless came from the same inspiration. The lamps and the candles were specially employed at funerals.

The grand liturgical act of the Sunday was a chef d'oeuvre of mystery and of understanding of the popular sentiments. It was already the mass, but the complete mass, not the flattened mass, if I dare to say so, crushed down as in our days; it was the mass living in all its parts, each part preserving the primitive signification which it later on so strangely lost. This mixture, skilfully composed of psalms, canticles, prayers, readings, professions of faith--this sacred dialogue between the bishop and the people--prepared their souls to think and feel in common. The homily of the bishop, the reading of the correspondence from foreign bishops and from persecuted churches, gave life and actuality to the peaceful assembly. Then came the solemn preface to the mystery, announced full of gravity, the recall of souls to contemplation, then the mystery itself, a secret canon, some prayers more holy even than those which had preceded; then the act of supreme brotherhood, the partaking of the same bread and the same cup. A sort of solemn silence fell upon the Church at that moment. Then when the mystery was finished life was renewed, the chants recommenced, the actions of grace even multiplied; a long prayer embraced all the orders of the Church, all the conditions of humanity, all the established powers. Then the president, after having exchanged with the faithful some pious desires, dismissed the assembly by the ordinary formula in judicial audiences, and the brethren separated full of edification for many days.

This assembly of the Sunday was in a manner the knot of all the Christian life. This sacred bread was the universal bond of the Church of Jesus. They sent it to the absent at their homes, to the confessors in prison, and from one church to the other, especially about the time of Easter; they gave it to the children, it was the grand sign of communion and brotherhood. The agape, an evening repast in common, not distinguished at first from the supper, became separated more and more and degenerated into abuse. The supper, on the contrary, became essentially a morning office, the distribution of the bread and wine was made by the elders and deacons. The faithful received it standing. In certain countries, especially in Africa, they believed because of the prayer, "Give us each day our daily bread," it was a duty to communicate every day. They carried away for that purpose a morsel of blessed bread, which they ate by themselves in the family after the morning prayer.

They were pleased, in imitation of the mysteries, to surround this supreme act with profound secrecy. Some precautions were taken that the initiated alone should be present in the church at the moment when it was celebrated. This was nearly the only fault which the budding Church committed. They believed because it sought the shade that it had need of it, and this, joined indeed to other indications, furnished appearances for the accusation of magic. The holy kiss was also a great source of edification and danger. The sage doctors recommended that it should not be repeated if any pleasure was felt in it, nor be taken twice, nor should the lips be open. They were not slow besides to suppress the danger by introducing the danger into the Church of the separation of the sexes. The Church had no temple, for they maintained as a fixed principle that God has no need of a temple, that his true temple is the heart of the righteous man. It had certainly no architecture which could make it recognised; it was at that time only a house apart. They called it "the House of the Lord," and the most tender sentiments of Christian piety commenced to cling to it. The assemblies at night, no doubt, because they were forbidden by law, had a great charm for the imagination. At bottom, although the true Christian held temples in aversion, the Church aspired secretly to become a temple; it became so completely in the middle ages. The chapel and the church of our days resemble much nearer the ancient temples than the churches of the second century.

An idea soon spread abroad contributed much to this transformation; it was represented that the eucharist was a sacrifice, since it was the memorial of the supreme sacrifice accomplished by Jesus. This imagination filled up a lacuna which the new religion appeared to present to the eyes of superficial people--I mean the want of sacrifices. Accordingly the eucharistic table became an altar, and it was a matter of offerings and oblations. These oblations were the very same bread and wine which the wealthy believers brought, that it should not be at the Church's expense, the remainder belonging to the poor and the servants of the cult. One can see how such a doctrine might become fertile in misunderstandings. The Middle Ages, which abused the mass so much by exaggerating the idea of sacrifice, arrived at this through a strange course. From transformations to transformations, they had come to the low mass, where a man, in a little recess, with an infant which took the place of the people, presided over an assembly consisting of himself alone, speaking in dialogue without ceasing with people who were not there, apostrophising absent auditors, taking the offering himself, giving the kiss of peace to it alone.

The Sabbath, at the end of the second century, was very nearly suppressed by the Christians. They appeared to find in it a mark of Judaism--a bad mark. The first Christian generations celebrated both Saturday and Sunday, the one in memory of the creation, the other as the souvenir of the resurrection; then everything concentrated itself on the Sunday. It was not that they looked exactly upon the second as a day of rest; the Sabbath was abrogated--not transferred; but the solemnities of Sunday, and especially the idea that this day ought to be one entirely for joy (it was forbidden to fast or to pray on one's knees), brought back the abstention from servile labour. It was much later that they came to believe that the precept of the Sabbath was applied to the Sunday. The first rules in this matter only concerned slaves, to whom from a feeling of pity they wished to secure some holidays. Thursday and Friday, dies stationum, were consecrated to fasting, to genuflexions and the souvenir of the Passion. The annual feasts were the two Jewish festivals, the Passover and Pentecost, with the transpositions known to them. As to the feast of Palms, it was half suppressed. The custom of shaking branches and crying Hosanna! associated as much good as evil with the Sunday before the Passover, in memory of a circumstance in the last week of Jesus. The anniversary day of the Passion was dedicated to fasting; on that day they abstained from the holy kiss.

The worship of the martyrs took already a place so considerable that the Pagans and the Jews made objections to it, maintaining that the Christians revered the martyrs more than Christ himself. They buried them in view of the resurrection, and they placed around them refinements of luxury which contrasted with the simplicity of Christian manners; they almost worshipped their bones. On the anniversary of their death they went to their graves; they read the story of their martyrdom; they celebrated the eucharistic mystery in remembrance of them. It was the extension of the commemoration of the departed, a pious custom which held a large place in the Christian life. They were nearly saying mass for the dead now. On the day of their anniversary they made the offering for them, as if they lived still; they brought their names into the prayers which preceded the consecration; they ate the bread in communion with them. The worship of the saints, by which Paganism resumed its place in the Church-- prayers for the dead, a source of the greatest abuse in the Middle Ages--was thus drawn from what, in primitive Christianity, was most elevated and pure.

The ecclesiastical chant existed from an early time, and was one of the expressions of the Christian conscience. It was applied to hymns whose composition was free, and of which we have a specimen in Clement of Alexandria's hymn to Christ. The rhythm was short and light; it was that of the songs of the time, of those for example to which Anacreon was set. There was nothing in common, in any case, between them and the recitative of the Psalms. We can find some echo in the Paschal liturgy of our churches, which has specially preserved its archaic air in the Judeo-Christian Victimæ paschali; in the O filii et filiæ and the Alleluia. The carmen antelucanum of which Pliny speaks, or the office in galli cantu is found probably in the Hymnum dicat turba fratrum, especially in the following strophe, of which the silvery sound nearly brings back to us the air to which it was sung:--

> Galli cantos, gall plausus
> Proximum sentit diem,
> Et ante lucem muntiemus
> Christum regem seculo.

Baptism had completely replaced circumcision, of which it was, in its origin among the Jews, only the preliminary. It was administered by a triple immersion in a separate place near the church: then the illuminated was introduced into the assembly of believers. Baptism was followed by the imposition of hands--the Jewish rite at the ordination of the rabbinate. It was what they called the baptism of the Spirit; without this baptism with water was incomplete. Baptism was nothing but a breaking with the past; it was by the imposition of hands that one became really a Christian. There were joined with this some anointings with oil, the origin of what is called confirmation, and a sort of profession of faith by questions and responses. All this constituted the definitive seal, the sphragis. The sacramental idea, the ex opere operato, the sacrament conceived of as a sort of magical operation, became thus one of the bases of the Christian theology. In the third century a species of novitiate in baptism, the catechumenate, was established; the faithful arrived at the threshold of the church only after having passed through the gradual orders of initiation. The baptism of infants began to appear about the end of the second century. It shall find up to the fourth century decided adversaries.

Penance was already regulated at Rome about the time of the pseudo-Hermas. That institution which supposed a society so strongly organised made some surprising developments. It is a wonder that it did not rend the budding Church. If anything proves how much the Church was beloved, and the intensity of the joy which was found in it, it is to see to what rude trials men submitted to re-enter and regain among the saints the place which they had lost. Confession or avowal of the fault, already practised by the Jews, was the first condition of Christian penance.

Never, we can see, was the material of a worship more simple. The vessels of the Supper became sacred only slowly. The saucers of glass, which were used there, were the first to be an object of a certain attention.

The adoration of the cross was a respect rather than a worship; the symbolism remained of extreme simplicity. The palm, the dome with the fish, the IXΘYΣ, the anchor, the phoenix, the AΩ, the T forming the cross, and probably already the chrisimon to mean Christ; such were nearly all the received allegorical figures. The cross itself was never represented, neither in the churches nor in the houses; on the contrary, the sign of the cross, made by bringing the hand to the forehead, was often repeated, but it cannot be that this usage was particularly dear.

The worship of the heart, on the other hand, was the most developed that had ever been. Although the liberty of the charismas had already been well reduced by the episcopate, spiritual gifts, miracles, direct inspiration, continued in the Church and made the life of it. Irenæus saw in these supernatural faculties which marked it as the Church of Jesus. The martyrs of Lyons still shared in them. Tertullian believed himself surrounded by perpetual miracles. It is not only among the Montanists that a superhuman character is given to the most simple acts. Theopneustism and thaumaturgy in the whole Church were the permanent state. They only spoke by female spirits, who made certain replies, and were like harps resounding under the touch of the divine bow. The soror, whose souvenir Tertullian has preserved to us, astonished the Church by her visions. Like the illuminati of Corinth of the time of St. Paul, she mingled her revelations with the solemnities of the Church; she read their hearts; she pointed out remedies; she saw the souls corporeally like some little beings of human form, aërial, brilliant, tender, and transparent. Some ecstatic children passed also for the interpreters whom the Divine Word had chosen.

Supernatural medicine was the first of these gifts, which they considered as the heritages of Jesus. The holy oil was the instrument of it. The Pagans were frequently healed by the oil of the Christians. As to the art of chasing away demons, everybody knows that the exorcist Christians had a great superiority; from all sides they brought the possessed, that they might be delivered absolutely, as the thing takes place to-day in the East. It even happened among those people who were not exorcised in the name of Jesus. Some Christians were indignant; but the majority rejoiced at it, seeing there a homage to truth. They did not stop in such a good path. As the false gods were nothing but demons, the power of chasing away demons implied the power of unmasking the false gods. The exorcist thus incurred the accusation of magic, which was reflected upon the entire Church.

The orthodox Church saw the danger of these spiritual gifts, remnants of a powerful primitive ebullition, that the Church must be disciplined, under pain of being extinguished. The sensible doctors and bishops were opposed to it: for these marvels, which charmed the irrational Tertullian, and to which St. Cyprian attached so much importance, gave place to evil reports, and there mingled with them some individual oddities which orthodoxy opposed. Far from encouraging them, the Church marked the charismas with suspicion, and in the third century, without disappearing, they became more and more rare. Ecstasy was doomed. The bishop became the depository of the charismas, or rather the charismas were succeeded by the sacrament, administered by the clergy, while the charisma is an individual matter, an affair between man and God. The synods inherited permanent revelation. The first synods were held in Asia Minor against the Phrygian prophets; brought into the Church, the principle of inspiration by the Spirit became a principle of order and authority.

The clergy were already a body distinct from the people. A great complete Church, besides the bishop and elders, had a certain number of deacons and assistant-deacons attached to the bishops and the ministers of his orders. It possessed, besides, a series of less functionaries, anagnostes or readers, exorcists, porters, singers or chanters, acolytes, who served in the ministry of the altar, filled the cups with water and wine, and carried the eucharist to the sick. The poor and the widows cared for by the Church, and who remained there more or less, were considered as people of the Church, and were inscribed on her rolls (matricularii). They filled the humblest offices, such as that of sweeping, later that of ringing bells, and lived along with the clergy from the surplus of the offerings of bread and wine. For the higher orders of the clergy, celibacy became more and more established; at least, second marriages were forbidden. The Montanists began soon to claim that the sacraments administered by a married priest were null. Castration was never anything but an excess of zeal, and was soon condemned. The sister-companions of the apostles, whose existence was established by well-known texts, were found among these thus introduced, a sort of deaconess-servants, who formed the origin of the concubinage avowed by the clergy in the Middle Ages. Rigorists demanded that they should be veiled, to prevent the too tender sentiments which might arise in the brethren in the ministry of love.

The graves became from the end of the second century an annexe of the Church, and the object of an ecclesiastical service. The mode of Christian burial was always that of the Jews, inhumation, which consisted of placing the body enveloped in a shroud in a sarcophagus formed like a trough, often surmounted by an arcosolium. Cremation always inspired great repugnance in the faithful. The Mithraists and other Oriental sects shared the same ideas, and practised at Rome what was called the Syrian mode of burial. The Greek belief in the immortality of the soul led to burning, the Oriental belief in the resurrection led to interment. Many indications point to the most ancient Christian burials in Rome near St. Sebastian on the Appian Way. There the Jewish and Mithraist cemeteries are found. It is believed that the bodies of the apostles Peter and Paul rest in this place, and that is why they have called it Catatumbas, "to the tombs."

About the time of Marcus-Aurelius a decided change took place. The question which preoccupied the great towns made an imperious demand. Just as the system of cremation was sparing in the matter of space consecrated to the dead, so inhumation in the Jewish, Christian, and Mithraist manner crowded the surface of the ground. One needed to be rich to purchase, while alive, a loculus in the dearest ground in the world, at the gate of Rome. When the great masses of population in comfortable circumstances wished to be interred in this way, it was necessary to go under ground. They dug to a certain depth to find black beds sufficiently firm; there they began to pierce horizontally, sometimes in many stages, those labyrinths in whose vertical walls were opened the loculi. The Jews, the Sabazians, the Christians simultaneously adopted this kind of burial, which agreed well with the congregational mind, and the taste for mystery which distinguished them. Now, the Christians having continued this kind of burial during the third, fourth, and a part of the fifth century, the collection of catacombs in the environs of Rome was nearly altogether a Christian work. From necessities analogous to those which caused these vast hypogea around Rome, they were produced likewise at Naples, Milan, Syracuse and Alexandria.

In the first years of the third century, we see Pope Zephyrin entrusting his deacon Callistus with the care of these great mortuary depôts. They were what is called cemeteries or "sleeping places;" for men believed that the dead slept there waiting for the day of resurrection. Many martyrs were interred there. From this time the respect which had been connected with the bodies of the martyrs was applied to the places where they were laid. The catacombs were soon holy places. The organisation of the burial service was complete under Alexander Severus. About the time of Fabian and Cornelius, this service is one of the principal preoccupations of Roman piety. To repose near the martyrs, ad sanctos ad martyres, was a privilege. Year by year, the mysteries were celebrated over these sacred tombs. Hence the cubicula or sepulchral chambers, which, grown larger, became subterranean chapels, where they assembled in times of persecutions. Besides, they added sometimes scholæ, serving as a triclinium for the agapes. Assemblies under such conditions had the advantage that they could be taken as funerals, which placed them under the protection of the law. The cemetery, which was subterranean or in the open air, became thus a place essentially ecclesiastical. The fossor in some churches was a clergyman of the second order, like the anagnost and the porter. The Roman authority, which in questions of sepulture gave large toleration, very rarely interfered with these subterranean places; they admitted, except at moments of furious persecution, that the property of these consecrated areæ belonged to the community, that is to say, to the bishop. The entrance to the cemeteries was, besides, nearly always masked on the exterior by some family burying ground, whose right was beyond dispute.

Thus the principle of burial by the brotherhood stood complete in the third century. Each sect built its subterranean passage and enclosed it. The separation of the dead became a common right. They were classed by their religion in the tomb; to remain after death with his brethren became a necessity. Up to that point, burial had been an individual or family matter; now it became a religious and collective matter; it supposed a community of opinions on divine things. It is not one of the least difficult that Christianity shall meet in the future.

From its first beginning, Christianity was thus as opposed to the development of the plastic art as Islam has been. If Christianity had remained Jewish, architecture alone would have developed, as has been the case with the Mussulmans; the Church would have been like the Mosque, a grand house of prayer--that would have been all. But religions are what the races who adopt them make them. Brought among people who were the friends of art, Christianity became a religion as artistic as it would have been little so if it had remained in the hands of the Judeo-Christians. Thus it was some heretics who founded Christian art. We have seen the Gnostics entering into that path, with an audacity which scandalised the true believers. It was still too much so; everything that recalled idolatry was suspected. The painters who were converted were looked on askance, as having seemed to turn away to graven images the homage due to the Creator. The images of God and Christ, I mean the isolated images which seemed like idols, excited apprehension, and the Carpocratians, who had busts of Jesus, and addressed Pagan honours to them, were considered profane. The Mosaic precepts against figured representations were obeyed to the letter in the churches. The idea of the uncomeliness of Jesus, subversive of Christian art, was widely spread. There were some painted portraits of Jesus, St. Peter, and St. Paul, but this custom was regarded as being unseemly. The making of the statue of the woman with the issue of blood appeared to Eusebius as having need of an excuse; that excuse was that the woman who witnessed thus belief in Christ acted from a remnant of Pagan habit and by a pardonable confusion of ideas. Otherwise Eusebius repelled as entirely profane the desire to have portraits of Jesus.

The arcosolia of the tombs some called pictures. They were made at first purely decorative, destitute of all religious significance; vines, leaves, vases, fruits, birds. Then Christian symbols were mixed with these; then they painted some simple scenes, borrowed from the Bible, and in which a special delight was found in the time of persecution; such as Jonah under his gourd, or Daniel in the den of lions, Noah and his dove, Psyche, Moses drawing water from the rock, Orpheus charming the beasts with his lyre, and especially the Good Shepherd, in which they could only copy one of the most widely spread types of Pagan art. The historical subjects of the Old and New Testaments did not appear till most recent times. The table, the sacred bread, the mystic fishes, some scene of angling, the symbolism of the supper, are, on the contrary, represented from the third century.

All this little painting of ornament, excluded still from the churches, and which was not tolerated because it tended to precedent, had absolutely nothing original in it. It would be wrong to see in those timid essays the principle of a new art. The expression was feeble; the Christian idea totally absent; the countenance generally undecided. The execution was not bad; there were some artists who had received a good enough instruction in the studio. It is very superior in any case to that which is found in the real Christian painting which was born much later. But what a difference in the expression! Among the artists of the seventh and eighth centuries one can follow a powerful effort to introduce into the scenes represented a new sentiment; the material means were quite wanting. The artists of the catacombs, on the contrary, are painters of the Pompeian kind, converted by some motives entirely foreign to art, and who apply their skill to what is suitable to the austere places which they decorate.

The Gospel history was only treated by the first Christian painters partially and slowly. It is here especially that the Gnostic origin may be seen with clearness. The life of Jesus, which the ancient Christian painters present, is exactly that which the Gnostics and the Docetists have set forth, that is to say, that the passion does not appear there. From the Prætorium to the resurrection all the details are suppressed, the Christ in this order of ideas not having really suffered. They disembarrassed themselves thus of the shame of the cross--a great scandal to the Pagans. At that time there were Pagans who pointed to the God of the Christians with derision as the crucified; the Christians defended themselves from this. By representing a crucifix they were afraid of provoking the blasphemies of the enemy, and to appear wedded to their own opinions. Christian art was born heretical; it bears traces of that for a long time; Christian iconography disengaged itself from the prejudices among which it was born. It only leaves it to submit to the apocryphal, themselves more or less born under a Gnostic influence. Hence a situation for a long time false. Even fully up to the Middle Ages some doctors of authority condemned art; art on its side even ranked with orthodoxy--permitted itself strange liberties. Its favourite subjects were borrowed from the condemned books, so much so that the representatives forced the gates of the church when the book which explained them had been for a long time expelled. In the west in the thirteenth century art emancipated itself all at once, but it was not the same in Oriental Christianity. The Greek Church and the Oriental churches never triumphed completely over that antipathy to images which has been carried to its acme in Judaism and Islamism. They condemned the relief, and shut themselves up into a hieratic imagery, out of which serious art shall have much difficulty to emerge.

We cannot see that in private life Christians made any scruple of using the products of ordinary industry, which bore no representation shocking to them. Soon, nevertheless, there were Christian workmen who, even on the usual objects, replaced the ancient ornaments by images appropriate to the taste of the sect (Good Shepherd, a dove, a fish, a ship, a lyre, an anchor). A sacred guild of gold-smiths and glass-workers was formed especially for the necessities of the supper. Ordinary lamps bore nearly all the Pagan emblems; there was soon in trade lamps with the representation of the Good Shepherd, which probably came from the same workshop as the lamps with the representations of Bacchus or Serapis. The sculptured sarcophagi, representing sacred scenes, appeared about the end of the third century. Like the Christian paintings, they did not differ except in the subject from the styles of the Pagan art of the same period.

CHAPTER XXX

CHRISTIAN MANNERS

The manners of the Christians were the best preaching of Christianity. One word summed them up--piety. It was the life of good little people without worldly prejudices, but of a perfect honesty. The Messianic expectation grew weaker every day, and they passed from the somewhat strained morality, which was suitable to a state of crisis, to the stable morality of a settled society. Marriage was invested with a high religious character. They did not require to abolish polygamy; the Jewish manners, if not the Jewish law, had, in fact, nearly suppressed that. The harem was not, to tell the truth, among the ancient Jews but an exceptional abuse--a privilege of royalty. The prophets always showed themselves hostile to it; the practice of Solomon and his imitators was a subject of blame and scandal. In the first centuries of our era the cases of polygamy became very rare among the Jews; neither the Christians nor the Pagans reproached them with it. By the double influence of the Roman and Jewish marriage, there arose also that high ideal of the family which is still in our days the basis of European civilisation, so much so that it has become an essential part of natural law. It is necessary to recognise nevertheless that upon this point the Roman influence was superior to the Jewish influence, since it is only through the influence of the modern codes, drawn from the Roman law, that polygamy has disappeared from among the Jews.

The Roman, or it may be the Aryan influence, is also more traceable than the Jewish influence in the disfavour with which second marriages were regarded. These appear to them like an adultery decently disguised. As to the question of divorce, in which certain Jewish schools had yielded a blamable relaxation, they did not show themselves less strict. Marriage could not be broken but by the adultery of the wives. Not to separate "that which God has united" became the basis of the Christian law. At last the Church placed itself in full contradiction to Judaism by the fact of considering celibacy and virginity as a preferable state to marriage. Here Christianity, preceded, besides, in that by the Therapeutists, came near no doubt to the ideas which among the ancient Aryan peoples presented the virgin as a sacred being. The synagogue always held marriage as obligatory; in its eyes the celibate is guilty of homicide; he is not of the race of Adam, for man is not complete except when he is united to the woman; marriage ought not to be deferred after the age of eighteen. They made an exception to him who gave himself up to the study of the law, and who feared that the necessity of ministering to the needs of a family would take him from his work. "Let those who are not like me, absorbed by the law, people the earth," said Rabbi ben Azai.

The Christian sects which remained connected with Judaism advised, like the synagogue, early marriages, and even wished that the pastors should keep an eye open upon the old men that they might be restrained from the danger of adultery. All at once, however, Christianity turned to the opinion of Ben Azai. Jesus, although he lived for more than thirty years, had never married. The expectation of an approaching end of the world rendered useless the desire for children, and the idea was established that there is no perfect Christian except through virginity. "The patriarchs had reason to see to the multiplication of their posterity; the world was young then; now, on the contrary, all things were declining and drawing to their close." The Gnostic and Manichean sects were only consistent in forbidding marriage and the act of generation. The orthodox Church, always moderate, avoided this extreme; but continence, even chastity in marriage, were recommended, and excessive shame attached to the execution of the natural desires; women took a foolish horror of marriage; the shocking timidity of the Church in everything relating to the legitimate relations of the two sexes shall provoke one day more than one well-founded jest.

Following the same current of ideas the state of widowhood was looked upon as sacred; the widows constituted an ecclesiastical order. Woman must always be subject; when she has no longer a husband to obey, she serves the Church. The modesty of Christian ladies answered to these severe principles, and in many communities they did not go out without being veiled. The custom of the veil covering the whole figure in the fashion of the East did not become universal for young or unmarried women. The Montanists looked upon this custom as obligatory; if it did not prevail it was because of the opposition which the excesses of the Phrygian or African sectaries provoked, and especially by the influence of Greek and Latin countries, which had no need to found a true reformation of manners on this hideous mark of physical and moral weakness.

Ornaments at least were entirely forbidden. Beauty is a temptation of Satan. Why add to the temptation? The use of jewels, of paint, of dye for the hair, and of transparent garments, was an offence against modesty. False hair was a still graver sin; it lost the benediction of the priest, which, falling upon dead hair taken from another head, could not tell where to rest. Indeed, the most modest arrangements of the hair were held to be dangerous. St. Jerome, going farther, considered women's hair as a simple nest for vermin, and recommended its being cut off.

The defect of Christianity appeared to be here. It was too singularly moral; beauty, according to it, is to be entirely sacrificed. Now, in the eyes of a complete philosophy, beauty, far from being a superficial advantage, a danger, an inconvenience, is a gift of God, like virtue. It is as good as virtue; the beautiful woman expresses an aspect of the divine purpose, one of the designs of God, like the man of genius or the virtuous woman. It knows him, and hence its pride. It feels instinctively the treasure which it bears in its body; it knows well that, without mind, talent, or great virtue, it is reckoned among the first manifestations of God. And why forbid her from putting into use the gift which has been given her, to set the diamond which has been cut? The woman by adorning herself accomplishes a duty; she practises an art, an exquisite art, in one sense the most charming of arts. We do not allow ourselves to be misled by the smile which certain words provoke among frivolous people. We decree the palm of genius to the Greek artist who knew how to solve the most delicate of problems, to ornament the human body, that is to say, to adorn perfection itself; and we do not see only a question of frippery in the attempt to work together in the finest work of God, in the beauty of woman! The toilette of the woman, with all its refinements, is a grand art in its way. The centuries and the countries which have succeeded in that are the great centuries, the great countries; and Christianity showed, by the exclusion with which it marked that kind of elegance, that the social idea it conceived would not become the framework of a complete society, as, indeed, it did later on, when the revolt of people of the world should have broken the firm yoke primitively imposed upon the sect by an exalted pietism.

It was, to tell the truth, everything which could be called luxury and worldly life which we see marked as forbidden. Spectacles were held as abominable and indecent, not only the bloody spectacles of the theatre, which all honest people detested, but even the more innocent spectacles. Every theatre, if for this only, that men and women assembled there to see and to be seen, is a dangerous place. There was no less horror for the thermæ, the gymnasia, the baths and the xysts, because of the nudities they produced. Christianity inherited there a Jewish sentiment. The public places were avoided by the Jews, because of circumcision, which exposed them to all sorts of disagreeables. If the games, the concourse, which make for a single day a mortal equal to the gods, and of which inscriptions preserve the memory, quite disappeared in the third century, Christianity was the cause of it. A blank was made by the disappearance of these ancient institutions; they taxed them with vanity. They were right; but human life is over when one has succeeded too well in proving to man that all is vanity.

The sobriety of the Christians equalled their modesty. The prescriptions relating to meats were nearly all suppressed; the principle "to the pure all things are pure" prevailed. Many, nevertheless, imposed abstinence from things that have had life. Fasts were frequent, and caused among many that nervous debility which caused many tears to flow. Readiness to weep was considered a heavenly favour, the gift of tears. The Christians wept unceasingly; a sort of sweet sadness was their habitual condition. In the churches, gentleness, piety, and love were marked on their faces. The rigorists complained that often, in leaving the holy place, that meditative attitude gave place to discipline; but in general they recognised the Christians by nothing but their air. They had in some sort some faces apart, good faces, impressed by a calm, not excluding the smile of an amiable contentment. That made a sensible contrast to the easy appearance of the Pagans, which often was wanting in distinction and reserve. In Montanist Africa, certain practices, in particular that of making at every turn the sign of the cross on the forehead, revealed still more clearly the disciples of Jesus.

The Christian was then essentially a separate being, vowed to a profession quite external to virtue, an ascetic indeed. If monastic life only appears about the end of the third century, it is because up till then the Church was a true monastery, an ideal city where perfect life was practised. When the century shall enter en masse into the Church, when the Council of Gangres in 325 shall have declared that the maxims of the Church upon poverty, upon renunciation of the family, and on virginity, are not addressed to the simple believers, the perfect ones shall create certain separate places, where the evangelical life, too high for common men, can be practised without reserve. Martyrdom had presented till then the means of putting in practice the most exaggerated precepts of Christ, particularly on the despising of the affections of blood relationship; the monastery will take the place of martyrdom, so that the counsel of Jesus may be practised somewhere. The example of Egypt, where the monastic life had always existed, might contribute to that result; but monachism was in the very essence of Christianity. Since the Church was opened to all, it was inevitable that there should be formed little churches for those who claimed to live as Jesus and the apostles at Jerusalem had lived.

A great struggle was thus indicated for the future. Christian piety and worldly honour shall be two antagonists which will rudely fight with each other. The awakening of the worldly spirit shall be the awakening of unbelief. Honour will be revolted, and maintain that it values more that morality which permits a man to be a saint without being always a gallant man. There shall be the voice of the sirens to rehabilitate all those exquisite things which the Church has declared profane in the first days. The Church, an association of holy people, shall preserve that character in spite of all its transformations. The worldling shall be its worst enemy. Voltaire will show that these diabolic frivolities, so severely excluded from a pietistic society, are in their way both good and necessary. Father Canaye will try indeed to show that. nothing is more gallant than Christianity, and that no one is more a gentleman than a Jesuit. He will not convince Hocquincourt. In any case, the people of mind will be unconvertible. They will never induce Ninon de l'Enclos, Saint-Evremond, Voltaire, Merimée, to be of the same religion as Tertullian, Clement of Alexandria, and the good Hermas.

CHAPTER XXXI

REASONS FOR THE VICTORY OF CHRISTIANITY

It is by the new discipline of life which it introduced into the world that Christianity conquered. The world had need of a moral reformation; philosophy did not provide it; the established religions in the Greek and Latin countries were struck by incapacity to improve man. Among all the religious institutions of the ancient world, Judaism alone raised against the corruption of the times a cry of despair. Eternal and unique glory this, which ought to make one forget even its follies and its violence! The Jews are the revolutionaries of the first and second centuries of our era. Respect their fever! Possessed by a high ideal of justice, convinced that this ideal ought to be realised on this earth, not admitting these compositions with which those who believe in Paradise and hell content themselves so readily, they had a hunger for good, and they conceived of it under the form of a little synagogical life of which the Christian life is only the ascetic transformation. Some numerous little groups of humble and pious people, leading among them a pure life, and awaiting together the great day which shall be their triumph, and shall inaugurate upon the earth the reign of the saints--that is, budding Christianity. The happiness which they enjoyed in these little guest-chambers became a powerful attraction. The people threw themselves by a sort of instinctive movement into a sect which satisfied their innermost aspirations, and opened up infinite hopes.

The intellectual exigencies of the time were very weak; the tender necessities of the heart were most imperious. Minds did not shine, but manners were sweetened. A religion was desired which should teach piety, myths which offered good examples, capable of being imitated, a sort of morality in action provided by the gods. An honest religion was desired, for Paganism was not that. Moral preaching proposes deism or monotheism; polytheism has never been a worship tending to morality. It was desired specially to have some assurances for a further life where the injustices of this should be repaired. The religion which promises immortality, and assures us that one day we shall see again those whom we have loved, always succeeds. "Those who have no hope" are very quickly conquered. A crowd of brotherhoods, where those consoling beliefs were professed, drew numerous adherents. Such were the Sabazian and Orphic mysteries in Macedonia, in Thrace the mysteries of Dionysius. In the second century, the symbols of Psyche took a funereal sense, and became a little religion of immortality, which the Christians adopted with earnestness. Ideas as to the other life, alas! as everything which is a matter of taste and sentiment, are those which subdue most easily the caprices of the world. The pictures which on this point have for a moment contented us pass quickly away; in making dreams beyond the tomb, we wish always something new, for nothing can long bear investigation. The established religion did not therefore give any satisfaction to the deep necessities of the age. The old god was neither good nor bad; he was a force. With time the adventures which were accounted concerning these divinities became immoral. The worship bordered on the grossest idolatry, sometimes the most ridiculous. It was not rare for philosophers in public to deliver themselves of attacks against the official religion, and that amid the applause of their auditors. The government, by wishing to mix themselves up with it, only brought it to the ground. The divinities of Greece, so long identified with the divinities of Rome, had their place by right in the Pantheon. The barbarian divinities suffered analogous identifications, and became Jupiters, Apollos, and Esculapiuses. As to the local divinities, they were saved by the cult of the Lares gods. Augustus had introduced into the religion a very considerable change, by restoring and regulating the cult of the Lares gods, especially the Lares of the streets, and by permitting to be joined to the two Lares consecrated by custom a third Lare, the Genius of the Emperor. The Lares gained by this association the epithet of August (Lares Augusti), and, as the local gods retained for the most part their legal right to their title of Lares, nearly all were thus described as August (numina augusta). Around this complex worship a clergy was formed, composed of the Flamen, a sort of archbishop representing the State, and some august sevirs, corporations of workmen and little tradesmen specially attached to Lares or local divinities. But the Genius of the Emperor naturally bore down its neighbours; the true religion of the State was the religion of Rome, of the emperor, and of the administration. The Lares remained very little personages. Jehovah, the only local god who resisted obstinately the august association, and whom it was impossible to transform into an innocent fetish of the cross, killed both the divinity of Augustus and all the other gods who lent themselves so easily to become the panders to tyranny. The struggle was from that point established between Judaism and the oddly-amalgamated cult which Rome sought to impose. Rome shall be stranded on this point. Rome shall give to the world government, civilisation, law, and the arts of administration; but it shall not give it religion. The religion which shall spread itself apparently in spite of Rome, in reality thanks to it, shall be in no wise the religion of Latium, or the religion patched up by Augustus; it shall be the religion which Rome has so often believed it has destroyed--the religion of Jehovah.

We have referred to the noble efforts of philosophy to meet the exigencies of the soul which religion no longer satisfied. Philosophy had seen everything and expressed everything in exquisite language; but it was necessary that this should be said under a popular, that is to say, a religious form. Religious movements are only made by priests; philosophy has too much reason. The reward she offers is not tangible enough. The poor, the person without instruction, who cannot approach it, are really without religion and without hope. Man is born so mediocre that he is not good except when he dreams. He needs some illusions that he may do what he ought to do for the love of good. This slave has need of fear and of lies to make him perform his duty. We can only obtain sacrifices from the masses by promising that they shall be paid in return. The self-denial of the Christian is nothing after all but a clever calculation, a placing of the Kingdom of God before the vision. Reason will always have few martyrs. We only devote ourselves for what we believe. Now, what we believe is the uncertain, the unreasonable; we submit to the reasonable, we do not believe it. That is why reason does not impel to action, it rather impels to abstention. No great revolution has been produced in humanity without very distinct ideas, without prejudices, without dogmatism; we are not strong except in the condition of deceiving ourselves with the whole world. Stoicism besides implied an error which injured it much before the people. In its eyes virtue and moral sentiment are identical. Christianity distinguishes between these two things. Jesus loves the prodigal son, the harlot, souls good at bottom, although sinners. To the Stoics all sins are equal; sin is unpardonable. Christianity has pardon for all crimes. The more one has sinned, the more it is his. Constantine shall become a Christian because he believes that the Christians alone have expiation for the murder of a son by his father. The success which at the beginning of the second century shall attend. the hideous bullock sacrifices, from which people came covered with blood, proves how the imagination of the time was set upon finding means to appease the gods who were supposed to be angry. The bullock sacrifice is, among all the Pagan rites, that which the Christians most dreaded as competing with them. It was in some sects the last effort of expiring Paganism against the merit, each day more triumphant, of the blood of Jesus. We might have hoped one moment that the confraternities of cultores deorum would give the people the religious aliment which they needed. The second century saw their rise and their decadence. The religious character disappeared then little by little. In certain countries they lost even their funereal destination and became Tontines, treasuries of assurance and retreat, associations for mutual help. Alone, the colleges devoted to the worship of the Oriental gods (religious pastophores, isiastes, dendrophores, of the Great Mother) kept some devotees. It is evident that these gods spoke much more to the religious sentiment than the Greek and Italian gods. People grouped themselves around them; their faithful became quickly brothers and friends, while men scarcely grouped themselves at all, at least in heart, around the official gods. In religion there are but few sects which cannot succeed in founding something.

It is so pleasant to regard ourselves as a little aristocracy of the truth, to believe that we possess, along with a group of the privileged, the treasure of goodness. Pride is found here; the Jew, the metuali of Syria humbled, ashamed of everything, are at bottom impertinent and disdainful. No affront hurts them, they are so proud among themselves of being the elect people. In our days such a miserable association of minds gives more consolation to its members than healthy philosophy. A mass of people find happiness in these chimeras, and attach their moral life to them. In its day the abracadabra procured religious pleasures, and with a little willingness we could find there a sublime theology.

The worship of Isis had its regular inroads into Greece from the fourth century before Jesus Christ. All the Greek and Roman world was literally overrun. This worship, such as we see it represented in the paintings of Pompeii and Herculaneum, with its tonsured and beardless priests, clothed with a kind of alb, resemble much our "offices." Every morning the timbrel, like the clock of our parishes, calls the devotees to a sort of mass accompanied by a sermon, prayers for the emperor and the empire, sprinklings with the water of the Nile. Ite missa est. In the evening the salutation takes place, they wish good night to the goddess, they kiss her feet. There were some bizarre, some ridiculous processions in the streets, where the brothers carried their gods upon their shoulders. At other times they begged in a foreign dress, which made the true Romans laugh. That resembled much the brotherhoods of penitents in southern countries. The Isaists had their heads shaved. They were clad in a linen tunic, in which they wished to be buried. There were some miracles added to this little society, some sermons, a "taking of the habit," ardent prayers, baptisms, confessions and bloody penances. After the initiation a lively devotion took place like that of the Middle Ages towards the Virgin; they felt a pleasure in nothing but seeing the image of the goddess. The purifications, the expiations kept the soul awake. It established, especially among the assistants in these pious comedies, a tender feeling of brotherhood; they became father, son, brother, sister to each other. These little freemasonries, with some passwords, such as IXΘXC of the Christians, created deep and secret bonds.

Osiris, Serapis, and Anubis shared the favour of Isis. Serapis in particular, identified with Jupiter, became one of the Divine names which the most of those who aspired to a certain Monotheism, and especially to intimate relations with heaven, affected. The Egyptian god has a real presence, they see him unceasingly; he communicates with them by dreams and by continual apparitions; religion in that way is a perpetual sacred kiss between the faithful and his deity. They were especially women who leant towards these foreign cults. The national worship was cold to them. The courtesans, notably, were nearly all devoted to Isis and Serapis; the temples of Isis were looked upon as places for amorous meetings. The idols in this sort of chapels were adorned like the Madonnas. Women had a part in the ministry, they bore sacred titles. Everything showed devotion, and contributed to the excitement of the senses: weepings, passionate chants, dances to the sound of the flute, representations commemorative of the death and resurrection of a god. The moral discipline, without being serious, had the appearance of it. There were fasts, austerities, and days of continence. Ovid and Tibullus complain of the injury which these enchantments did to their amusements, in a tone which shows that the goddess asked nothing of these devoted beauties except the most limited mortifications.

A multitude of other gods were accepted without opposition, even with welcome. The heavenly Juno, the Asiatic Bellona, Sabazius, Adonis, the goddess of Syria, had their believers. The soldiers were the vehicle of these different cults, thanks to the habit they had of embracing one after another the religions of the countries through which they passed. Coming home, they consecrated a temple, an altar to their recollections of the garrison. Hence these dedications to Jupiter of Baal-bek, to Jupiter of Dolica, which are found in all parts of the empire. An oriental god especially held for a moment in the balance the fate of Christendom, and became the object of one of those cults of universal propaganda which seize upon the entire portions of humanity. Mitra is in Arian primitive mythology one of the names of the sun. This name became among the Persians of the Achemeniidan times a god of the first order. We hear mention of him for the first time in the Græco-Roman world about the year 70 before Christ. The fashion gradually leant towards him; it is only in the second and third century that the worship of Mithra, knowingly organised upon the type of the mysteries which had already so deeply moved ancient Greece, obtained an extraordinary success.

The resemblances of this cult to Christianity were so striking that St. Justin and Tertullian saw in it a Satanic plagiarism. Mithraism had baptism, the eucharist, the agapes, penitence, expiations and anointings. Its chapels much resembled little churches. It created a bond of brotherhood among the initiated. We have said it twenty times, it was the great need of the age. Congregations were desired where people could love each other, sustain each other, observe one another, some brotherhoods offering a narrow field (for man is not perfect) for all sorts of little vain pursuits, the inoffensive development of childish ambitions in the synagogues. From many other points of view, Mithraism resembled freemasonry. There were certain grades, orders of initiation, bearing odd names, some gradual trials, a fast of fifty days, terrors and flagellations. A lively piety was developed through these exercises. They believed in the immortality of the initiated, in a paradise for pure souls. The mystery of the cup, so like the Christian Supper, certain evening gatherings analogous to those of our pious congregations, in "caves" or "little oratories," a numerous clergy, to which women were admitted, some expiations by the sacrifice of bullocks, frightful, but thrilling, answered well to the aspirations of the Roman world towards a sort of materialistic religiosity. The immorality of the Phrygian Sabazites had not disappeared, but was marked by a veneer of pantheism and mysticity, sometimes by a quiet scepticism in the style of Ecclesiastes.

We may say that if Christianity had been arrested in its growth by some mortal malady, the world would have been Mithraistic. Mithra lent himself to all the confusions, with Attis, with Adonis, with Sabazius, with Mên, who had been already in possession for a long time back, to make the tears of women flow. The soldiers also affected this worship. In going back to their homes, they carried it to the frontier on the Rhine and the Danube. Thus Mithraism resisted Christianity more than the other cults. It needed, to destroy it, the terrible blows struck at it by the Christian empire. It was in the year 376 that we find the greatest number of monuments raised by the adorers of the great goddess of Mithra. Some very respectable senatorial families remaining attached to her rebuilt at their own expense the destroyed altars, and, by force of legacies and foundation, essayed to give eternity to a religion which was moribund.

The mysteries were the ordinary form of these exotic cults and the principal cause of their success. The impressions which the initiations left were very deep, like that of freemasonry in our day; although it was clumsy, it served as an aliment for the soul. It was a sort of first communion; one day, there was a pure being, privileged, presented to the pious public as a blessed one, as a saint, with the head crown, and a taper in the hand. Some strange spectacles, some appearances of gigantic puppets, some alternations of light and darkness, visions of the other life which they believed real, inspired a fervour of devotion whose souvenir was never effaced. There was mingled with them more of an equivocal

sentiment, whose evil manners of antiquity they abused. As in the Catholic confraternities, they
believed themselves bound by an oath; they held to it even when they scarcely believed it, for there was
attached to it the idea of a special favour, of a character which separated them from the vulgar. All these
Oriental cults involved more money than those of the West. The priests had there more importance than
in the Latin cult; they formed a clergy with different orders, a sacred soldiery, retired from the world,
having its own rules. These priests had a grave, and as we say now, an ecclesiastical air; they had the
tonsure, mitres, and a separate costume.

Religion founded like that of Apollonius of Tyana upon the belief in a journey upon the god to the
earth had special chances of success. Humanity seeks for the ideal; but it wishes the ideal to be a person,
it does not love an abstraction. A man-incarnation of the ideal, and whose biography would serve as a
framework to all the aspirations of the time, that is what religious opinion demanded. The gospel of
Apollonius of Tyana had only a half success; that of Jesus succeeded completely. The necessities of the
imagination and the heart which the nations cultivated were just those to which Christianity gave a
complete satisfaction. The objections which the Christian belief presents to minds led by rational culture
to the impossibility of admitting the supernatural did not then exist. Generally it is more difficult to
prevent a man from believing than to make him believe. No century indeed has ever been more
credulous than the second. Everybody admitted the miracles to be the most ridiculous; the current
mythology, having lost its primitive sense, reached the last limits of absurdity. The sense of the
sacrifices which Christianity demanded from reason were less than Paganism supposed. To be
converted to Christianity is not therefore an act of credulity; it is almost an act of relative good sense.
Indeed from the rationalist's point of view Christianity might be looked upon as an advancement; it was
the man religiously enlightened who adopted it. The believer in the ancient gods was the paganus, the
peasant always inclined against progress behind his age; as one day perhaps in the twentieth century the
last Christians will in their turn be called pagani, "rustics."

On two essential points, the worship of idols and the bloody sacrifices, Christianity answered to
the most advanced ideas of the time, as we would say to-day, and made a sort of junction with stoicism.
The absence of images which in the Christian worship on the part of the people made a kind of
accusation of atheism was pleasing to good minds revolted by the official idolatry. The bloody
sacrifices involved also the most offensive ideas as to the Divinity. The Essenes, the Elkasaïtes, the
Ebionites, and the Christians of every sect, inheritors in this of the ancient prophets, had on this point an
admirable sentiment of progress. Flesh was seen to be excluded even from the paschal feast. Thus the
pure worship was founded. The lower side of religion--these are the customs which have been
considered to operate themselves. Jesus, by the rôle there has been given him, if not by his personal act,
has marked the end of these practices. Why speak of sacrifices? That of Jesus is worth all the others. Of
the passover? Jesus is the true paschal lamb. Of the Thora? The example of Jesus is worth much more. It
is by this reasoning that St. Paul has destroyed the law--that Protestantism has killed Catholicism. The
faith in Jesus has thus replaced everything. The very excesses of Christianity have been the principle of
its force; by this dogma that Jesus has done all for the justification of his faithful, works have been put
aside as useless, every other worship than the faith has been discouraged.

Christianity had therefore an immense superiority over the religion of the State which Rome
patronised and over the different religions she tolerated. The Pagans comprehended it vaguely.
Alexander Severus having had the idea of raising a temple to Christ, they brought before him some old
sacred texts from which it was made plain that if he followed out his idea all would become Christians,
and that the other temples would be abandoned. In vain Julian shall try to apply to the official cult the
organisation which made the strength of the Church; Paganism shall resist a transformation contrary to
its nature. Christianity shall impose itself over the whole empire. The religion which Rome will spread
in the world shall be just that which she has the most strongly combated, Judaism under the Christian
form. Far from being surprised at the success in the Roman empire, it is much more astonishing that this
revolution has been so slow in being accomplished.

That which was deeply affected by Christianity was the maxims of the State, the basis of Roman
polity. These maxims defended themselves vigorously during a hundred and fifty years, and retarded the
coming of the worship destined to victory. But that coming was inevitable. Melito was right.
Christianity was destined to be the religion of the Roman Empire. The West still showed itself
refractory; Asia Minor and Syria, on the contrary, reckoned dense masses of Christian populations,
increasing every day in political importance. The centre of gravity of the empire drew them from that
side; they felt already that an ambitious man would have the temptation to sustain himself upon these
crowds which mendicity placed in the hands of the Church, and which the Church in its turn would
place in the hand of the Cwsar who should be the most favourable to it. The political position of the
bishop does not date from Constantine. From the third century the bishop of the great towns of the east
is shown us as a personage analogous to what in our days the bishop is in Turkey, among the Christian
Greeks, Armenians, &c. The depôts of the faithful, the testaments, the tutorship of pupils, processes, all
the administration, in a word, are confided to him. He is a magistrate alongside of the public

magistrature, benefiting by all the faults of that institution. The Church in the third century is already a vast agency of popular interests. It is felt that one day, when the empire falls, the bishop will be its heir. When the State refuses to occupy itself with social problems, these shall solve themselves apart by means of associations which demolish the empire.

The glory of Rome is to have attempted to solve the problem of human society without theocracy, without supernatural dogma. Judaism, Christianity, Islamism, and Buddhism are, on the contrary, great institutions, embracing the whole human life under the form of revealed religions. These religions are human society itself; nothing exists outside of them. The triumph of Christianity was the extinction of civil life for a thousand years. The Church is the community, if you will, but under a religious form. To be a member of that commune it is not enough to be born; a metaphysical dogma must be professed, and if your mind refuses to believe that dogma, so much the worse for you. Islamism only applies the same principle. The mosque, like the synagogue and the Church, is the centre of all life. The Middle Ages, ruled by Christianity, Islamism, and Buddhism, are indeed the era of the theocracy. The stroke of genius of the Renaissance has been to return to the Roman law, which is essentially the laic law--to return to philosophy, science, true art, and reason outside of all revelation. Let us keep it there. The supreme goal of humanity is the liberty of the individual. Now the theocracy and revelation never will create liberty. The theocracy made of the man clothed with power a functionary of God; reason makes of him a mainstay of the wills and the rights of each.

CHAPTER XXXII

SOCIAL AND POLITICAL REVOLUTION ADVANCED BY CHRISTIANITY

Thus in degree as the empire fell Christianity arose. During the third century Christianity sucked ancient society like a vampire, drawing out all its forces and creating that general enervation against which the patriotic empires vainly struggled. Christianity had no need to attack it with lively vigour; it had only to shut itself up in its churches. It revenged itself by not serving the State, for it kept nearly to itself alone certain principles without which the State cannot prosper. It is the grand battle which we see to-day waged in the State by our Conservatives. The army, the magistracy, the public services, require a certain amount of seriousness and honesty. Where the classes which can furnish that seriousness shut themselves up in abstention, the whole body suffers.

The Church in the third century, by monopolising life, drained civil society, bled it, made it empty. The little societies killed the great society. The ancient life, a life all exterior and manly; a life of glory, of heroism, of patriotism; a life of the forum, the theatre, and the gymnasium is conquered by the Jewish life--a life anti-military, a friend of shade, a life of pale immured people. Politics are not served by men too much withdrawn from the world. When a man decides to aspire only to heaven, he is no longer of the country here below. A nation cannot be made up of monks, or of Yoguis; the hatred and despisal of the world do not prepare for the struggle of life. India, which of all known countries is the most versed in asceticism, has not been since time immemorial anything but a land open to all conquerors. It was the same in some respect with Egypt. The inevitable consequence of asceticism is to make one consider everything which is not religious frivolous and inferior. The sovereign, the warrior, compared with the priest, are only rustic and brutal; civil order is taken for a vexatious tyranny. Christianity softened the manners of the ancient world; but, from the military and patriotic point of view, it destroyed the ancient world. The city and the State will not accommodate themselves later on to Christianity otherwise than by making it submit to the most profound modifications.

"They dwell on the earth," said the author of the Epistle to Diognetes, "but really their country is in heaven." When they ask the martyr as to his country, "I am a Christian," he says. The country and the civil laws, behold the mother, the father, which the true Gnostic, according to Clement of Alexandria, ought to despise that he may sit down at the right hand of God. The Christian is embarrassed, incapable, when the affairs of the world are concerned; the Gospel found believers, not citizens. It was the same of Islamism and Buddhism. The advent of these great universal religions puts an end to the old idea of native country: one was no longer a Roman, an Athenian; they were Christian, Mussulmans and Buddhists. Men henceforth are to be taught according to their cult, not according to their native land; they shall divide over heresies, not over questions of nationality.

This is what Marcus-Aurelius saw perfectly, and this renders him so favourable to Christianity. The Church appeared to him a State in a State. "The camp of piety," that new "system of native land founded on the divine Logos," had nothing to see in the Roman camp, which does not pretend to form subjects for heaven. The Church, in fact, avows itself to be a complete society, quite superior to civil society: the pastor is worth more than the magistrate. The Church is the native land of the Christian, as the synagogue is the native country of the Jew: the Christian and the Jew live in the country where they look upon themselves as strangers. The Christian has scarcely any father or mother. He owes nothing to the empire, but the empire owes everything to him, for it is the presence of the faithful scattered through the Roman world which stays the heavenly anger, and saves the State from its ruin. The Christian does not rejoice in the victories of the empire; the public disasters appear to him a confirmation of the prophecies which condemn the world to perish by the barbarians and by fire. The cosmopolitanism of the Stoics has as many dangers; but an ardent love of civilisation and of Greek culture served as the counterpoise to the excess of their indifference.

In many points of view, certainly, the Christians were loyal subjects. They never revolted; they prayed for their persecutors. In spite of their complaints against Marcus-Aurelius, they did not take any part in the revolt of Avidius Cassius. They affected the principles of the most complete legitimism. God giving power to whom he pleases, it is necessary to obey, without examination, him who possesses it officially. But this apparent political orthodoxy was at bottom only the cult of success. "There has never been among us any partisan of Albin, or of Niger," said Tertullian with ostentation, under the reign of

Septimus Severus. But, really, in what was Septimus Severus more legitimate than Albin, and than Pescennius Niger? He succeeded better than they, that is all. The Christian principle, "We must acknowledge him who exercises the power," ought to contribute to establish the worship of an accomplished fact, that is to say, the worship of force. Liberal policy owes nothing, and will never owe anything, to Christianity. The idea of representative government is the contrary of that which Jesus, St. Peter, and Clement of Rome expressly professed.

The most important of civic duties, military service, the Christians could not fulfil. That service implied, besides the necessity of shedding blood, which appeared criminal to the enthusiasts, certain acts which timorous consciences considered idolatrous. There were, no doubt, many Christian soldiers in the second century; but very quickly the incompatibility of the two professions disclosed itself, and the soldier laid down his sword or became a martyr. The antipathy was decided; in becoming a Christian, he quitted the army. "One cannot serve two masters," was the principle repeated without ceasing. The representation of a sword or a bow on a ring was forbidden. "It is the same to fight for the emperor as to pray for him." The grand weakness which was remarked in the Roman at the end of the second century, and which is visible especially in the third century, has its cause in Christianity. Celsus perceived the truth here with wonderful sagacity. The military courage which, according to the German, alone can open the Walhalla, is not in itself a virtue in the eyes of the Christian. If it is employed for a good cause, it is right; if not, it is only barbarity. Certainly a man very brave in war may be a man of mediocre morality; but a society of perfect people would be so weak! By being too consistent, the Christian East lost all military valour. Islam has profited by it, and has given to the world the melancholy spectacle of that eternal Christian of the East, always the same in spite of the difference of race, always beaten, always massacred, perpetually offering its neck to the sabre, a very uninteresting victim, for he does not revolt and does not know how to hold a weapon even when one puts it into his hand.

The Christian shunned likewise the magistracy, the public offices, and civil honours. To pursue these honours, to exercise ambition for these functions, or only to accept them, was to give a mark of faith in a world which, as principles, they declared condemned and stained by idolatry to the very depths. A law of Septimus Severus permits the "adherents of the Jewish superstition" to attain to honours with a dispensation from obligations contrary to their creed. The Christians could certainly have profited by these dispensations; they did not. To crown one's door with the announcement of festival days, to take part in the amusements and public rejoicings, was apostasy. They were even forbidden to go to the tribunals. Christians ought never to carry their cases there, they ought to hand them over to their pastors for arbitration. The impossibility of mixed marriages erected a wall that was insurmountable between the Church and the society. It was forbidden to the faithful to promenade in the streets, or to mingle in public conversations; they must live only among themselves. Even the taverns could not be in common: Christians on a journey went to the church, and there shared in the agapes, in the distributions of the remainder of the sacred offerings.

A crowd of arts and trades, whose profession drew with it association with idolatry, were forbidden to the Christians. Sculpture and painting, especially, came nearly to be objectless; they were treated as enemies. Here is the explanation of one of the most singular facts of history--I mean the disappearance of sculpture in the first half of the third century. What Christianity killed first in the old civilisation was art. It slowly killed riches, but in that respect its action has not been less decisive. Christianity was, before everything, an immense economic revolution. The first became the last, and the last first. That was really the realisation of the kingdom of God, according to the Jews. One day Rab Joseph, son of Rab Josua Ben Levi, having fallen into a lethargy, his father asked him, when he came to himself, "What have you seen in heaven, my son?" "I have seen," replied Joseph, "the world upside down; the most powerful were in the last rank; the most humble in the first." "It is the normal world which you have seen, my son."

The Roman empire, by humbling the nobility and by reducing almost to nothing the privilege of blood, increased, on the other hand, the advantages of chance. Far from establishing effective equality among the citizens, the Roman empire, opening to two knockers the doors of the Roman city, created a deep difference -- that of honestiores (the notables, the rich) and the humiliores or tenuiores (the poor). In proclaiming the equality of all, they introduced inequality into the law, especially the penal law. Poverty rendered the title of "Roman citizen " nearly useless, and the great majority were poor. The error of Greece, which had been to despise the workman and the peasant, had not disappeared. Christianity at first did nothing for the peasant; it even hurt the rural populations by the institution of the episcopate, in the influence and benefit of which the towns alone had part; but it had an influence of the first degree in the rehabilitation of the artisan. One of the recommendations which the Church made to the tradesman was to acquit himself in his occupation with taste and industry. The word operarius appears again; in their epitaphs the workman and workwoman are praised for having been good workers.

The workman honestly gaining his livelihood every day--this was indeed the Christian ideal.

Avarice was a supreme crime in the eyes of the Primitive Church. Now the most frequent avarice was simply economy. Almsgiving was a strict duty. Judaism had already a precept as to it. In the Psalms and prophetical books the ebion is the friend of God, and to give to the ebion is to give to God. Almsgiving in Hebrew is synonymous with justice (sedaka). The earnestness of pious people needed to be limited to justify itself in this way: one of the precepts of Ouscha forbids that more than a fifth of one's goods should be given to the poor. Christianity, which at its origin was a society of ebionim, fully accepted the idea that the rich, if he did not give of his superfluity, is keeping back the property of others. God gives all his creation to all. "Imitate the equality of God, and no one will be poor," we read in a text which was for some time held as sacred. The Church herself became an establishment of charity. The agapes and the distributions made of the superfluity of offerings kept the poor and travellers.

It was the rich man who all along the line was sacrificed. Few of the rich entered the Church, and their position there was most difficult. The poor, proud of the evangelical promises, treated them with an air which might appear arrogant. The rich man's fortune required to be pardoned, as if it were some derogation from the spirit of Christianity. By right the kingdom of God was closed to him, at least unless he purified his riches by almsgiving when he did not expiate it by martyrdom. They held him for an egotist, who fattened on the sweat of others. The community of goods, if it ever existed, existed no longer; it was called "the apostolic life," that is to say, the ideal of the Primitive Church of Jerusalem was a dream lost in the distance; but the property of the believer was only half property; he held little of it, and the Church really shared it as much as he.

It was in the fourth century that the struggle became great and desperate. The rich classes, nearly all attached to the ancient religion, fought energetically; but the poor carried the day. In the East, where the action of Christianity was even more complete, or rather, less opposed than in the West, there were scarcely any rich at the beginning of the middle of the fifth century. Syria, and especially Egypt, became quite ecclesiastical and monastic countries. The Church and the monastery--that is to say, the two forms of the community--were the only rich there. The Arabian conquest, throwing itself on these countries, after some battles on the frontier, found nothing more than a flock to lead away. Liberty of worship being once assured, the Christians of the East submitted to all tyrannies. In the West, the Germanic invasions and other causes did not allow pauperism to triumph completely. But human life was suspended for a thousand years. Great industry became impossible; consequently false ideas spread as to usury; all the operations of banking and assurance were interdicted. The Jew alone could handle money; they forced him to be rich; then they reproached him with that fortune to which they had condemned him. Here was the greatest error of Christianity. It would not have been so bad to say to the poor, instead of "Enrich yourselves at the expense of the rich," "Riches are nothing." It cut capital by the root; it forbade the most legitimate thing, the interest of money, by having the air of guaranteeing to the rich his riches; it took away its fruits from him; it rendered it unproductive. This fatal error spread across all the society of the Middle Ages, for the pretended crime of usury was the obstacle which opposed for more than ten centuries the progress of civilisation.

The amount of work in the world diminished considerably. Some countries, such as Syria, where the comfortable was not connected with so much pleasure as pain, and where slavery was a condition of material civilisation, were lowered to a considerable degree in the human ladder. The ancient ruins remained there like the vestiges of a world that had disappeared and had been misunderstood. The joys of the other life, not acquired by work, were dwelt upon as much as that which leads man to action. The bird of heaven, the lily do not toil nor spin, and yet they occupy through their beauty a rank of the first order in the hierarchy of creatures. Great is the joy of the poor when they thus announced to him happiness without work. The mendicant whom you tell that the world is going to be his, and that, passing his life in doing nothing, he is a noble in the Church, so much so that his prayers are the most efficacious of all--this mendicant soon becomes dangerous. We see this in the movements of the last Messianists of Tuscany. The peasants, indoctrinated by Lazaretti, having lost the habit of work, did not wish to resume their habitual life. As in Galilee, as in Umbria in the time of Francis d'Assisi, the people imagined that they could conquer heaven by poverty. After such dreams they did not resign themselves to take up the yoke again. They acted the apostle sooner than take up the chain which had been broken. It is so hard to bend every day under a humiliating and ungrateful task.

The goal of Christianity was not in any way the perfecting of human society, nor the increase of the sum of happiness of the individuals. Man strives to endure the least evil possible upon the earth when he looks seriously at the earth and the few days that he will pass there. But when he has been told that the earth is upon the point of finishing, and that life is nothing but a day's trial, the insignificant preface of an eternal idea, what good is there in beautifying it? They do not set themselves to adorn it, and to render comfortable the hovel where they must wait but an instant. It is especially in the relation of Christianity that this appears with clearness. Christianity eminently contributed to comfort the slave and to make his lot better. But it does not work directly to suppress slavery. We have seen that the great school of jurisconsultes, arising from the Antonines, is entirely possessed by this idea that slavery is an abuse which must be gently suppressed. Christianity never said, "Slavery is an abuse." Nevertheless, by its exalted idealism, it serves powerfully the philosophical tendency which for a long time back has made itself felt in the laws and manners.

Primitive Christianity was a movement essentially religious. Everything which in the social organisation of the time was not associated with idolatry appeared to it good to keep. The idea never came to the Christian doctors to protest against the established fact of slavery. That would have been a fashion of acting in a revolutionary way altogether contrary to their spirit. The rights of men were not in any way a Christian affair. St. Paul completely recognised the legitimacy of a master's position. No word occurs in all the ancient Christian literature to preach revolt to the slave, nor to advise the master to manumission, nor even to agitate the problem of public law which has been produced among us concerning slavery. There were some dangerous sectaries, like the Carpocratians, who spoke of suppressing the differences between people. The orthodox admitted the property as fixed, as it had for its object a man or a thing. The terrible lot of the slave does not touch them nearly so much as us. For the few hours that life lasts what matters the condition of man? "Hast thou been called a slave? care not for it; if thou canst free thyself, profit by it. . . . The slave is the Lord's freeman; the freeman is the slave of Christ. In Christ, there is no more Greek nor Jew, slave nor freeman, male nor woman." The words servus and libertus are extremely rare on the Christian tombs. The slave and the freeman are equally servus Dei, as the soldier is miles Christi. The slave, on another side, calls himself proudly the freeman of Jesus.

Submission and conscientious attachment of the slave towards the master, gentleness and brotherhood on the part of the slave--by this is bounded, in practice, the morality of primitive Christianity on this delicate point. The number of slaves and of freedmen was very considerable in the Church. Never is the master Christian, who has Christian slaves, counselled to free them: it is not forbidden even to use corporal chastisement towards them, and this is the nearly inevitable consequence of slavery. Under Constantine the favour of liberty appeared to retrograde. If the movement which dates from the Antonines had continued in the second half of the third century, and in the fourth century, the suppression of slavery would have come about as a legal measure and by redemption money. The ruin of the liberal polity, and the misfortunes of the times, caused all the ground which had been gained to be lost. The Fathers of the Church speak of the ignominy of slavery, and the baseness of slaves, in the same terms as the Pagans. John Chrysostom, in the fourth century, is almost the only doctor who formally counsels the master to enfranchise his slave as a good action. Later on the Church possessed slaves, and treated them like everybody else, that is to say, harshly. The condition of the Church slave was governed, indeed, by one circumstance, viz., the impossibility of alienating the property of the Church. Who was his proprietor? Who could enfranchise him? The difficulty of solving this question eternised ecclesiastical slavery, and brought about this singular result, that the Church, which really had done so much for the slaves, had been the last to possess slaves. The enfranchisements were generally made by will; now the Church had no wills to make. The ecclesiastical freeman remained under the patronage of a mistress who did not die.

It is in an indirect fashion, and by way of consequence, that Christianity contributed powerfully to change the situation of the slave, and to suppress slavery. The rôle of Christianity in the question of slavery has been that of an enlightened Conservative who serves Radicalism by his principles, while holding very reactionary language. While showing the slave to be capable of virtue, heroic in martyrdom, equal to his master, and probably his superior in point of view of the Kingdom of God, the new faith made slavery impossible. To give a moral value to the slave is to suppress slavery. The gatherings in the church, and they alone, were sufficient to ruin this cruel institution. Antiquity had not preserved slavery, except by excluding the slaves from the cults of the country. If they had sacrificed with their masters, they would have been morally elevated. Frequenting the church was the most perfect lesson of religious equality. What shall be said of the eucharist, of martyrdom endured in common? From the moment that the slave has the same religion as his master, prays in the same temple as he, slavery is nearly at an end. The sentiments of Blandina and her "carnal mistress" are those of a mother and daughter. In the Church the master and the slave were called brethren. Even on the most delicate matter, that of marriage, we see some miracles--certain freedmen marrying noble ladies, some feminæ clarisimæ.

As it is natural to suppose, the Christian master led his slaves more frequently to the faith, without committing any indiscretion which would people the Church with unworthy subjects. It was a good action to go to the slave market, and, allowing oneself to be guided by grace, to choose some poor creature to purchase to make sure of his salvation. "To purchase a slave is to gain a soul" became a current proverb. A kind of proselytism, more common and more legitimate, still consisted in receiving foundlings, who became the alumni Christians. Sometimes certain churches ransomed at their expense one of their members from a servile condition. This excited the desires of the unfortunate ones less favoured. The orthodox doctors did not encourage these dangerous pretensions: "Let them continue to serve for the glory of God, that they may obtain from God a much better liberty." The slave, or rather the freedman, rose to the most important ecclesiastical functions, provided that his patron or his master made no opposition.

What Christianity founded is equality before God. Clement of Alexandria and John Chrysostom especially did not lose an occasion of consoling the slave, of proclaiming him the freeman and as noble as he, if he accepts his condition and serves for God willingly and from the heart. In its liturgy the Church has a prayer "for those who pine in bitter slavery." Already Judaism on the same subject had professed some relatively humane maxims. It had thus opened as widely as possible the door for ransoms. Slavery among the Hebrews was much ameliorated. The Essenes and the Therapeutists went further; they declared servitude contrary to natural law, and did entirely without servile work. Christianity, less radical, did not suppress slavery, but it suppressed the manners of slavery. Slavery is founded on the absence of the idea of brotherhood among men; the idea of brotherhood is the dissolving of it. At the beginning of the fifth century, enfranchisement and the ransom of captives were the acts of charity most recommended by the Church.

Those who have pretended to see in Christianity the revolutionary doctrine of the rights of man, and in Jesus a precursor of Toussaint Louverture, are completely deceived. Christianity has inspired no Spartacus; the true Christian does not revolt. But let us hasten to say it, it was not Spartacus who suppressed slavery; it was much more done by Blandina; it is especially the ruin of the Græco-Roman world. Ancient slavery has never really been abolished; it has fallen, or rather it is transformed. The inertia into which the East sunk at the beginning of the complete triumph of the Church, in the fifth century, rendered slavery useless. The barbarian invasions in the West were an analogous effect. The kind of general indifference in which humanity was wrapped after the fall of the Roman empire led to numerous manumissions. The slave was a surviving victim of Pagan civilisation, a nearly useless remnant of a world of luxury and leisure. It was believed that a man could ransom his soul from the terrors of the other life by delivering this suffering brother here below. Slavery, besides, became especially rural, and implied a bond between man and the earth, which should one day become property. As to the philosophic principle that man ought not to belong to any but himself, it is much later when it appears as a social dogma. Seneca and Ulpian had proclaimed it in a theoretical way; Voltaire, Rousseau, and the French Revolution have made from it the basis of the new faith of humanity.

CHAPTER XXXIII

THE CHRISTIAN EMPIRE

Some ancient and profound reasons would have it, notwithstanding the contrary appearances, that the empire should become Christian. The Christian doctrine on the origin of power seemed to be made expressly to become the doctrine of the Roman state. Authority loves authority. Some men as Conservative as the bishops came to have a terrible temptation to reconcile themselves with the public force, whose action they realised had been often exercised for good. Jesus had laid down the rule. The effigies on the coin was for him the supreme criterion of the legitimism, beyond which there was nothing to seek for. In the midst of Nero's reign, St. Paul wrote--"Let every one be subject to the higher powers; for there is no power which does not come from God. The powers which be are ordained of God; so that he who resisteth the powers that be resists the order established by God." Some years after Peter, or he who wrote in his name the epistle known under the name of Prima Petri; expresses himself in a nearly identical way. Clement is likewise a subject who cannot be more devoted to the Roman empire. Lastly, one of the features of St. Luke, as we have seen, is his respect for the imperial authority, and the precautions he takes not to wound it.

There had, no doubt, been certain fanatical Christians who had thoroughly shared the Jewish rage, and waited for the destruction of the idolatrous town identified by them with Babylon. Such were the authors of the Apocalypse and the authors of the Sibylline writings. For them Christ and Cæsar are two irreconcilable terms. But the believers in the Great Churches had quite different ideas. In 70, the Church of Jerusalem, with the most Christian and patriotic feeling, abandoned the rebellious town and went to seek quietness beyond the Jordan. In the revolt of Bar-Coziba, the separation was still more marked. Not a single Christian would take part in that attempt of blind desperation. St. Justin, in his Apologies, never combats the principle of the empire; he would have the empire examine the Christian doctrine, prove it, countersign it in some sort, and condemn those who calumniate it. We have seen the first doctor of the time of Marcus-Aurelius, Melito, bishop of Sardis, making offers of service still more distinct, and representing Christianity as the foundation of an empire of heredity and divine right. In his treatise on the Word, preserved in Syriac, Melito expresses himself in the style of a bishop of the fourth century, explaining to Theodosius that his first duty is to procure the triumph of the truth (without telling us, alas! by what mark the truth is to be recognised). All the apologists flatter the favourite idea of the emperors, that of heirship in a direct line, and assure them that the effect of the Christian prayers will be that their sons shall reign after them. Only let the empire become Christian, and those persecuted to-day will consider that the interference of the State is perfectly legitimate.

Hatred against Christianity and the empire was the hatred of people who should one day be beloved. Under the Severi, the language of the Church remains what it was under the Antonines, plaintive and tender. The apologists declare for a kind of legitimism, the pretension with which the Church always saluted the emperor at first. The principle of St. Paul bore its fruits. "Every power comes from God; let him who holds the sword hold it from God for good."

This correct attitude as to power held quite as much to external necessities as to the very principles which the Church had received from its founders. The Church was already a grand association; it was essentially conservative; it needed order and legal guarantees. That is admirably seen in the act of Paul of Samosata, bishop of Antioch under Aurelian. The bishop of Antioch would already pass, at that period, for a high personage. The property of the Church was in his hand; a large number of people lived on his favours. Paul was a brilliant man, mystical, worldly, a great secular lord, seeking to render Christianity acceptable to people of the world and to the authorities. The pietists, as would have been expected of them, considered him heretical and dismissed him. Paul resisted and refused to leave the episcopal mansion. It is by an act like this that the haughtiest sects are caught, for who could regulate a question of property or enjoyment if not the civil authority? The question was laid before the emperor, who was at Antioch at the time, and we see there this original spectacle of an unbelieving sovereign and persecutor charged with deciding who was the true bishop. Aurelian showed in these circumstances a layman's remarkably good sense. He made them bring to him the correspondence of the two bishops, marked him who was in relation with Rome and Italy, and concluded that he was the bishop of Antioch.

The theological argument which took place in this affair Aurelian would attribute to certain objections, but one fact became plain, and that was that Christianity could not live without the empire, and that, on the other hand, the empire could do nothing better than adopt Christianity as its religion. The world wished a religion of congregations, of churches or synagogues, of chapels; a religion where the essence of the worship was reunion, association, brotherhood. Christianity fulfilled all these conditions. Its admirable worship, its pure morality, its clergy skilfully organised, assured its future.

Frequently, in the third century, this historical necessity made itself realised. It was seen, especially in the time of the Syrian emperors, that their character as strangers and the baseness of their origin brought under their shelter certain prejudices; and, in spite of their vices, they inaugurated a breadth of ideas and a tolerance unknown till then. The same thing appears again under Philip the Arabian, in the East under Zenobia, and generally under the emperors whose origin was outside of Roman patriotism.

The struggle redoubled in fury when the great reformers, Diocletian and Maximian, believed they could give the empire a new life. The Church triumphed by its martyrs; Roman pride bent; Constantine saw the internal strength of the Church, the populations of Asia Minor, of Syria, Thrace, Macedonia, and, in a word, of the oriental part of the empire, already more than half Christian. His mother, who had been a servant in a tavern at Nicomedia, dazzled his eyes with an empire of the East, having its centre at Nicea, and whose sinews should be the favour of the bishops and those multitudes of poor enrolled in the Church, who, in the large towns, created opinion. Constantine inaugurated what he called "the peace of the Church," and this was really the domination of the Church. From the Western point of view this astonishes us; for the Christians were still, in the West, only a weak minority; in the East, Constantine's policy was not only natural, but imperative, Julian's reaction was a caprice without result. After the struggle came close union and love. Theodosius inaugurated the Christian empire--that is to say, the thing which the Church, in its long life, has most longed for--theocratic empire, of which the Church is the essential framework, and which, after having been destroyed by the barbarians, remained the eternal dream of the Christian conscience, at least in Roman countries. Many, in fact, believed that with Theodosius the goal of Christianity was reached. The empire and Christianity were identified to such a point, the one with the other, that many doctors looked on the end of the empire as the end of the world, and applied to this event the apocalyptic images of the last catastrophe. The Oriental Church, which was not troubled in its development by the barbarians, never withdrew from that ideal; Constantine and Theodosius remained its two poles; they hold the same yet, at least in Russia. The great social enfeeblement, which was the necessary consequence of such a regime, soon showed itself. Devoured by monachism and theocracy, the Eastern Empire was like a prey offered to Islam; the Christian in the East became a creature of a lower order. We arrive accordingly at this singular result, that the countries which have created Christianity have been the victims of their work. Palestine, Syria, Egypt, Cyprus, Asia Minor, Macedonia, are to-day countries lost to civilisation, subjected to the very hard yoke of an unchristian race.

Fortunately things came about in the East in a different manner. The Christian empire of the West soon perished. The city of Rome received from Constantine the heaviest blow which had ever struck it. What succeeded with Constantine, no doubt, was Christianity; but this was, before all the East. The East--that is to say, the half of the empire speaking Greek--had, after the death of Marcus-Aurelius, taken more and more the upper hand over the West, speaking Latin. The East was more free, more lively, more civilised, more political. Already Diocletian had removed the centre of affairs to Nicomedia. By building a New Rome on the Bosphorus, Constantine reduced ancient Rome to be nothing more than the capital of the West. The two halves of the empire became thus nearly strangers to each other. Constantine was the real author of the schism between the Latin and the Greek churches. We may say, also, that he was the distant cause of Islamism. Christians speaking Syriac and Arabic, persecuted or looked upon askance by the emperors of Constantinople, became an essential element in the future clientèle of Mahomet.

The cataclysms which followed the division of the two empires, the invasions of the barbarians, who spared Constantinople and fell upon Rome with their whole force, reduced the ancient capital of the world to a limited, often humble, rôle. That ecclesiastical primacy of Rome, which shone so clearly in the second and third centuries, survived no longer since the East had a separate existence and capital. The Christian empire was the empire of the East, with its oecumenical councils, its orthodox emperors, its courtly clergy. That lasted till the eighth century. Rome, during this time, took its revenge by the earnestness and profoundness of its spirit of organisation. What men were St. Damasius, St. Leo, and Gregory the Great! With admirable courage, the Papacy wrought for the conversion of the barbarians; it drew them to her, made them her clients, her subjects.

The chef-d'oeuvre of its policy was its alliance with the Carlovingian House, and the bold stroke by which it re-established in that family the empire of the West--dead since 324. The empire of the West, in fact, was only destroyed in appearance. Its secrets lived in the higher Roman clergy. The Church of Rome kept in some sort the seal of the old empire, and it used it to authenticate surreptitiously the unheard-of act of Christmas Day of the year 800. The dream of the Christian empire recommenced. With the spiritual power was needed a secular arm, a temporal vicar. Christianity, not having in its nature that military spirit which is inherent in Islamism, for example, could not draw an army from its bosom; it was necessary, therefore, to demand it from outside, in the empire, among the barbarians, in a royalty constituted by the bishops. From that to the Mussulman caliphate there is an infinite distance. Even in the Middle Ages, when the Papacy admitted and proclaimed the idea of a Christian army, neither the pope nor his legates had ever been military chiefs. A holy empire, with a barbarian Theodosius, holding the sword to protect the Church of Christ--that was the ideal of the Latin Papacy. The West only escaped, thanks to Germanic indocility and the paradoxical genius of Gregory VII. The pope and the emperor quarrelled to the death: the nationalities whom the Christian empire of Constantinople had stifled were able to develop themselves in the West, and a door was opened for liberty.

That liberty was in almost nothing the work of Christianity. The Christian royalty came from God: the king made by the priests is the Lord's Anointed. Now the king of divine right can scarcely well be a constitutional king. The throne and the altar become thus two inseparable terms. The theocracy is a virus from which they are not purged. Protestantism and the Revolution were necessary that we should arrive at the possibility of conceiving of a liberal Christianity, and that liberal Christianity, without pope or king, has not yet had trial enough for one to have the right to speak of it as of an accomplished and durable fact in the history of humanity.

CHAPTER XXXIV

ULTERIOR TRANSFORMATIONS

Thus a religion made for the internal comfort of quite a small number of elect ones became, by an unheard-of chance, the religion of millions of men constituting the most active part of humanity. It is especially in the victories of religious orders that it is true to say that the conquered make the law to the conquerors. The crowds by entering into the little churches of saints carried with them their imperfections, sometimes their impurities. A race by embracing a religion which has not been made for it transformed itself according to the demands of its imagination and its heart.

In the primitive Christian conception a Christian was perfect; the sinner, simply because he was a sinner, ceased to be a Christian. When entire towns came to be converted en masse everything was changed. The precepts of devoutness and evangelical self-denial became inapplicable; some advice was given designed only for those who aspire to perfection. And where is this perfection to be realised? The world, such as it was, absolutely excluded it; he who in the world practised the Gospel to the letter played the part of a dupe and an idiot. The monastery remains. Logic demanded its rights. The Christian morality, the morality of a little church and people retired from the world, created itself the means which was necessary for it. The Gospel must join with the convent; a Christianity having its complete organisations cannot do without convents--that is to say, places where the evangelical life, impossible elsewhere, can be practised. The convent is the perfect church; the monk is the true Christian. Thus the most effectual works of Christianity have only been executed by the monastic orders. These orders, far from being a leprosy which should attack from the outside the work of Jesus, were the internal and inevitable consequences of the work of Jesus. In the West they had more advantages than inconveniences, for the Germanic conquest maintained in the face of the monk a powerful military caste; the East, on the contrary, was really consumed by a monachism which had only the most deceptive appearance of Christian perfection.

A mediocre morality, and a natural leaning towards idolatry, such were the gloomy dispositions which brought into the Church the masses who entered it partly by force after the close of the fourth century. Man does not change in a day; baptism has not instantaneous miraculous effects. These Pagan multitudes, scarcely evangelised, remained what they were before their conversion; in the East wicked, egotistical, corrupt; in the West gross and superstitious. As to what regards morality, the Church had only to maintain its rules already written in books held to be canonical. As to what regards superstition, the task was much more delicate. Changes in religion are in general only apparent. Man, whatever his conversions or apostasies may be, remains faithful to the first worship which he has practised, and more or less loved. A multitude of idolaters, in no way changed at heart, and transmitting the same instincts to their children, entered the Church. Superstition began to flow in full stream in the religious community which up till that time had been most exempt from it.

If we except some Oriental sects, the primitive Christians were the least superstitious of men. The Christian, the Jew, might be fanatics, they were not superstitious as a Gaul or a Paphlagonian were. Among them were no amulets, no images of saints, no object of worship beyond the divine hypostases. The converted Pagans could not lend themselves to such a simplicity. The worship of the martyrs was the first concession forced by human weakness from the gentleness of a clergy who wished to be all in all to gain all to Jesus Christ. The holy bodies had miraculous virtues, they became talismans, the places where they reposed were marked by a holiness more special than the other sanctuaries consecrated to God. The absence of all ideas to the laws of nature soon opened the door to an unbridled thaumaturgy. The Celtic and Italian races, which formed the basis of the population of the West, are the most superstitious of races. A crowd of beliefs, which the first Christianity would have considered sacrilegious, thus passed into the Church. It did what it could; its efforts to improve and to elevate the gross catechumens form one of the most beautiful pages of human history. During five or six centuries the Councils were occupied in combating the ancient naturalistic superstitions; but the priests went beyond that. St. Gregory the Great took his part in it, and counselled the missionaries not to suppress the rites and the holy places of the Anglo-Saxons, but only to consecrate them to the new worship.

Thus a singular phenomenon came about; the thick vegetation of Pagan fables and beliefs which primitive Christianity believed itself called upon to destroy was preserved to a large extent. Far from succeeding like Islam in suppressing the times of ignorance, that is to say, the former souvenirs, they concealed them under a light Christian varnish. Gregory of Tours is as superstitious as Elian or Elius Aristides. The world in the sixth, seventh, eighth, ninth, and tenth centuries was more grossly Pagan than it had ever been. Up till the advancement in primary instruction at the present day, our peasants had not abandoned a solitary one of their little Gallic gods. The worship of the saints has been the cover under which polytheism has been established. This encroachment of the idolatrous spirit has sadly dishonoured modern Catholicism. The follies of Lourdes and Salette, the multiplication of images, the Sacred Heart, the vows, the pilgrimages, make of contemporary Catholicism, at least in certain countries, a religion as material as a worship such as that of Syria combated by John Chrysostom, or suppressed by the edicts of the emperor. The Church had, in fact, two attitudes in regard to the Pagan cults--sometimes a struggle to the death, like that which took place in Aphaca and in Phoenicia; sometimes a compromise, the old creed accepting more or less complacently a Christian shade. Every Pagan who embraced Christianity in the second or third century had a horror of his old religion: he who baptized him asked him to detest his ancient gods. It was not the same with the Gallic peasant, with the Frank or Anglo-Saxon warrior; his old religion was such a small affair that it was not worthy of being hated or seriously opposed.

The complacency which Christianity, become the religion of crowds, showed for the ancient cults, it had also for many Greek prejudices. It seems to have been ashamed of its Jewish origin, and tried to conceal it. We have seen the Gnostics and the author of the Epistle to Diognetes affecting to believe that Christianity was born spontaneously, without any relation with Judaism. Origen and Eusebius did not dare to say so, for they knew the facts too well; but St. John Chrysostom, and, in general, the fathers who had received a Hellenic education, did not know the true beginnings of Christianity, and did not wish to know them. They rejected all the Judeo-Christian and millenarian literature; the orthodox Church eagerly sought their works: books of this sort were not known except when they were translated into Latin or the Oriental tongues. The Apocalypse of John escaped only because it held by its roots in the very heart of the canon. Some essays of Unitarian Christianity, without metaphysic or mythology-- of a Christianity little distinguished from Jewish rationalism, such as were the attempts of Zenobia and Paul of Samosata--were cut to the ground. These attempts would have produced a simple Christianity, a continuation of Judaism, something analogous to what Islam produced. If they had succeeded, they would have no doubt prevented the success of Mahomet among the Arabs and Syrians. What fanaticism would thus have been shunned! Christianity is an edition of Judaism accommodated to the Indo-European taste; Islam is an edition of Judaism accommodated to the taste of the Arabs. Mahomet did nothing in short but return to the Judeo-Christianity of Zenobia, by a reaction against the metaphysical polytheism of the Council of Nicea and the Councils which followed.

The separation, more and more deep, between the clergy and the people was another consequence of the conversions en masse which took place in the fourth and fifth centuries. These ignorant crowds could not but listen. The Church came to be little more than a clergy. Far from this transformation having contributed to elevate the intellectual average of Christianity, it lowered it. Experience proves that little Churches without clergy are more liberal than the large. In England, the Quakers and the Methodists have done more for ecclesiastical liberality than the Established Church. Contrary to what happened in the second century, we see this good and reasonable authority of the Episcopi and Presbyteri keeping back excesses and follies; henceforth those things which shall be law among the clergy, these are the demands of the basest party. The Councils obeyed the maniacal crowds in their deep fanaticism. In all the Councils it is the most superstitious dogma which carries the day. Arianism, which had the rare merit of converting the Germans before their entrance into the empire, and which could have given to the world a Christianity susceptible of becoming rational, was stifled by the grossness of a clergy which willed the absurd. In the Middle Ages this clergy became a feudalism. The democratic Book par excellence, the Gospel, is confiscated by those who claim to interpret it, and those prudently conceal its boldness.

The lot of Christianity has therefore been almost to founder in its victory, like a ship which nearly sinks by the fact of the number of passengers who crowd it. Never has a founder had votaries who have so little resembled him as Jesus. Jesus is much more a great Jew than a great man; his disciples have made out that he was more of an anti-Jew--a God-man. The additions made to his work by superstition, metaphysics and politics, have entirely masked the Great Prophet--so much so, that reform of Christianity consists apparently in suppressing the graces which our Pagan ancestors have added to it to return to Jesus as he was. But the gravest error which can be committed in religious history is to believe that religions are to be valued for themselves in an absolute manner. Religions are to be estimated by the people who accept them. Islamism has been useful or fatal according to the races who have adopted it. Among the debased peoples of the East Christianity is a very mediocre religion, inspiring very little virtue. It is among our Western races--Celtic, Germanic and Italian--that Christianity has been really fruitful.

A product entirely Jewish in its origin, Christianity has gradually come to be stripped, with time, of all which it holds by its origin, so much so that the theory of those who consider it the Aryan religion par excellence is true from many points of view. During the centuries we have imported into it our ways of feeling, all our aspirations, qualities, and defects. The exegesis according to which Christianity should be carved from the interior of the Old Testament is the falsest in the world. Christianity has been the rupture with Judaism--the abrogation of the Thora. St. Bernard, Francis d'Assisi, St. Elizabeth, St. Theresa, Francis de Sales, Vincent de Paul, Fenélon and Channing were nothing like Jews. These are people of our race, feeling with our hearts, thinking with our brain. Christianity has been the traditional notion upon which they have embellished their poem, but the genius is their own. St. Bernard interpreting the Psalms is the most romantic of men. Every race attaching itself to the discipline of the past claims it, makes it its own. The Bible has thus borne fruits which are not its own; Judaism has only been the wild-stock upon which the Aryan race has produced its flower. In England, in Scotland, the Bible has become the national book of the Aryan branch which resembles the Hebrews least. This is how Christianity, so notoriously Jewish in origin, has been able to become the national religion of the European races, which have sacrificed to it their ancient mythology. The renunciation of our old ethnic traditions in favour of Christian holiness, a renunciation little serious at bottom, has been apparently so absolute that it has taken nearly fifteen hundred years to produce this result as an accomplished fact. The grand awakening of national minds which was produced by it in the nineteenth century, this kind of resurrection of dead races, of which we are the witnesses, cannot fail to bring the recollection of our abdication before the sons of Shem, and to provoke in that respect some reaction. Although assuredly no one beyond the cabinets of comparative mythology could longer think of recalling the Germanic, Pelasgian, Celtic and Slav Mythologies, it would have been much better for Christianity if those dangerous images had been suppressed altogether, as was done in the establishment of Islam. Races which claim nobility and originality in everything are not wounded by being in religion the vassals of a despised family.

The impetuous Germanists have not concealed their shame, some Celto-maniacs have manifested the same feeling. The Greeks, finding again their importance in the world by the souvenirs of ancient Hellenism, have no longer concealed the fact that Christianity has been for them an apostasy. Greeks, Germans, and Celts have consoled themselves by saying that if they have accepted Christianity they have at least transformed it, and made it their national property. It is not less true that the modern principle of races has been hurtful to Christianity. The religious action of Judaism is apparently colossal. We see the defects of Israel at the same time as its greatness. We have been ashamed of being made Jewish in the same way that fanatical German patriots have believed themselves obliged to treat so badly the seventeenth and eighteenth French centuries, to which they owe so much.

Another cause has strongly undermined, in our days, the religion which our ancestors practised with such perfect contentment.

The negation of the supernatural has become an absolute dogma for every cultured spirit. The history of the physical and moral worlds would appear to us like a development having its causes in itself and excluding miracle. That is to say, the intervention specially reflected wills. Now from Christianity's point of view, the history of the world is nothing but a series of miracles. The creation, the history of the Jewish people, the rule of Jesus, all passed through the crucible of the most liberal exegesis, leave a residuum of the supernatural, which no operation can suppress or transform. The Semitic-Monotheistic religions are at bottom enemies of physical science, which would appear to them a diminution, nearly a denial, of God.

God has done everything and does everything still; that is their universal explanation. Christianity, not having carried this dogma to the same exaggerations as Islam, implies revelation; that is to say, a miracle, a fact such as science has never proved. Between Christianity and science the struggle is therefore inevitable; one of the two adversaries must succumb.

From the thirteenth century, the moment when, following upon the study of the works of Aristotle, Averroès, the scientific spirit, commenced to awake in the Latin countries, up to the sixteenth century, the Church, using the public strength, succeeded in defeating her enemy, but in the seventeenth century scientific discovery has been too striking to be stifled. The Church is still strong enough to trouble gravely the life of Galileo, to disquiet Descartes, but not to prevent their discoveries from becoming the law of the intellectual. In the eighteenth century reason triumphs; about the year 1800 A.D. scarcely any educated man believed in the supernatural. The reactions which have followed have not been hindrances of any consequence. If many timid minds, fearing great social questions, have refused to be logical, the people in the town and country are wandering more and more from Christianity, and the supernatural loses some of its adherents every day.

What has Christianity done to put itself on guard against the formidable assault which shall sweep it away if it does not abandon certain desperate positions? The reform of the sixteenth century was assuredly a deed of wisdom and conservatism. Protestantism diminished the supernatural daily; it returned in a sense to the primitive Christianity, and reduced to a small matter the idolatrous and Pagan part of the creed. But the principle of miracle, especially in what regards the inspiration of "the books," was preserved. This reform, besides, could not extend over all Christendom; it has gained life through rationalism, which will probably suppress the matter to be reformed before the reformation is made. Protestantism will only save Christianity if it arrives at complete rationalism, if it make a junction with all free spirits, whose programme may perhaps thus be summed up:--

"Great and splendid is the world, and, in spite of all the obscurities which surround it, we see that it is the fruit of a deep tendency towards good--a supreme goodness. Christianity is the most striking of those efforts, which are drawn up in history for the birth of an ideal of light and justice. Let it be that the first slip has been Jewish, Christianity has become with time the common work of humanity; each race has given to it the special gift with which it has been endowed, whatever was best in it. God is not exclusively present there, but he is more present there than in any other religious or moral development. Christianity is, in fact, the religion of civilised people; each nation admits it in different senses, according to its degree of intellectual culture. The free-thinker, who is satisfied at once, is in his right; but the free-thinker constitutes a highly respectable individual case; his intellectual and moral position cannot yet be that of a nation or of humanity.

"Let us preserve then Christianity with admiration for its high moral value, for its majestic history, for the beauty of its sacred books. These books assuredly are books. We must apply to them the rules of interpretation and criticism we apply to all books, but they constitute the religious archives of humanity; even the weak parts which they include are worthy of respect. It is the same with dogma; let us revive, without making ourselves their slaves, those formulas under which fourteen centuries have adored the Divine wisdom. Without admitting either particular miracle or limited inspiration, let us bow before the supreme miracle of this great Church, the inexhaustible mother of unceasingly varied manifestations. As to worship, let us seek to eliminate from it some shocking dross; let us hold it in any case as a secondary thing, not having any other value than the sentiments which are infused into it."

If so many Christians have entered into such sentiments, we may hope for a future for Christianity. But, the Protestant liberal congregations apart, the great Christian masses have in no way modified their attitude. Catholicism continues with a species of desperate fury to bury itself in the miraculous; orthodox Protestantism remains immovable. During this time popular rationalism, the inevitable consequence of the advancement in public instruction and democratic institutions, caused the temples to be deserted and multiplied purely civil marriages and funerals. We shall not bring back the people of the large cities to old churches, and the people of the country will not go there from habit. Now, a Church does not exist without people, the Church is the place for the people. The Catholic party on the other hand has committed in these last years so many faults that its political power is nearly gone. A tremendous crisis will take place in the bosom of Catholicism. It is probable that a part of that great body will persevere in its idolatry, and remain at the side of the modern movement like a counter-current of stagnant and dead water. Another party shall live, and, abandoning the supernatural errors, shall unite itself to liberal Protestantism, to enlightened Israelitism, to ideal philosophy, to march towards the conquest of pure religion in spirit and in truth. What is beyond doubt, whatever may be the religious future of humanity, is that the place of Jesus shall be very high. He has been the founder of Christianity, and Christianity remains the bed of the great religious river of humanity; some tributaries coming from the most opposite points in the horizon have mingled with it. In this confluence no source can say, "This water is mine." But let us not forget the primitive brook of the beginnings, the spring on the mountains, the upper course whence a river, becoming at once as large as the Amazon, flowed at first into a bend of the earth of little extent. It is the picture of this higher course which I have wished to draw; happy shall I be if I have presented in its truth what there was on these high summits of vigour and force--sensations, sometimes hot, sometimes icy, of divine life and fellowship with heaven. The creators of Christianity occupy with good right the first rank in the homage of men. These men were very inferior to us in the knowledge of the real; but they have never been equalled in conviction, in devotion. Now it is that which makes the foundation. The solidity of a construction is in proportion to the amount of virtue, that is to say of sacrifices, which have been laid as its foundations.

In this edifice, demolished by time, what excellent stones besides are there which could be re-employed, such as they are, to the profit of our modern constructions. What better than Messianistic Judaism could point us to irrefragable hope and a blessed future--faith in a brilliant destiny for humanity under the government of an aristocracy of the righteous? Is the kingdom of God not the perfect expression of the final goal which the idealist pursues? The Sermon on the Mount remains the completed code of it; reciprocal love, gentleness, goodness, disinterestedness will be always the essential laws of perfect life. The association of the weak is the legitimate solution of the larger part of the problems which the organisation of humanity suggests. Christianity can give upon this point some lessons to all the ages. The Christian martyr will remain up to the end of time the type of the defender of the rights of conscience. At last the difficult and dangerous art of governing minds, if it is one day recovered, shall be upon the models furnished by the first Christian doctors. They had some secrets which can be learned only in their school. There have been professors of virtue more austere, perhaps firmer, but there never have been like masters in the science of goodness. The joy of the soul is the grand Christian art, to such an extent that civil society has been obliged to take precautions lest humanity should bury itself there. The fatherland and the family are the two great natural forms of human associations. They are both necessary, but they are not sufficient. There needs to be maintained alongside of them the place for an institution where one may receive nourishment for the soul, comfort, advice; where charity can be organised, where one shall find spiritual masters or directors. That is called the Church. We shall never pass from that without the danger of reducing life to a desperate dryness, above all for women. What is needful is that ecclesiastical society should not enfeeble civil society, that it should be only a liberty, that it should display no temporal power, that the State should not concern itself with it, nor control it, nor patronise it. During two hundred and fifty years Christianity gave in these little free reunions faultless models.

www.ingramcontent.com/pod-product-compliance
Lightning Source LLC
Chambersburg PA
CBHW021237090426
42740CB00006B/578